Helene
965- 3234

Up Came Hill

The Story of the
Light Division and
Its Leaders

Up Came Hill

The Story of the
Light Division and
Its Leaders

By

Martin Schenck

THE STACKPOLE COMPANY

HARRISBURG, PENNSYLVANIA

Library of Congress Catalog Card Number: 58-13303

Butternut Press, Inc.
12137 Darnestown Road
Gaithersburg, Maryland 20878

Contents

page

Chapter 1—A Weapon is Forged 1

2—The Brigades and Their Commanders 25

3—The First Battle 43

4—Gaines' Mill 65

5—Frayser's Farm and Malvern Hill 79

6—Aftermath of the Seven Days 99

7—Personalities Clash 117

8—Cromwell and the Cavalier 131

9—Battle of Slaughter's Mountain 147

10—Holding the Line at Manassas 159

11—Victory at Heavy Cost 177

12—Saving the Army at Sharpsburg 187

13—Lee the Mediator 205

14—Preparation Along the Rappahannock 215

15—Victory and Tragedy 227

16—"Let Us Cross Over the River—" 243

17—Two Successors to the Light Division 261

18—Debut as Corps Commander 269

19—Keeping the Enemy Moving 285

20—Bristoe Station and The Wilderness 295

21—The End Approaches 311

22—Death of a Hero 329

Appendix 337

Bibliography 339

Index 341

Maps

page

Map 1 Theater of Operations 10
Map 2 The Peninsular Campaign 13
Map 3 Location of A. P. Hill's Brigades in June, 1862 21
Map 4 Routes of Branch and Jackson on June 26, 1862 51
Map 5 Battle of Mechanicsville 55
Map 6 Battle of Gaines' Mill 69
Map 7 Lee's Plan of Pursuit, June 30-July 1, 1862 81
Map 8 Movements of Light Division, June 30-July 8, 1862 100
Map 9 Battle of Slaughter's Mountain 153
Map 10 Campaign of Second Manassas Gets Under Way 162
Map 11 Movements of Light Division, August 24-28, 1862 166
Map 12 Second Battle of Manassas, August 29, 1862 172
Map 13 Last Day of Second Manassas 181
Map 14 Battle of Sharpsburg (Antietam) 199
Map 15 Battle of Fredericksburg—Action on South Flank 231
Map 16 Repulse of Federal Attack Against Marye's Heights 235
Map 17 Battle of Chancellorsville—Jackson's Flank Attack 247
Map 18 First Day at Gettysburg—Initial Contact 275
Map 19 Situation about 10:30 a.m., July 1, 1863 276
Map 20 Situation about 7:30 p.m., July 1, 1863 278
Map 21 Actions on the Three Days at Gettysburg 281
Map 22 Engagement at Bristoe Station 298
Map 23 Battle of The Wilderness 306
Map 24 Wilderness to Petersburg 312

Illustrations *(Following page 24)*

Captain Ambrose Powell Hill
Lieutenant General James Longstreet
General Robert E. Lee
Major General Richard H. Anderson
Lieut. Gen. Thomas J. Jackson
Major General A. P. Hill
Brigadier General James J. Archer
Brigadier General Joseph R. Anderson
Brigadier General William Dorsey Pender
Brigadier General L. O'Brien Branch
Brigadier General Maxcy Gregg
Brigadier General Charles W. Field

Brigadier General Henry Heth
Colonel R. Lindsay Walker
Brigadier General Edward L. Thomas
Major General Cadmus M. Wilcox
Brigadier General James H. Lane
Brigadier General G. Moxley Sorrell
Brigadier General Samuel McGowan
Brigadier General W. W. Kirkland
Major General William Mahone
Brigadier General Abner Perrin
Brigadier General A. M. Scales
Brigadier General H. H. Walker
Brigadier General John R. Cooke
Brigadier General Joseph R. Davis

To my wife, Barbara, and my friend, Dan, without the aid and counsel of both of whom I would never have become so well acquainted with A. P. Hill.

A Weapon Is Forged

*I*T HAD RAINED the day before, so that the infantry shuffled silently along the dirt road leading east through the forest. The soft, damp earth, its pungency faintly nostalgic to South Carolina boys far from home, felt good to tired feet, for many of McGowan's men, in common with the rest of Lee's Army, were practically shoeless. Dusk was turning into night. The gloom was accentuated by the tangles of blackjack and underbrush crowding in from the roadsides while the pine boughs seemed to meet overhead, making the road a virtual tunnel. Presently an orange glow appeared through the trees ahead. The men first thought a farmhouse or hay shed had been set afire by the recent shelling. It was, however, the May full moon. Now its reflection glinted from scabbard and musket. An aroused whippoorwill in a nearby thicket set up his maddeningly repetitious call.

The troops were a part of A. P. ("Powell") Hill's famous Light Division, coming up rapidly from a reserve position at the rear of Stonewall Jackson's column to take over from General Rodes the spearhead of the Confederate envelopment of the Union forces near Chancellorsville. Rodes' Division, overrunning Howard's Federal corps west of Chancellorsville, had become disorganized by its own headlong rush through the darkening forests. Jackson himself was at the very front, reconnoitering the situation and telling Hill what he wanted done.

Suddenly the men heard a scattering of small-arms fire a few hundred yards to the front followed by angry shouts.

1

At once Lane's North Carolina Brigade, deploying along the edge of a clearing ahead, poured volley after volley into the eastern darkness. Long tearing sheets of musketry fire lighted up forest and lane, the echoes resounding and filling the warm air with acrid clouds of smoke. In a moment the enemy replied with a terrific burst of artillery fire. Grape-shot and shell screamed through the trees, slashing off branches and creating a tremendous uproar punctuated by the venomous impact of iron balls and shell fragments. The woods magnified the terror, throwing the dreadful sounds back again and again. Even veterans of two years' campaigning cowered in the brush. Never, they thought, had they been under such fire. Some had been cut down by the first volley, others were safely prone while the bursts continued overhead. During intervals in the cannonading there came from the front frenzied cheers, wild and fierce.

There followed a more protracted lull, broken only by occasional rifle shots.

Several dim figures came slowly and awkwardly down the road from the front. At once suspicious soldiers sprang up, alert, challenging. Low, evasive answers were made. A soldier elbowed his way into the little group to stare at the central figure who was half supported by two others. "Great God!" he cried, at the sight of the pale, bearded face, "It's General Jackson!"

A muffled protest came from one of the group. Then a litter was brought up on which the wounded leader was carried to the rear.

Again a hurricane of enemy fire swept down the road. In a few moments General Hill, the division commander, whom the men were accustomed to see in the thick of every fight, came limping from the front, sword in hand. Evidently he had been struck in the calf of the leg and was in pain. But this did not stop him from raging at the men. He stood in the middle of the road, hurling furious rebukes because they had fired at unidentified sounds in the night, wounding members of the reconnaissance party and disclosing the imminence of the division's attack.

2

There was a tense silence. The concern of the commander was instantly transmitted in a mysterious way to the listening men. Then suddenly the atmosphere was cleared and relaxed by a drawling comment from the inevitable wag of Company B, 18th North Carolina Infantry: "Everybody knows the whole damyankee army cain't run the Light Division, and one little general needn't try it!"

Chuckles ran along the line in the edge of the woods. A. P. Hill subsided at once, grinning in his red beard. He hobbled off down the road, his thoughts returning to his wounded corps chief, Stonewall Jackson.

Though the men did not know it then, the Light Division had just lost the leader who had fashioned it and made it into a fine, tempered blade, justly renowned throughout the Confederacy. A. P. Hill, about to be given command of a corps, never again directly commanded the Light Division.[1]

The Light Division was just two years old when it entered the Battle of Chancellorsville. In the preceding months it had fought in a series of desperate engagements, becoming what many believed to be the best division in the Army of Northern Virginia. It had taken its tone from its commander, who had transmitted to his subordinates and his men something of his own impetuous courage and deft skill. The quality of A. P. Hill and his division was recognized by Jefferson Davis and Robert E. Lee and was acclaimed in the contemporary press in the South.

With the passage of decades since the war, however, the memory of A. P. Hill and the Light Division has become dim. He is now a shadowy figure on the stage of history, the spotlight being on others who have captured the fancy of the scribes. To recover some measure of the worth of

---

[1] The foregoing description is based on J. F. C. Caldwell, *The History of a Brigade of South Carolinians Known as "Gregg's" and Subsequently as "McGowan's Brigade,"* page 78. Philadelphia: King and Baird, 1866; and on "The 18th Regiment," *Histories of North Carolina Regiments,* Vol. 2, ed. by Walter Clark, Raleigh, 1901. A more detailed description of the fatal wounding of Jackson is given in Freeman's *Lee's Lieutenants,* Vol. 2, Chap. XXXIII. Chas. Scribner's Sons, N.Y., 1943.

Hill and his subordinate leaders in the hard-hitting Light Division is the purpose of this story.

Ambrose Powell Hill, known familiarly as Powell, was born on November 9, 1825, of a well-to-do family of Culpeper, Virginia. The Hill family stemmed from Shropshire, England. The first of Powell's ancestors to be noted by history was Henry Hill, a captain of horse in the army of Charles II, during the civil war occasioned by Oliver Cromwell. Captain Hill and his brother William were among the monarchists to flee to America before Cromwell's vengeance after the fall of the king. William Hill established himself in Virginia and it is from him that Powell descended. Powell's grandfather, Henry, served as a colonel in the American Revolution under Lighthorse Harry, father of Robert E. Lee. This Henry Hill married Ann Powell, daughter of Captain Ambrose Powell, another descendant of the original cavaliers. Despite this background, however, Thomas Hill, Powell's father, was a businessman whose only active military involvement was as a militiaman in 1812. Nevertheless, Thomas, always conscious of his ancestry, maintained a burning interest in military matters and had his heart set on sending a son to the Military Academy at West Point.

Powell's mother was Fanny Russell Baptist, a descendant of the Earl of Gainsboro in Charles II's reign. Mrs. Hill, however, was not as imbued with the cavalier spirit as her husband. She was, furthermore, something of a hypochondriac, a trait that led her to attempt to shelter her children too much and to regard them as babies long after they outgrew that stage. As a result, Powell's early boyhood was confined more to reading and other indoor pursuits than was common for a lad growing up in the open, rolling country of central Virginia. It is significant, in the light of his future, however, that one of his favorite studies was the military career of Napoleon. His mother also exercised a peculiar religious influence upon him that is reflected in his subsequent somewhat negative attitude upon that sub-

4

ject. Fanny Hill had been reared in the Episcopalian faith. Her children were brought up accordingly until she became almost fanatically interested in the Baptist "new light" movement of 1840. Powell, who had been even closer to his mother than were his brothers and sisters, became exposed to a rather violent conflict in religious concepts that was aggravated by his mother's increasing neuroticism. He became, as a result, somewhat irreligious and found it difficult to comprehend fully the devoutness of some of the extremely religious men with whom he would serve during the war, notably Jackson and Dorsey Pender.

His mother's objections to his attending West Point fell far short of his father's enthusiasm for such a course. As a result, amidst the plaudits of friends and neighbors, Powell bade farewell to his parents, brother Edward, and sisters, Margaret, Evelyn, and Lucy, and boarded a train for the North.[2] The slim seventeen-year-old boy entered West Point in 1842. Among his classmates later to become famous were Thomas J. Jackson, George E. Pickett, and Fitz John Porter. His roommate was George B. McClellan, with whom he formed a friendship that was to endure despite their later becoming rivals in love and in war.

Powell did reasonably well in his studies during the plebe year, but was forced to drop out because of illness. This ailment, the exact nature of which is not recorded, seems to have been what was once called "biliousness," probably some disability of the biliary tract. In Hill's case the trouble was aggravated by yellow fever contracted during his service in the Everglades of Florida in the early fifties; he may have even suffered from a virus infection of the liver, today recognized as hepatitis.[3] At any rate his illness recurred throughout his life, and often proved a severe handicap to him.

[2] A. P. Hill had two other brothers. One, Thomas Theophilius, died in infancy. The other, John Henry Hill, went to Alabama in the 1830's and apparently was never heard of again by anyone in the family.
[3] This theory as to the nature of Hill's complaint is strengthened by a statement of Colonel Willard Webb, Chief of the Reader and Stack Division of the Library of Congress, who states that he has seen a surgeon's report on Hill which ascribed the latter's illness to chronic liver inflammation.

5

A. P. Hill reentered the Academy, and graduated with the Class of 1847, too late to see much active service in the Mexican War. Two of his classmates, Harry Heth and Ambrose Burnside, will receive further notice in this narrative. Heth, Burnside, and Hill became the social leaders of the class. Their escapades became celebrated among the legends of the Corps of Cadets. That all graduated, especially the ebullient Burnside, almost seemed a miracle. Their careers at the Academy were in marked contrast to that of the stolid, plodding Jackson, to whom, in common with most cadets, they paid little attention.

Hill was commissioned a brevet second lieutenant in the First U. S. Artillery Regiment, and was sent to Mexico shortly before the end of the war there. Later he campaigned against the Seminoles in Florida, and was briefly stationed in Texas. Then for seven years he was on duty in the Office of the Superintendent of U.S. Coast Survey in Washington, D.C. While on this assignment, he met and paid ardent suit to Nellie Marcy who was, however, not the first "flame" of the romantic young officer. Shortly after leaving West Point, Powell had become very much enamored of Emma Wilson of Baltimore, a classmate of his favorite sister, Lucy, at a Maryland school. This romance was not sufficiently hardy to withstand the years of separation required by Hill's service in distant outposts. He never forgot Emma, however, nor became seriously involved, despite many flirtations, until he met Miss Marcy.

Nellie was the belle of the Army, the daughter of Randolph B. Marcy, noted western explorer who later became Chief of Staff to General McClellan, and after the war was Inspector General of the U.S. Army. Marcy discouraged Hill's suit, with the result that Nellie broke off with the Culpeper blade and married his former roommate, George McClellan. "Little Mac," who had been associated with Marcy as a Topographical Engineer, was about to resign from the Army. Soon he became vice president of the Illinois Central Railroad. His fortunes appeared to Marcy to have more promise than those of Hill. Though Hill's quick

6

pride was bruised by this outcome, he bore no grudge, and even attended McClellan's wedding. Within a year he had fallen in love with an attractive young widow from Louisville, Kentucky, the former Katherine Morgan. Kitty, or "Dolly" as she was known to her intimates, came from a wealthy and respected family. She had several brothers who served with distinction in the war, the most famous becoming General John Morgan. Her sister married General Basil Duke, who served under Morgan.

Powell Hill and his bride were happy together during the few years remaining for him on this earth, despite the unattractive features of service in the pre-Civil War Army. Pay was poor, promotion agonizingly slow, and living conditions substandard. Many able officers, destined to wear stars during the Civil War, had already resigned to seek employment in civil life. Hill was considering taking this step, too, when outbreak of the war became certain.

Powell and Dolly had a daughter, Henrietta, born to them in 1860. He was more interested in establishing a sound home life than he was in the national political discord of that year. Hill, like Robert E. Lee, was not an advocate of slavery. Lee stated the view of many Virginians, including a great number of the cavalier families, such as the Hills, when he said:

"If the millions of slaves in the South were mine, I would free them with a stroke of the pen to avert this war."[4]

At about the same time, Hill became violently and profanely enraged at news of a lynching in Culpeper. He wrote to his brother that "every b—— connected with that outrage should be hung."

Nevertheless, Lee and Hill were Virginians, possessing that loyalty to state which was based upon their cavalier heritage and which was found no place else in the country, not even in South Carolina, the hotbed of secession. Powell therefore resigned his captaincy in the U.S. Army in March, 1861, not to become a civilian but to accept appointment

[4] *Southern Historical Society Papers,* Vol. 14, p. 461, hereinafter cited as *S.H.S.P.*

as colonel in the Virginia Volunteers.

One old lady in Culpeper, who remembered him as tied to the apron strings of his now deceased mother, shook her head as she sighed, "Heaven help us if Powell Hill is going to be a colonel in the Confederate Army!"

Initially he was assigned to station at Harpers Ferry, where he received favorable notice for his skill and energy in organizing and training the 13th Virginia Volunteer Regiment.

General Joseph E. Johnston, Confederate commander in West Virginia, was quick to observe the capabilities of young Colonel A. P. Hill. Within a very few weeks of the outbreak of hostilities, he added the 3d Tennessee Regiment to Hill's own 10th Virginia and sent them to Romney in Hampshire County to observe and check a reported Union ffanking movement. Hill now gave the first indications of his brilliance at the swift, skillful maneuvers which will always be associated with his name. He handled his augmented command so well in staging a demonstration before Romney that the Federal threat to Johnston's flank was eliminated.[5] Hill received honorable mention in the reports and it was expected that a promotion to brigadier general would be forthcoming. But the situation was still in such confusion with respect to the organization of the Army that the government, now established at Richmond and alert to the jealousy among the sister states of the new Confederacy, decided that Virginia already had enough general officers, for the time being at least.

Hill was disappointed but quickly went about his task of organizing and drilling the raw recruits who continued pouring into Johnston's command. His military experience in many fields from the date of his graduation from West Point until the start of his tour of duty in Washington now stood him in good stead. Not only did he build his own regiment into the best one in Johnston's army, but he worked tirelessly and successfully in whipping other raw units into military cohesion.

---

[5] *20 S.H.S.P.*, 379.

In July, when the Confederate army in Virginia, then commanded by Beauregard, engaged McClellan's Northern forces at Manassas in the first major engagement of the war, Hill and his regiment were ordered to a reserve position on the Confederate right flank. The fact that Hill commanded a Johnston regiment in a battle which Beauregard had planned and started didn't enhance the Colonel's chances of getting into the thick of things where he wanted to be. At any rate, Powell Hill had to curb his impetuosity and "sit out" the first major conflict of the war. This of course, put a further damper upon his aspirations for immediate promotion.

After Manassas, Hill's regiment, together with other troops being trained by him, was added to the 1st Maryland Regiment, forming a brigade under Brigadier General Arnold Elzey. It was with this brigade that Powell continued his training duties for the remainder of 1861 and the early part of 1862.

Even at this stage of his career one of his outstanding traits became apparent. The men who came under his command began to esteem Powell Hill above all other Confederate officers for the manner in which he treated them and concerned himself with their needs. This consideration for his troops and the intense loyalty which it engendered was to play a prominent part in the story of Hill's activities throughout the war. Nevertheless, he maintained an air of aloofness and, even while making the welfare of his men his chief concern, never lapsed into undue familiarity with them.

The theater of action in Virginia shifted during the winter of 1862 to "the Peninsula," that portion of the state between Richmond and Fortress Monroe. The army was reorganized after Manassas. Beauregard had been transferred to the western sector of the war and Johnston was in command in Virginia. Manassas had not been a victory for either the North or the South but had served to frighten Washington sufficiently so that a campaign against Richmond was determined upon to relieve pressure against the

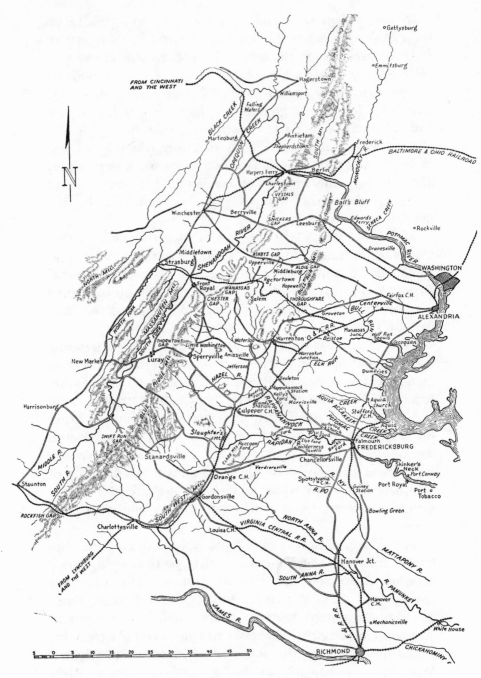

MAP 1. THEATER OF OPERATIONS

Northern capital. McClellan was given the task of mounting the Peninsular campaign with what at first appeared to be an overwhelmingly superior force.

The first Confederate reaction to the new threat was a concentration of forces at Yorktown near the lower end of the Peninsula. James Longstreet, affectionately known as "Old Pete" to his troops, had so distinguished himself during the early phases of the war that the reorganization of Johnston's army saw him promoted from the command of a brigade to that of a division. Powell Hill, on February 26th promoted to the rank of brigadier general, was placed in command of Longstreet's old brigade consisting of the 1st, 7th, 11th, and 17th Virginia Regiments.[6] Hill assumed his new command at Orange Court House, only a few miles from his beloved Culpeper. There was, however, no time for any amenities at the old homestead. McClellan was at the tip of the Peninsula. Richmond was threatened. Hill hastened with his troops to join the brigades of Richard H. (Dick) Anderson and George E. Pickett at Yorktown. These three brigades comprised Longstreet's Division as the Peninsular campaign opened. Hill was thus reunited with one of his old friends and classmates, Pickett. Anderson also was a West Pointer but had graduated in 1842, the year that Hill and Pickett entered the Academy.

Hill's brigade had little to do but maneuver during the early stages of the campaign. Johnston was feeling out McClellan and the latter, even more cautious, was in no hurry to commit himself.

Having permitted McClellan to become established on the Peninsula, the Southern command was left with no choice to make except the determination of the line along which to defend Richmond. Yorktown becoming untenable, Johnston, on May 3, 1862, commenced a withdrawal up the Peninsula.

The movement started in haste and confusion. No less than 56 heavy guns, 53 in perfect condition, together with ammunition and supplies, were left to fall into McClellan's

---

[6] 20 *S.H.S.P.*, p. 379.

hands.[7] And so it was that the campaign which was to see some of the most savage and brilliant fighting of the war opened on a note of confused, hasty retreat and abandoned equipment.

The retreat from Yorktown as such, however, took on a new aspect for Longstreet's Division within forty-eight hours. Old Pete was given the task of setting up a rear-guard defense to fight a delaying action at Fort Magruder on the road from Yorktown toward Williamsburg. On the morning of May 5th, Anderson's Brigade held Fort Magruder. As this comparatively small force became engaged, Longstreet sent Powell Hill and Cadmus Wilcox, another acquaintance of West Point days, now attached to Longstreet's Division, to Anderson's relief. Hill received his orders shortly before 8 AM.[8] He immediately moved his brigade into action. The regiments in his command were under the following officers, respectively: 7th Virginia, Colonel J. L. Kemper; 11th Virginia, Colonel Samuel Garland; 17th Virginia, Colonel M. D. Corse; 1st Virginia, Colonel Louis B. Williams. G. Moxley Sorrell, later to become an outstanding general staff officer and highly regarded chronicler of the war, then a captain, served as A. P. Hill's assistant adjutant general.

Arriving on the field under heavy artillery fire, Hill characteristically made a personal reconnaissance which disclosed that Wilcox's sector was in need of reinforcement. Wilcox, after coordinating with Hill, opened a counter-attack designed to disrupt Federal attempts to mass in such force as to overrun Fort Magruder and resume the advance. Hill hurled Kemper's regiment into a frontal supporting assault. It was the first close-range fighting in which the men had engaged but they plunged in without hesitation. The training and discipline so patiently inculcated into his troops now paid their first dividends. The men charged with a cheer and then methodically pushed back the Union

[7] *Official Records of the Union and Confederate Armies* (hereinafter called *O.R.*) 11, Pt. 1, pp. 18, 337.
[8] *Ibid*, pp. 575-579, for Hill's report of the entire action near Fort Magruder.

12

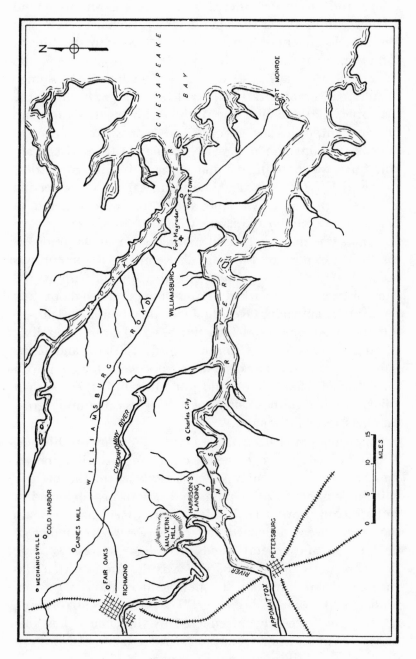

CHESAPEAKE BAY

FORT MONROE

YORK RIVER

YORKTOWN

Fort Magruder

WILLIAMSBURG

WILLIAMSBURG ROAD

JAMES RIVER

Charles City

CHICKAHOMINY RIVER

MECHANICSVILLE

COLD HARBOR

GAINES MILL

HARRISON'S LANDING

MALVERN HILL

FAIR OAKS

RICHMOND

PETERSBURG

APPOMATTOX RIVER

N

0   5   10   15
MILES

MAP 2. THE PENINSULAR CAMPAIGN

13

forces until Kemper ordered a halt at a position behind a fence within 45 yards of the enemy. Colonel Corse's 17th Virginia Regiment was next sent by Hill into the line to form a prolongation of Kemper's left. This regiment also underwent its baptism of close-range fire admirably although it suffered comparatively heavy losses in establishing the new line. Garland and the 11th Virginia then came up on the right. Williams' Brigade had been switched over to Wilcox's command temporarily, so that Hill's entire available force was now in line and engaged in pitched battle.

Powell Hill, for the first time in his career, was directing a brigade in action. Garland and Corse were ordered to open up savagely on the flanks with full firepower.

"Then was the time!" Hill exulted even in the midst of his formal report of the battle.[9] Kemper's Regiment was ordered to charge the center. This the 7th did with all the flamboyance that marked Hill's forces throughout the Peninsular campaign. Over the fence they bounded, led personally by Kemper, and into the heart of the Union line, driving it back. Almost simultaneously Garland and Corse moved out on the flanks. The enemy were forced into a retreat from which they could not rally until they reached a field of felled timber where their reserves came up in great numbers to make a stand.

For two hours Hill's Brigade faced the enemy on this new line at 30 yards' range, each side delivering its full firepower upon the other. Colonel Williams returned to the brigade with his regiment at this point. Now, with his command at full strength, Powell Hill ordered a bayonet charge. Again the enemy were dislodged and driven back. A number of field pieces and several stands of colors as well as some prisoners were the prize of this assault. Ammunition was running short, however; the new gain could not be consolidated for want of firepower. The 17th Virginia, having taken ground recently surrendered by the enemy, was able to obtain ammunition from the cartridge boxes of Northern dead, who, as Hill picturesquely puts it in his report, "were

---

[9] *Ibid*, p. 576.

plentifully and opportunely strewn around." Kemper and Garland, however, were not so fortunate in finding a resupply. They had to withdraw to the point at which they had first overrun the Union line in order to find sufficient fallen enemy to fill their needs.

In the meantime the pressure of superior enemy numbers was rapidly building up. It was clear that the field would soon be untenable. Longstreet ordered a withdrawal; hence the delaying-action task force, its mission accomplished, drew back toward Williamsburg.

When Hill filed his report on May 10 from a new position along the Chickahominy, he characterized the fight as "one of the most obstinately contested battles ever fought." Hill was then new to both battles and report writing. He was to see many engagements far more savagely contested and on a far greater scale. This was the first, however, the baptism of fire; and his enthusiasm is understandable. There was one other statement somewhat gratuitously included in that report to which Hill never ceased to adhere and which keynoted his plans of action throughout the war, at least as long as he commanded a brigade or division in the line. He wrote of the bayonet charge: "The superior nerve and enthusiasm of our men will ever drive them back when the bayonet is resorted to."

Proud as he was of the heroism and exploits of his men, Hill's innate modesty always prevented him from including in his reports any reference to his own individual exploits on the battlefield. At Williamsburg, for example, he engaged in hand-to-hand combat with the enemy. On two occasions he personally saved the lives of enlisted soldiers.[10] He didn't hesitate to use his sword in the same manner as he expected his men to employ their bayonets. The *Official Records* do not disclose such incidents, but letters written home by Confederate soldiers are replete with them.

The Fort Magruder phase of the Battle of Williamsburg dwindles into insignificance in the light of subsequent engagements. Hill's total losses amounted to only 326 men,

---

[10] Pollard, *Lee and His Lieutenants,* p. 447.

15

yet this was the heaviest loss among all the Confederate forces engaged at and near Williamsburg. For A. P. Hill, however, it was a victory, a cause for exultation despite his heartfelt regret at the casualty list then looming so high before him. Hill's losses were always to be high, just as his victories were to be many, because the men who fought with A. P. Hill were never out of the thick of battle.

Longstreet paid tribute to A. P. Hill's Brigade in his report on the Williamsburg fighting: "Its organization was perfect throughout the battle and it was marched off the field in as good order as it entered it ."[11] Hill had finally been given his opportunity and he had not failed to grasp it. Recognition was now his. Further promotion was inevitable.

Longstreet was ordered to a position on the Chickahominy near Long Bridge, dividing with Major General Gustavus W. Smith the subordinate command of the army under Johnston. Longstreet took up a position with the bridges across the Chickahominy conveniently to his rear, his headquarters being at Baltimore Cross Roads. The Chickahominy thus was the line of defense upon which the next stand against McClellan would be based.

Johnston now had complete and unquestioned command, although constant interference from Richmond made his lot difficult. The new position was reasonably sound from a tactical standpoint. The York River Railroad supplied the troops from Richmond. The ironclad, *Virginia* (or *Merrimac* as it had previously been known), provided protection at the mouth of the James on the lower side of the peninsula. The control of the James by naval vessels was promptly dissipated, however. In an apparent moment of panic the *Virginia* was scuttled, ostensibly to keep it from falling into Northern hands. Federal gunboats promptly advanced up the James. Although they were repulsed by shore batteries, this sortie indicated that a coordinated Union land and naval advance up the James River and the lower side of the Peninsula could pose a real threat to Richmond.

Between Johnston and Davis an excess of caution now

---

[11] 11 *O.R.*, Pt. 1, p. 567.

prompted plans for a further withdrawal. The concentration on the Chickahominy was, therefore, centered further north along the stream. McClellan's advance guard then began probing across the lower reaches of the Chickahominy near Charles City. This brought the enemy within 10 miles of Richmond. The desperate situation also aroused some overdue activity in the lethargic Confederate Senate. Johnston had been imploring for more major generals to command divisions. Appointments were, at last, forthcoming. They included the two brigadiers who, perhaps more than any others, had distinguished themselves at Williamsburg —Lafayette McLaws and A. P. Hill.[12]

The following orders [13] directed the formation of Powell Hill's new division:

SPECIAL ORDERS,)　　　HDQRS. DEPT.
　　　　　　　　　) OF NORTHERN VIRGINIA,
No. 119　　　　　) *Richmond, Va., May 27, 1862.*

The troops serving under Brig. Gen. J. R. Anderson and Brig. Gen. L. O'B. Branch will form a division, to the command of which Maj. Gen. A. P. Hill is assigned.
By command of General Johnston:

A. P. MASON
Assistant Adjutant General

On this same day, May 27, Charles W. Field's Virginian and Maxcy Gregg's South Carolinian Brigades were also assigned to Hill's Division. These two brigades, with Joseph R. Anderson's Georgians, had formed a provisional division under command of the latter. They had been stationed near Guiney's Station (today spelled Guinea), south of Fredericksburg, keeping an eye on McDowell who, with a corps of some 30,000 men, had been on the point of moving south to augment McClellan's army on the Peninsula. After the threat from McDowell subsided (see below), the three Confederate brigades marched south, being met en route by orders assigning them to A. P. Hill's Division. At this time

---

[12] Hill assumed command May 27, 1862. 11 *O.R.,* Pt. 3, p. 554.
[13] *Ibid,* p. 555.

17

they were in the vicinity of Hanover Junction.[14] Branch's Brigade had previously been attached to Ewell's Division of Stonewall Jackson's Valley command. On May 27 it had just been driven back in an engagement with part of Fitz John Porter's V Corps (Federal) and was in reserve west of Hanover Court House. This gave Hill four brigades, three of which were comparatively fresh and inexperienced, and one (Branch's North Carolina Brigade) which had just been roughly handled in battle.

At about this time General Joseph E. Johnston decided to overwhelm McClellan's right flank near Mechanicsville before McDowell could come up as reinforcement to the already very numerous Northern forces facing Richmond. In furtherance of this he ordered Major General G. W. Smith, commanding his left wing, to assemble Whiting's division and Hill's new division in the area northwest of Meadow Bridges,[15] for the purpose of rolling up McClellan's flank by sweeping down the Chickahominy from the northwest. Hill accordingly sent orders to his brigades to march on Ashland, in which vicinity he would join them. Apparently the plans for the attack contemplated a wide envelopment, with Hill on the extreme flank.

On May 28 Johnston learned that the Federal high command, still worried over the threat to Washington posed by Stonewall Jackson, had recalled McDowell. Johnston therefore called off his proposed attack and assigned A. P. Hill the mission of guarding the bridges on the Chickahominy north of Richmond. Hill then ordered Gregg, Anderson, and Field to continue their march south but left Branch where he was for the time being.

On May 31 Johnston launched the divisions of D. H. ("Harvey") Hill, Huger, and Longstreet against the Federal forces on the right. This engagement, called the Battle of

---

[14] *Ibid*, p. 554.

[15] Also called Meadow Bridge. Prior to McClellan's arrival there had been two bridges there, one for the railroad and the other for the highway. Upon the approach of the enemy the Confederates had burned both bridges, which the Federal engineers very obligingly rebuilt then failed to destroy when the Confederates attacked late in June.

Seven Pines, lasted until the following day, when the Confederates returned to their positions inside the defenses of Richmond, having lost 6,100 officers and men as against 5,000 for the Federals. During the confused fighting, in which, to put it charitably, General Smith failed to distinguish himself, Joe Johnston was wounded. Smith was subsequently relieved and later resigned. President Jefferson Davis, who had long been at odds with Johnston, immediately replaced him with General Robert E. Lee. Lee had had no command, being military adviser to the Confederate Government.

Powell Hill, not involved in the Seven Pines engagement, was already busily reorganizing his brigades and welding them into a division. He decided to call his new command the Light Division, the first dispatch bearing this heading being dated June 1, 1862.[16] There is no record as to exactly why this unique name was selected; it was unusual because the other divisions, and most of the brigades, were designated by the names of their commanders. It is possible that Hill had in mind a title which would differentiate his division from that of Daniel Harvey Hill. Also, being a student of military history, he may have been inspired by the British Light Brigade, which eight years before had made itself immortal by its gallant charge at Balaclava, in the Crimea. It is even more reasonable to suppose that Powell intended, by means of the name "Light Division," to set up a *leitmotiv* for his unit—one which would epitomize its characteristics of being nimble footed, fast marching, hard hitting. One member of the division remarked later, and somewhat wryly, "We are lightly armed, lightly fed, but march rapidly, fight frequently!" [17]

Be that as it may, the name was a happy one. It seems to have captured the fancy of the Southern press, who gave much excellent publicity to the new unit. Perhaps Hill was shrewd enough to have foreseen this.

---

[16] 11 *O.R.*, Pt. 3, p. 567.
[17] *Battlefields of the South*. By an English combatant. New York, John Bradburn, 1864. Pp. 307-320.

Contemporary reports and maps show only in a general way the initial location of the Light Division. General G. W. Smith's account [18] indicates that on May 30 it was south of the Chickahominy and between the Meadow Bridge Road and Brook Turnpike. In the succeeding days Hill's brigades, moving down from the north, were assigned sectors along the river. Field was near Meadow Bridges.[19] Gregg, followed by Anderson and Field, had reached the Richmond area "without any injury except stiff joints and the loss of some superfluous baggage." [20] Gregg camped at Smith's farm, west of Nine Mile Road, while Anderson apparently occupied that portion of the line between Gregg and Field. On June 11 Hill directed Branch to move down from the Hanover Court House area and occupy a new camp site west of Brook Turnpike, some 3½ miles north of the outskirts of Richmond. This placed Branch's Brigade on the left flank of the division. On this same day General Lee transferred to the Light Division two additional brigades, William Dorsey Pender's and James J. Archer's, which, under Magruder had participated in the Battle of Seven Pines (also called Fair Oaks). These units were placed on the right of Gregg, connecting up with Magruder's left at about the line of earthworks at Mrs. Price's farm.[21] The foregoing reconstruction of events establishes the initial location of the Light Division, about as shown on Map 3.

In the meantime, General Lee on June 2 had assembled all the division and brigade commanders at a place called "The Chimneys" near the scene of the fighting which had just been concluded.[22] This gave him an opportunity to meet his general officers and to brief them on his general plans for further operations. He announced that no further retreat toward Richmond would be made, that the mission of the newly named Army of Northern Virginia would be

---

[18] *Battles and Leaders of the Civil War.* Century Co., N.Y., 1884, Vol. 2, p. 227.
[19] *Ibid*, p. 277.
[20] Caldwell, *op. cit.*, p. 10.
[21] 11 *O.R.*, Pt. 3, pp. 591-2.
[22] Maurice, *An Aide-de-Camp of Lee.* Comprising an edition of the papers of Col. Charles Marshall of Lee's staff. P. 77.

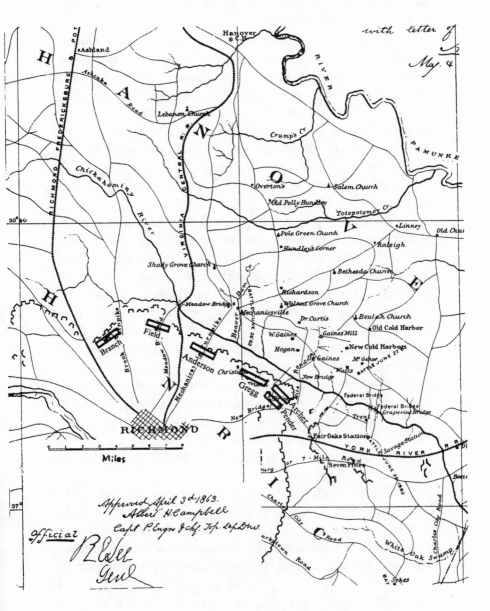

MAP 3. LOCATION OF A. P. HILL'S BRIGADES IN JUNE, 1862

aggressive. Pending a resumption of the offensive, Lee ordered a line somewhat in advance of the present front, to be laid out and fortified.

In furtherance of this plan, Lee directed his Chief of Engineers, Major W. H. Stevens, to reconnoiter for the location of the new line and to form a corps of pioneers consisting of 300 men from each division to commence work on it. He also pointed out that the enemy was capable of bringing up siege artillery via the Richmond and York Railroad. Orders were issued to improvise some howitzers on flatcars to oppose any such move, pending the construction, under the Navy Department, of armored heavy guns mounted on railway cars.

Lee then took steps to improve the condition and morale of his army. He pointed out to the Quartermaster General that few of the units had tentage, that the men were throwing blankets—certainly not waterproof—over rails in lieu of tents. He wished to have shelter tents, or at least tent flies, made and issued. Special attention was paid to the problem of desertion. The ration was augmented. It was directed that "whiskey rations be issued by division commanders when deemed essential to the health of the men from inclemency of the weather or exposure in the swamps." That the weather was quite inclement is indicated by the fact that it soon became necessary to reinforce the provost guard in Richmond by special "flying squads" of cavalry to arrest drunks and to return AWOL's to their commands.[23]

A. P. Hill, taking his cue from General Lee, as well as following his own convictions, spent the next three weeks in reorganizing and refitting his brigades and regiments. Replacements were secured for those units which had been depleted by the recent fighting, administration and discipline were tightened up, and attention was given to all the numerous minor details necessary in the establishment of a first-rate fighting outfit. In those days—before the era of Plans and Training Officers, Army Training Programs,

---

[23] 11 *O.R.*, Pt. 3, pp. 571, 573, 574, 577, 585.

22

and supervised instruction—little attention was paid to formal training except for a certain amount of close-order drill. As the troops generally maneuvered and fought in close order, such drill was beneficial, even if inadequate as a substitute for a complete training program.

It might have been worthwhile to have had some target practice. Very little musketry had been taught in the "old Army," however, and there was no time and little ammunition available for it after the war started. Lee directed that all extra ammunition in possession of the men be turned in to prevent loss. No great harm probably resulted from this lack of practice firing, for most of the Southern boys were accustomed to the use of firearms. As a country boy said, with a grin, "Why, I used to have to get my supper with a rifle." Furthermore, in battle, most firing was done at very short, almost point-blank, range, and delivered on command by battalion or regimental volleys. In this kind of work many Confederate soldiers at first were convinced that a shotgun loaded with buckshot was the surest and most deadly weapon. Many of them were so armed. Others had a variety of rifles, smoothbores, and ancient fowling pieces. A few had been issued muskets made at the former U.S. Arsenal at Fayetteville, North Carolina. It was only later that they were able to re-equip themselves with more up-to-date weapons, many obtained from the enemy.

Health conditions were poor by modern standards. Sanitation in the field was very inadequate. It was not then known that many diseases, thought to be inevitable in military camps, were transmitted by flies and other insects, and by impure water, food, and milk. Dysentery was common, as was malaria. Most of the men sooner or later contracted childhood diseases such as mumps, measles, and chicken pox, if they had not already had them before entering the army. Vaccination against small pox, however, had been practiced since the Revolutionary War. Malaria was not attributed to the mosquito, but to "miasma" from the swamps.

Still, the fact that the men were outdoors, and were working hard throwing up earthworks, as well as performing arduous picket duty distant from their base camps, kept them reasonably hard and fit. Observers visiting the front commented in glowing terms on the excellent condition of Hill's division. As one of the brigade historians wrote, "Our unit was large, well drilled, thoroughly disciplined, and in the highest spirits." [24]

[24] Caldwell, *op. cit.*, p. 10.

CAPTAIN AMBROSE POWELL HILL, 1ST U.S. ARTILLERY

National Archives
LIEUTENANT GENERAL JAMES
LONGSTREET
Commanding the First Corps, Army of
Northern Virginia.

Library of Congress
GENERAL ROBERT E. LEE
Commanding the Army of Northern
Virginia.

Valentine Museum
MAJOR GENERAL RICHARD H. ANDERSON
Commanding a division under Hill,
later a corps.

Library of Congress
LIEUTENANT GENERAL THOMAS J.
JACKSON
Commanding the Second Corps, Army
of Northern Virginia.

MAJOR GENERAL A. P. HILL

Commanding the Light Division, later the Third Corps.

BRIGADIER GENERAL JAMES J. ARCHER

BRIGADIER GENERAL JOSEPH R. ANDERSON

BRIGADIER GENERAL WILLIAM DORSEY PENDER

BRIGADIER GENERAL L. O'BRIEN BRANCH

BRIGADIER GENERAL MAXCY GREGG

BRIGADIER GENERAL CHARLES W. FIELD

BRIGADIER GENERAL HENRY HETH

COLONEL R. LINDSAY WALKER
Artillery Commander of the Light
Division.

National Archives

National Archives

BRIGADIER GENERAL EDWARD L. THOMAS   MAJOR GENERAL CADMUS M. WILCOX

Library of Congress

Valentine Museum

BRIGADIER GENERAL JAMES H. LANE   BRIGADIER GENERAL G. MOXLEY SORREL

Valentine Museum

BRIGADIER GENERAL SAMUEL McGOWAN

Valentine Museum

BRIGADIER GENERAL W. W. KIRKLAND

National Archives

MAJOR GENERAL WILLIAM MAHONE

Valentine Museum

BRIGADIER GENERAL ABNER PERRIN

BRIGADIER GENERAL A. M. SCALES

BRIGADIER GENERAL H. H. WALKER

BRIGADIER GENERAL JOHN R. COOKE

BRIGADIER GENERAL JOSEPH R. DAVIS

CHAPTER 2

The Brigades and
Their Commanders

*B*Y MID JUNE the organization of the Light Division had been completed, and was as shown on the accompanying table. Owing to the Confederate slipshod manner of maintaining strength records and rendering returns, it is virtually impossible to determine the strength of any unit accurately. The Light Division probably had some 23,000 officers and men on its rolls at this time, with 14,000 of them listed as "effectives" —possibly 15,000.[1] The strength of the brigades varied. Gregg's Brigade was said to have had 5,000 present and absent, of whom only about 3,000 were fit for duty.[2] Branch's Brigade, also stated to have been unusually large, could muster only 870 rifles. Archer reports that there were 1,228 in his brigade at the Battle of Mechanicsville. Some of the other brigades were smaller, others larger. In any event, the new division was the largest in the army, even upon the basis of "effectives." The orders assigning the brigades to Hill, having been issued within a two-week period, chronology of their respective appearances in the story of the Light Division is of little meaning.

Field's Brigade consisted of three Virginia regiments— the 40th, 55th, and 60th—which had not yet been tested in battle despite their service near Fredericksburg; and the 47th which, as part of Pettigrew's Brigade, had fought at

---

[1] *Numbers and Losses in the Civil War*, by Thomas L. Livermore. Indiana University Press, Bloomington, 1957 (reprint of 1900 book). See also 11 *O.R.*, Pt. 3, p. 645.

[2] Caldwell, *op. cit.*, p. 8.

25

Seven Pines on May 31-June 1, and then had been transferred to Field on June 11 when Pettigrew's Brigade was broken up. The first three were assigned to A. P. Hill on May 27.

Charles W. Field had something in common with Powell Hill. They shared a Culpeper heritage. Field's father was born in Culpeper where the family had lived for several generations.[3] Charles, however, was born in Woodford County, Kentucky, where the family had migrated shortly before his birth in 1828. The elder Field made some good political connections in Kentucky, including one with Henry Clay. It was through the intervention of Andrew Jackson, during the presidency of Polk, that Charlie was appointed to West Point in 1845. After graduation from the Academy in 1849, he served as a second lieutenant of cavalry in the Indian campaigns of the West. Later he was in the Second Cavalry of which Colonel Albert Sidney Johnston was commander with Lieutenant Colonel Robert E. Lee second in command. In 1856 Field was assigned to the United States Military Academy as chief cavalry instructor. He was serving in that capacity with the rank of captain at the beginning of 1861. As the inevitability of war developed, he resigned and went to offer his services to the Confederacy. Although he was a Kentuckian, destiny brought him back to the state of his ancestry where he was placed in command of an all-Virginian brigade.

While serving under A. P. Hill in the Second Manassas campaign, he was severely wounded, losing a leg. He was confined to his bed for nearly a year, but managed to get back into military harness, serving in Longstreet's corps until Appomattox. During the last days of the war he appeared as a spectacular division commander, engaging the enemy in a number of surprisingly successful skirmishes right up to the final surrender. Field was something of a jolly character who afforded Powell Hill considerable amusement at times when the stress of battle, interspersed with

---

[3] Edwin A. Pollard, *"Lee and His Lieutenants,"* p. 520, et seq affords a colorful, although somewhat inaccurate, biography of Field.

26

TABLE OF
ORGANIZATION OF A. P. HILL'S LIGHT DIVISION*

FIRST BRIGADE
Brig. Gen. C. W. Field
40th Virginia, Col J. M. Brockenbrough
47th Virginia, Col. R. M. Mayo
55th Virginia, Col. Francis Mallory
60th Virginia, Col. W. E. Starke

SECOND BRIGADE
Brig. Gen. M. Gregg
1st South Carolina, Col. D. H. Hamilton
12th South Carolina, Col. Dixon Barnes
13th South Carolina, Col. O. E. Edwards
14th South Carolina, Col. Samuel McGowan
1st South Carolina Rifles, Col. J. F. Marshall

THIRD BRIGADE
Brig. Gen. Joseph R. Anderson
14th Georgia, Lieut. Col. R. W. Folsom
35th Georgia, Col. Edward L. Thomas
45th Georgia, Col. Thomas Hardeman
49th Georgia, Col. A. J. Lane
3d Louisiana Battalion, Lieut. Col. Edmund Pendleton

FOURTH BRIGADE
Brig. Gen. L. O'B. Branch
7th North Carolina, Col. R. P. Campbell
18th North Carolina, Col. R. H. Cowan
28th North Carolina, Col. J. H. Lane
33d North Carolina, Lieut. Col. R. F. Hoke
37th North Carolina, Col. Chas. C. Lee

FIFTH BRIGADE
Brig. Gen. J. J. Archer
5th Alabama Battalion, Capt. A.S. Van de Graaf
19th Georgia, Lieut. Col. T. C. Johnson
1st Tennessee, Lieut. Col. J. C. Schackleford
7th Tennessee, Col. J. F. Goodner
14th Tennessee, Col. W. A. Forbes

SIXTH BRIGADE
Brig. Gen. W. D. Pender
2d Arkansas Battalion, Maj. W. N. Bronaugh
16th North Carolina, Lieut. Col. J. S. McElroy
22d North Carolina, Col. James Conner
34th North Carolina, Col. R. H. Riddick
38th North Carolina, Col. W. J. Hoke
22d Virginia Battalion, Capt. J. C. Johnson

ARTILLERY
Lieut. Col. Lewis M. Coleman†

Maryland Battery, Capt. R. S. Andrews
South Carolina (German) Battery, Capt. W. K. Bachman
Virginia Battery (Fredericksburg), Capt. C. M. Braxton
Virginia Battery, Capt. W. G. Crenshaw
Virginia Battery (Letcher), Capt. G. Davidson
Virginia Battery, Capt. Marmaduke Johnson
Master's Battery, Capt. L. Masters
South Carolina Battery (Pee Dee), Capt. D. G. McIntosh
Virginia Battery (Purcell), Capt. W. J. Pegram

---

* *Battles and Leaders,* 2, pp. 316, 317. For the organization on July 23, 1862, see 11, *O.R.,* Pt. 3, pp. 649-50.
† Coleman was temporarily in place of Major R. Lindsay Walker, absent sick.

27

Hill's bickering with Jackson, kept his nerves under constant strain. Field was the type of man to arouse the comic-actor instinct in others. Just before the Second Manassas campaign, Jeb Stuart, with Fitz Lee and some of their troopers, in a daring raid captured Pope's plumed hat and great cloak. Lee observed Field and his staff riding down the road a short while later. Fitz went into the bushes, put on Pope's hat and cloak, and rushed out to hail Field with grandiose gestures. Field led the others in an uproar of laughter that lasted for minutes and provided a mirth-provoking story for many months thereafter.[4]

Field was a good "professional" of the type that Powell Hill liked to have in his command, although he certainly never disparaged the work of that great "amateur," Maxcy Gregg. The popular "Charlie," as he became generally known among the troops, later proved his worth as a military authority and as a hail-fellow-well-met type of politician. He spent part of his postwar life as Inspector General of the Egyptian Army, and the rest of it in various political posts in the United States, including that of doorkeeper of the House of Representatives. Hill appreciated Field. He later experienced more difficulty in successfully filling his place than he did in the case of any other brigadier vacancy in the history of the division.

May 27 was also the date upon which Maxcy Gregg and his then untried South Carolinians were ordered to Powell Hill's embryonic command. Maxcy Gregg was a scholarly lawyer from Columbia, South Carolina. He was a bachelor, forty-seven years old, and slightly deaf. Undoubtedly he would have enjoyed a long and fruitful career in law and politics. A man of courtly manners, and being of considerable wealth, he had established himself in a comfortable, bookish way of life. He owned slaves and believed in the institution of slavery. He was regarded as an authority on ornithology, astronomy, and other scientific subjects. But when the war came, he felt all the passionate devotion to the new cause that stamped all South Carolinians. He gave

---

[4] *Battles and Leaders,* Vol. 2, p. 528 (story by Major Roy Mason).

up everything he held dear when he left Columbia as a colonel of the 1st South Carolina volunteer regiment, which he organized himself. He lacked prior active military service although he had held a commission during the Mexican War. He probably was no braver than other men of his age and substance who found different ways of serving. He was, however, so charged with patriotism that only the vigorous action of combat could make him feel that he was offering his best upon the altar of his cause. He became a savage fighter on the battlefield but at all other times maintained his gentle calm. He imbued all who were privileged to know him with a feeling of confidence on the eve of battle, and produced a soothing effect on the taut nerves of the men who surrounded him.

Gregg was one of the two officers who would always be welcome intruders upon Powell Hill's loneliness as a division commander. The other was William Dorsey Pender. Hill was by nature convivial, but his position tended to isolate him. There were many evenings of quiet talk while Gregg and Dorsey Pender joined their chief in a late pipe. Gregg's death at Fredericksburg was probably more of a personal blow to Hill than the loss of any other of his officers. There were none whom Hill eulogized with greater sincerity in his official reports.[5]

The regiments of Gregg's South Carolina Brigade had been raised near Columbia in July 1861, trained in that area for three months, then sent to the coast near Pocotagligo where the brigade was organized. In April 1862 it was sent by rail to Virginia, joining J. R. Anderson's provisional division in the Fredericksburg area. On May 24 the unit moved toward Richmond by rail and marching, finally joining the Light Division on May 30, as previously described. Prior to this time the men had never been in battle.

Pender's Brigade, which joined the Light Division about two weeks after Gregg's and Field's, came from several sources. It was organized as a brigade in June 1862, shortly

⁵ 21, *O.R.*, p. 646.

after Pender was made a brigadier general. Hampton's Brigade and Pettigrew's Brigade had been broken up after the Battle of Seven Pines. Pender's Brigade received the Second Arkansas Battalion and the Twenty-second North Carolina Regiment from Pettigrew's command, although the Arkansas unit was to remain with Pender only for a week. From Hampton's Brigade Pender received the Sixteenth North Carolina. Both of these Tarheel regiments had been organized near Raleigh in June 1861 and were shipped to Richmond the following month. Here the men caught their first sight of Robert E. Lee, who a year later was to become their army commander. Their impression is worth relating:

> His (Lee's) person was the finest we had ever seen. There was only a bold hint of silver in his hair. His eye, lustrous and clear as a mountain brooklet, seemed in its normal line of vision never to fall below the distant horizon, and yet our souls were pierced by the mingled pathos and nobility of his look. He was the most magnificent horseman we had ever seen; the most perfect citizen-soldier and the manliest man. The General had his field glass and was making a survey of the surrounding country, when a member of the 16th North Carolina, a shrewd, inimitable fellow, stepped up to him and, paying the usual homage, promptly asked him for a chew of tobacco. General Lee as promptly turned to a member of his staff, who supplied the much coveted quid. [6]

This incident, aside from its somewhat florid description, is indicative of the graciousness of Lee, who despite a manner always dignified, possessed the common touch and thus won the hearts of his men. He was no "stuffed shirt."

After being moved frequently during the winter of 1861-62, these two regiments were sent to the Peninsula in April, participated in the fighting during the withdrawal from Williamsburg, and finally were in the Battle of Seven Pines. The other two regiments, the Thirty-fourth and the Thirty-eighth North Carolina, after being organized during the

---

[6] *North Carolina Regiments,* Vol. 1, pp. 751-769; Vol. 2, pp. 21, 161, 466 ff, 582, 662.

summer of 1861, spent the winter in training near Raleigh and High Point, being sent to the Richmond area in the spring of 1862. They had not been in battle prior to joining Pender's Brigade.

William D. Pender was born and brought up in Edgecombe County, North Carolina.[7] At the outbreak of war he was in his twenty-eighth year. He had graduated from West Point in 1854, spending the next six years with the Army in the West. As in the case of Powell Hill, romance blossomed for Dorsey Pender in the late 1850's, but he seems to have been one of the few handsome, eligible young officers who never became involved in the pursuit of the affections of Nellie Marcy. He had a friendship of some year's standing with Mary Frances Shepperd of Salem, North Carolina. Friendship turning to love, they were married in 1859. Between them developed perhaps the closest bonds of any couple that would pass through the ordeals of the coming years, bonds that would be broken only by the fatal wound that Dorsey would suffer at Gettysburg before he reached his thirtieth birthday. The almost daily letters that he wrote to his beloved Fanny attested the sincerity and depth of his devotion.

In 1861, however, the Penders were just another Army couple with a baby. Neither was from a slave-holding family. Neither had the passionate love of state that constantly flamed in the hearts of Virginians. It was probably as much sheer geography, together with exposure to the Southern viewpoint as any sense of burning conviction of the right of the cause which he determined to follow, that brought Dorsey Pender into the Confederate fold. He had considered the problem carefully. He talked it over with other Army officers, some from the North, who were to remain loyal to the Washington Government, and some from the South to whom the conception of secession became an exciting tonic. He wrote to Fanny when duty took him away during this transition period, frankly stating his doubts as to what to do, as well as expressing the views of his

[7] *William Dorsey Pender Papers,* courtesy University of North Carolina.

colleagues who urged him to follow their respective paths. His family and Fanny's, however, were caught up in the whirlpool of secession. Not as violently, perhaps, as families in the adjoining states of Virginia and South Carolina, but, nevertheless, sufficiently to communicate to Dorsey the feeling that the exercise of his loyalty to his native land would best be served by adherence to the Confederacy. The Southern cause would, he realized, embrace his kin by blood and marriage and his home. The Confederacy would include the countryside that he knew. It would be supported by the neighbors among whom he had grown up, who had cheered his departure to West Point, and who welcomed him home on his leaves from the Army.

So it was that, even before the final die was cast, Dorsey Pender slipped into Maryland and began unobstrusively to recruit men for the Confederacy. In early March he reported to the new headquarters at Montgomery, Alabama, where he was commissioned a captain of "regulars" in the Confederate Army. The system of state autonomy that was always to hamper the proper organization of the Southern Army, however, brought him back to Raleigh in March, where he was appointed a lieutenant colonel of volunteers. It might have been that he first entered the Confederacy's service with something of personal indifference. Now, however, he was a dedicated adherent to the cause.

It seems that, regardless of the manner in which West Pointers of all ages joined the South, or the reasons which they had for breaking their allegiance to the Stars and Stripes, the men who took that course without exception immediately went all out in every respect in behalf of their new government and the "bonnie blue flag" which was its first emblem. Just as Lee hastened to expound his views of strategy to the heads of the new civil government, and as A. P. Hill was to vehemently exhort the governor of Virginia a few months later, Dorsey Pender did not hesitate to publicly criticize Governor Ellis of North Carolina for not keeping pace with his rapidly quickening pulse for a strong and determined course of action.

Pender had been commissioned a lieutenant colonel by Governor Ellis in late April. By early May he was finding fault with the governor for what he felt was inaction and niggardliness. He spoke publicly to his fellow officers and to the troops on the subject. From his recruiting and training station at Raleigh, he wrote his views to his wife in no uncertain terms, expressing not only his criticism of Ellis, but his opinion as to a flaw in the makeup of North Carolinians generally:

> If they do not act soon North Carolina is a ruined state. Everyone readily admits that we are totally deficient in military preparedness and that the volunteers are bad at the best. I am disgusted with North Carolina and am convinced that nothing can be done until we are badly whipped. Governor Ellis got $300,000 appropriated last session to buy munitions of war and after getting it has only spent $27,000, having the state withhold powder enough to fight half of our battles and if we did not have the arms that have been taken, we would have hardly enough to arm a company. I have told you often that we as a people, and in many cases as individuals, are too mean to spend money. The Governor is very much blamed for not having spent the money for arms. I have never seen a public officer so mean in money matters. Even now, any proposal that is made, that involves the outlay of a few dollars, is answered by the reply, it will cost too much.

The carefree young officer of the 1850's was becoming an embittered partisan in the spring of 1861. Good natured, easygoing in his personal life, affectionate toward his family almost to a fault, Dorsey Pender early in the war became a tough fighting man. He was an unrelenting champion of his new cause, who would not hesitate to throw barbs at his superiors if he felt they were remiss in their duties. He would, however, never express serious criticism of the general under whom he would serve during practically all of his military career and whom he and Harry Heth would eventually succeed as commanders of the troops who constituted A. P. Hill's Light Division.

Dorsey Pender stood loyally with Powell Hill through

the bitter battles that followed those days of decision in the spring of 1861.

As in the case of Hill, Pender's early years had remained free from effective religious influence. Dorsey did not have Powell's formal Episcopalian background. Nor did he have to go through a period of anything like the fanaticism that engulfed the Hill family when Powell's mother became a Baptist disciple. Young Powell Hill, years before, seemed to have developed an inner resistance to open and formal manifestations of religion which stayed with him until his death. It prompted him to exhibit something akin to contempt at Jackson's rather ostentatious demonstrations of piety, as when Stonewall refused to engage in battle on the Sabbath at Savage Station.[8]

Pender's early indifference to religion was, therefore, a different proposition from Hill's seeming antagonism to churchly ritual. Dorsey did not develop the chip-on-shoulder attitude that marked Powell. He was, as a result, more responsive to the religious urges and the thirst for divine help and guidance that in all wars have developed among soldiers who in peacetime were little more than perfunctory in church attendance or private prayer. Pender reached such a point of devoutness by October 1861 that he arranged for his baptism in the sight of his entire regiment. This occasion seemed to start a ground swell of religious revival that spread through the entire army.

Hill was never anything but God fearing despite his dislike of religious show and ceremony. Robert E. Lee, a devout man, was pleased to be asked to be godfather to one of the Hill children during the dark latter days of the war. He would not have done this for an ungodly family. The fact remains, however, that Hill never had any interest in encouraging religious observance among his troops. So it was somewhat ironical that Pender, his best known lieutenant, did as much as anyone to spark the religious flame that blazed through Southern camps until the very end at Appomattox four years later.

---

[8] See Chapter 5, infra.

34

Dorsey Pender turned out to be a resourceful soldier upon whom Hill increasingly relied in battle. His religious influence upon his chief was more subtle. It was nevertheless present. Hill was free with profanity. He did not kneel in prayer on the eve of battle as has been the custom of many great soldiers of many creeds in many armies. He did, however respect the right of his men to take time to worship. He never tried to discourage them. He became a friend of the chaplains who served with him.[9] In all this he was guided, consciously or not, by the example which Dorsey Pender constantly set him. Hill probably ridiculed Jackson's devoutness because he didn't like Jackson as a man, although he demonstrated respect for him as a military strategist on many occasions. Dorsey Pender's presence during the bloody days to follow often caused Hill to hold in check his scorn for the demonstratively religious Jackson.

Then there was the occasion when Hill looked into Jackson's tent on the eve of Chancellorsville. Observing Stonewall on his knees praying, he turned with a somewhat contemptuous smile to Ewell, who was accompanying him to receive orders for the following day, and remarked caustically, "There goes Jackson praying again."

Pender would probably have dropped to his knees and joined Jackson. On the other hand, he would not have criticized Hill's conduct. Dorsey understood Hill probably better than any of his contemporaries. He knew that Hill swore somewhat excessively and drank occasionally to the limits of moderation. But he felt these were actions of a sensitive, high-strung personality, and a negative reaction to the overdoses of religious medicine to which he had been subjected in his youth. He knew that there was not a trace of spiritual weakness in the man who would lead him and the others of the Light Division during the following months that were to be the most soul testing of any ever experienced on the North American continent. Pender followed Hill into battle with a respect that he could never feel for Stonewall Jackson, a man whose outward views

[9] Rev. J. William Jones several times mentions Hill favorably.

and manifestations of religion nevertheless coincided closely with his own.

Pender initially was a stranger to both Hill and Jackson that first spring of the Confederacy. Just as the two older men threw themselves into their troop-training chores under Johnston, Pender was engaged in like duties with North Carolinians at Garysburg, North Carolina. By late May, however, he was ordered into Virginia, nearer the lines of battle. He wrote to Fanny of his love for her and his longing for their son Turner. But, like Hill and Jackson, Dorsey Pender was now champing at the bit for action and the promotion that success would bring. The inexorable finger of destiny was already pointing to the paths that would bring these three men together in their brightest and darkest hours. The journey would not be long before the first great climax in their relationship was reached. The last name that Jackson would mention in his lifetime would be A. P. Hill's. Stonewall's last battlefield order would be to Pender.

Branch's Brigade, one of the four to comprise Hill's original division command under orders dated May 27, was mustered into the service in Alamance County, North Carolina, in August 1861. From there it was shipped by rail to the New Bern area where, on March 31, 1862, it participated in the Battle of New Bern. Early in May it went by rail to Richmond, thence to the Shenandoah Valley where it joined Jackson's command and was attached to Ewell.[10] On May 27th the brigade got its first heavy engagement at Slash Church, near Hanover Court House. Although Branch commanded the largest brigade in the army at that time, he found himself overmatched in confronting an entire Union division. This battle was as severe a test as the baptism of fire of Hill's Brigade at Williamsburg. Branch handled an impossible situation adroitly but eventually was forced to withdraw before overwhelming numbers. His

---

[10] *N. C. Regts.*, Vol. 1, p. 362.

losses were heavy, but his troops so hurt the Northern division opposing them that there was no immediate pursuit. Branch's Brigade was thus enabled to withdraw in good order towards its designated reserve position. While marching toward that area on the afternoon of the 27th, Branch received his orders to join A. P. Hill. He reported personally to his new commander at once, leaving his unit at Ashland.[11]

The two generals met at a place called Stony Run,[12] apparently on Brook Turnpike near Yellow Tavern. Branch instinctively liked Hill, but he could not repress a faint flicker of amusement at the latter's uniform. Powell was wearing a bright red hunting shirt. On his head was a rather ornately decorated kepi of the French style. His legs were encased in hip-length, soft leather boots. The kepi was not unusual headgear for Confederate officers, though later in the war it was generally replaced by slouch hats. Lee early adopted the hat for field wear, and most of the other generals followed suit—except Stonewall Jackson. A. P. Hill, somewhat like Jeb Stuart, loved to dress colorfully. The red shirt was his trademark, dating back to the Mexican War. Although he usually wore it only in action, he donned it for the present meeting with his brigade commanders, as being the distinguishing feature by which they could readily recognize him on the battlefield. The uniform had a striking effect, as was intended by Hill.

Powell Hill, who, except when in temper, habitually wore a slight, pleasant smile, was laughing when he shook hands with Branch. Branch saw him as a man of medium height, neatly built, with a full brown beard which had a reddish tinge. His rather long hair was of the same hue. Although of average size, Hill was often referred to as "Little" A. P. Hill. He sat his horse gracefully, erect and military in his bearing at all times. His face had always been thin, but at this time was not as gaunt as it later became, when his liver ailment, aggravated by the rigors of campaign, troubled

<hr>

[11] For Branch's report of this action, see 11 *O.R.*, Pt. 1, pp. 740-42.
[12] 11 *O.R.*, Pt. 3, p. 554.

him more seriously. He was generally described as being a handsome man.[13]

Lawrence O'Brien Branch (called familiarly by his middle name) was a mature gentleman of forty-one, a Princeton graduate who had entered the Confederate Army from civil life. A former congressman from North Carolina, he had early organized a volunteer brigade, of which he retained command until he was killed at Antietam. Although not a professional soldier, he did well as a commander, and was highly regarded by Hill. His early photographs taken when his unit was formed show him to have been a fine-looking man with a small spade beard which, however, he later shaved off.

Branch kept a journal in which he occasionally expressed his matter-of-fact views of things he did not like. He felt that his troops were constantly short of rest, despite A. P. Hill's intense efforts to make the men of the Light Division the best cared for in the Army. He blamed the situation on Jackson. Stonewall was credited with "traveling light," thus enabling him to make the fast marches for which he was noted. Branch said the supposition that Jackson carried very little baggage was not true. "I think he carries too much," wrote O'Brien. "The secret of the celerity with which he moves is that he spends very little time in camps." Branch knew that Jackson was a great battle leader, however, and he never failed him, rested or tired, although he would have preferred to see the higher command in the hands of his popular immediate superior, A. P. Hill.

James J. Archer's Brigade joined A. P. Hill pursuant to orders from the new commanding general, Robert E. Lee, on June 11th. The three regiments constituting the basis of Archer's Brigade had been formed in Ten-

---

[13] One interested in obtaining a pen picture of Hill must search diligently through numerous obscure sources. Even Dr. William J. Jones, a lifelong friend who delivered a eulogy of Hill at the establishment of his statue, is content to say, "It seems but yesterday that I saw in Culpeper and Washington the young artillery officer whom I so much admired,"—without giving particulars. *Confederate Veteran*, 1, pp. 233-36.

nessee in May 1861 and grouped as a brigade under Colonel (later Brigadier General) Robert Hatton, a former politician. After a short service in West Virginia the brigade was briefly under Stonewall Jackson in the upper Shenandoah. Following Manassas it became a part of Joseph E. Johnston's army, participating in the retreat from Yorktown. In the Battle of Seven Pines it suffered severely. One regiment, the Seventh, sustained casualties of fifty percent, including eight of its ten company commanders. General Hatton was killed, being replaced a few days later by Brigadier General James J. Archer, formerly colonel of the Fifth Texas of Hood's Brigade. The brigade was so greatly depleted by its losses and by sickness that General Lee added to it the 5th Alabama Battalion and the 19th Georgia Regiment, the latter having been a part of Hampton's Brigade which had also fought at Seven Pines. So much filling and reorganization of the brigade was necessary that General Lee, in assigning it to A. P. Hill on June 11, suggested that it be given only light duty initially.[14]

Archer, the second oldest of Hill's brigadiers, was forty-five years of age and a seasoned Regular Army veteran. He had fought in Mexico and had served many years in the United States Army as a captain. Like Powell Hill, he had been the victim of the sluggish promotion system in the peacetime service. His resentment at the conditions which had apparently ruined his career by leaving him stalemated as a captain at forty-three, was instrumental in bringing him into the Confederacy. Now, as a brigadier general, he was to demonstrate some real battlefield ability. He was on the firing line under A. P. Hill in every battle of the Light Division until he was taken a prisoner of war at Gettysburg. Exchanged and returned to duty, his constitution, weakened by many months of frontline action, could not withstand the hardships undergone in prison camp. He died shortly after his release.

---

[14] *The Military Annals of Tennessee—Confederate.* Edited by John Berrien Lindsley. J. M. Lindsley & Co., Nashville, 1886. See also 11, *O.R.*, Pt. 3, pp. 569, 574, 589.

While he lived to fight, Archer was a cool, competent, forceful leader. He was not as spectacular as Gregg or Pender, but he had an experienced, professional way of handling his command that made him invaluable to Hill. The scholarly Maxcy Gregg came close to being a fanatic on the field, with the result that his troops attained brilliant, even superhuman, heights in the attack. His losses were correspondingly heavy. Pender, although a professional soldier, lacked Archer's seasoning. Dorsey, too, was a savage offensive fighter. Archer, on the other hand, always maintained a calm sense of balance. When he thought the time was ripe he could lead a charge with the best of them. His all-around generalship was often better than that of the others.

Despite Archer's age and soundness as a tactician, his lack of that peculiar element known as "color," in which Pender so exuberantly abounded, compelled A. P. Hill to make him subordinate to Dorsey in the Light Division's command chain.

Joseph R. Anderson, the commander of the Georgia Brigade, which was the first unit designated in the orders of May 27 to A. P. Hill's command, was a native of Virginia who had graduated from West Point in 1836 and resigned the following year.[15] A competent officer, he had been well regarded by the Confederate War Department from the start. He had first been placed in command of the Wilmington, North Carolina, District and later of the Department of North Carolina.[16] As in the case of every officer and man in the Light Division, he saw plenty of action during the Seven Days, his career coming to a temporary halt when he was wounded at Frayser's Farm on June 30. In this battle he was performing in an outstanding manner at the head of his Georgia brigade when he was incapacitated by what he described as a blow on his forehead. The injury was not serious and he returned to duty shortly after Malvern Hill.

---

[15] *Register of Graduates and Former Cadets, USMA.*
[16] 9, *O.R.*, p. 460.

40

Frayser's Farm, however, was his last battle. He resigned before the next campaign in order to accept assignment as director of the Tredegar Iron Works in Richmond. Production of munitions was already becoming such an important factor in the Confederacy that line officers with experience in heavy manufacturing, such as Anderson possessed, were being returned to their civilian specialties. After the war, Anderson remained in the iron manufacturing business and was extremely successful, acquiring considerable wealth, a rather unusual feat for an industrialist in the post-bellum South.

The six brigades that formed A. P. Hill's proud new division had very little time for training before they were hurled into a week of as savage fighting as any division would see during the war. Some of the troops had yet to receive their baptism of fire. Others, especially some of Archer's and Branch's men, had engaged in heavy battle. All had one thing in common, however. In the short time available, A. P. Hill had succeeded in instilling into them a glowing *esprit de corps*—especially remarkable for a basically green division.

Hill liked his officers. He had strong confidence in them, even in those who lacked combat experience. That confidence was reciprocated by the brigade commanders and flowed down the chains of command through every unit to the privates of the last squad. These soldiers were Southerners, they respected the Southern gentlemen who would lead them, and, being early volunteers for the most part, they had the fervent patriotism that is the best substitute for experience or proper training. Powell Hill knew that the Light Division would be a good one—the best in the army if it got a chance. He knew, furthermore, that with McClellan moving down the Peninsula, ever closer to Richmond, it would soon get that chance.

CHAPTER 3

The First Battle

GENERAL LEE realized, even before he assumed command of the Army of Northern Virginia, that Richmond would not be able to withstand a lengthy siege. Without a steady inflow of such vital necessities as food and ammunition the troops would soon become ineffective. Furthermore, the Federal army was drawing so close that it soon could cause great destruction with its numerous and powerful artillery. The only solution, as Lee saw it, was to take the offensive and drive McClellan away. This was entirely in line with Lee's natural inclinations. He was ever a *fighter,* definitely—in a military sense— offensively minded. Therefore he began to formulate plans to begin an attack as soon as he could concentrate sufficient forces to guarantee a reasonable chance of success.

Lee's plan, not dissimilar from that conceived by Johnston, followed sound military principles. It contained a blueprint for a classical battle of annihilation, and was typical of the boldness which characterized him throughout the war. He proposed to concentrate secretly the bulk of his army, together with the Valley command of Stonewall Jackson, on the west Federal flank. An assault would then be launched with great violence, sweeping down between the Chickahominy and the Pamunkey, rolling up the enemy flank and cutting McClellan's line of communications. The blow would fall initially on the V Corps of Fitz John Porter, which numbered some thirty thousand men and was in a strong position with excellent artillery support. But Porter was separated from the rest of the Army of the Potomac by the Chickahominy, which with its swamps was generally unfordable and over which there were only a few reconstructed bridges.

As a preliminary move, early in June General Lee sent General Jackson instructions to prepare to leave the Valley and come to the Peninsula. Before Jackson was ordered to actually move east, however, Lee had a rumor circulated that Jackson was to advance north against Washington. This rumor was effectively substantiated by sending Whiting's Division from the Peninsula toward the west in an ostentatious manner so that the movement was observed by a number of Union prisoners who were about to be sent north in an exchange. The stratagem worked. The government at Washington and McClellan both went on the assumption that Stonewall would move north and would not figure in the Peninsular campaign. Actually, an order went to Jackson on the 16th to come immediately to the Peninsula. Whiting's forces, of course, after making their feint turned around and headed back toward Richmond with Jackson's men.[1]

General Lee held a conference on June 23 at his headquarters on Nine Mile Road, at which he outlined to his division commanders his plan for the coming operation. Jackson was present, having ridden all night accompanied only by a single orderly. Since the timing of the attack depended almost entirely on the hour at which he could arrive with his command for the jumpoff, Jackson was asked to state when he would be in position for the attack. He replied that he would be ready by the 25th. Longstreet, a little skeptical, urged Jackson to take more leeway; so "daylight on the 26th" was finally determined upon as the time to commence the attack with Jackson in line. Since Jackson was making the main attack, or at least would constitute the hammerhead of the swinging blow, Lee desired to make his force as strong as possible. Therefore the plan called for D. H. Hill to reinforce Jackson. Instead of having D. H. Hill's Division make an exhausting march far around the left to join Jackson in the Ashland area, it was planned to

---

[1] Maurice, *An Aide-de-Camp of Lee*, p. 84.

have him march straight up the Mechanicsville Turnpike and unite with Jackson somewhere to the east of the head-waters of Beaver Dam Creek (see Map 4). Since General Porter's Federal corps was in a fortified position along that stream, the envelopment then would strike Porter's right and rear, possibly forcing him out without the necessity for an all-out assault. Lee envisioned the advance from that point as occurring so swiftly as to cause Porter to recoil across the defiles formed by the crossings over the Chicka-hominy to his rear, and throw the over-cautious McClellan into complete confusion. Upon successful completion of the maneuver annihilation of the Union army would be-come possible.

But D. H. Hill could not hasten up the Mechanicsville Turnpike until the high ground at Mechanicsville was cleared of the reinforced regiment which Porter had sta-tioned there as outposts for his main position back of Beaver Dam Creek. The clearing of Mechanicsville and the approaches to the Federal position was the mission given to A. P. Hill. It was important that Hill's attack be coordi-nated with the advance of Jackson, that it be launched soon enough to accomplish its mission before Jackson arrived north of the creek, but not so far in advance as to "give away the show." It was not desired nor planned that Hill's Division alone make the attack against Porter's strong posi-tion. The idea was that Porter was to be forced out by the arrival of Jackson on his right and rear, combined with frontal pressure exerted by the Light Division. This ex-cellent plan was to be spoiled, however, by Jackson's ex-cessively tardy arrival, by A. P. Hill's premature advance, and by Jackson's failure to attack even when he did arrive.

Longstreet was assigned a less spectacular role in the operation. He was to support A. P. Hill, but was to march in right echelon to the Light Division, not attacking until that division had commenced its assault. In general, the attack was to take place successively from the left: first Jackson (except for A. P. Hill's preliminary clearing of Mechanicsville), then the Light Division, then Longstreet.

This is primarily the story of the Light Division. It is manifestly impossible here to analyze in any detail the grand strategy of the war or even to delve into operations in other sectors of battles in which our spotlight is turned upon Hill and the Light Division. It is equally impossible to attempt anything more than the briefest sketches of the officers with whom Hill came in contact. In the case of the much chronicled Stonewall Jackson it would scarcely be necessary in any event to recount the saga of the man's deeds or to analyze his character. In connection with the great battle that was about to ensue on the Peninsula and which would rage for seven days, however, brief reference might be in order with respect to Jackson's activity in the months preceding this event. His conduct during the early stages of the Seven Days was somewhat enigmatic to say the least, and the background from which he emerged to step upon the stage of the Peninsula might divulge some clues in this respect.

On the face of it, Jackson's Shenandoah Valley campaign had been spectacularly successful. With a force of 17,000 men when at full strength, which it rarely was, Jackson had practically cleared the enemy from the Valley. He was hailed as the "hero of the South," being at the time even more renowned than Lee. He was respected by many of his men but feared by most. While A. P. Hill was beloved by troops who would follow him into any hazard because of their devotion to him, Jackson maintained his leadership upon the basis of fear, engendered by cold, hard discipline. Capital punishment was resorted to by Jackson more often than by any other Confederate officer. One of Stonewall's soldiers later wrote that the first army order read to his company after being attached to Jackson's corps was "the shooting to death by musketry of two men who had stopped on the battlefield to carry off a wounded comrade."[2]

In the Valley Jackson had been almost completely on his own. He mapped and personally directed each campaign.

[2] *Co. Aytch,* by Sam R. Watkins, Private, C.S.A.

He would brook no interference, if he could get away with it, either from Richmond or from officers of equal or higher rank. He drove himself and he drove his officers and men. He was penurious in his praise of subordinates although he did not have the wordly vanity that sought or expected praise for his own deeds. He was deeply religious, perhaps fatalistically so. He placed his entire faith in God and his own ability as a soldier. He was, therefore, resentful of any threatened encroachment of his sovereignty over his command.

This trait of Jackson's character is forcibly illustrated by an incident which occurred on April 3rd while McClellan's invasion of the Peninsula was still in its incipiency. Longstreet, who ranked Jackson, was in command on the Rapidan under conditions analogous to Jackson's authority in the Valley. Old Pete devised a plan to counteract McClellan's move against Richmond which apparently received sanction from the capital provided he could obtain Jackson's cooperation. He sent a note by courier to Jackson suggesting they combine forces for a quick blow toward Washington which, if even partially successful, would cause the usual panic in the Northern capital and would result in withhdrawal of at least part of McClellan's troops. Longstreet insisted in the letter, however, that it was necessary for him personally to accompany the detachment which, it was proposed, would join Jackson.[3] This, of course, meant that Jackson would be outranked on the expedition although he presumably would still be commander of the Valley district. Jackson refused point blank. One report of the incident relates that Stonewall was sucking a lemon when Longstreet's courier gave him the note. According to this source, Jackson read the message without removing the lemon from his mouth and then calmly tore the message to pieces without any comment to the courier or reply to Longstreet.

Regardless of the detailed truth of the aforesaid incident, it was clear that Jackson very much wanted to be in charge of any field upon which he was to be engaged. One other

---

[3] Longstreet, James, *From Manassas to Appomattox*, p. 65.

phase of Jackson's campaigns in the Valley might also be commented upon in appraising his conduct at the outset of the Seven Days' Battle. This was the fact that, although he had been successful in the Shenandoah, his opposition had been pronouncedly second rate. The Union troops in the early Valley campaigns were the poorest the North had to offer. McClellan, the master organizer and drillmaster, was training the best for his own campaign against Richmond. The Union officers in the Shenandoah were as poor as their troops. Headed by Nathaniel Banks, one of Lincoln's less fortunately selected political generals, they included another political appointee, R. H. Milroy, together with a veteran Irish soldier of fortune, James Shields. The latter was the best of an inferior lot by Confederate standards.

It is not intended here to disparage Stonewall Jackson nor to belittle the victories he had already won and those he would win before his all too brief career reached its tragic climax at Chancellorsville the following spring. The point is, however, that the man upon whom all Southern eyes were turned as his troops approached the Richmond front had still not been tested against the Federal's best. And, even more important, he was, for the first time, to act as a cog in a delicately balanced plan of attack requiring the utmost by way of cooperation and coordination. Robert E. Lee commanded the field. Thomas J. Jackson was now cast in a supporting role which, as far as the new campaign was concerned, did not predominate over that of the "rookie" division commander with whom he was to "team," Ambrose Powell Hill.

It should not be inferred that Jackson undertook his assignment in any but a cooperative and capable manner. The destination of his troops as they left the Valley was a well-kept secret, at least from the officers involved.[4] Whiting, for example, thought Jackson was a fool for turning his division around and taking it right back towards Richmond with him. Even Jackson's capable senior major general,

---

[4] McClellan, however, was aware of it, 11, *O.R.*, Pt. 2, p. 19.

48

"Old Baldy" Ewell, was angered at not being taken into confidence relative to the secret move to the Peninsula. Jackson did not spare himself, riding, in fourteen hours without rest, the last fifty-two miles of the journey to the rendezvous with Lee on Nine Mile Road. He accepted the plan of attack without protest and unhesitatingly acceded to Longstreet's request that his time of arrival be postponed a day to the 26th. Apparently he cheerfully accepted A. P. Hill as his "team mate," although he knew him only slightly from casual acquaintance at West Point together with a brief period of service in the lower Valley, during which their activity was confined largely to troop training.

Jackson was less familiar with Lee's overall plan than were the others who had been engaged throughout the Peninsular campaign to date. He seemed, however, to agree to the details of the method by which he would make contact with Hill and would then swing into the action on the latter's left in the major assault against McClellan's right. Jackson was to communicate with Hill on June 25 when he reached a position southeast of Ashland on the Hanover Court House Road. On the morning of the 26th he was to advise Branch, now one of Hill's brigadiers, of his position. Branch's Brigade would then become the liaison between Jackson and the rest of Hill's Division. When Hill received word that Jackson was in line on the left he was to cross the Chickahominy and strike out at Mechanicsville. Both divisions would then make for Cold Harbor where it was anticipated that McClellan's line of supply could be cut. As already pointed out, Longstreet would support Powell Hill, and D. H. Hill would be in support of his brother-in-law, Jackson. The plan was clear to the men who had already been on the field. It might have been confusing to Jackson, but he said nothing to this effect and left the conference in an apparent atmosphere of mutual understanding.

Powell Hill also returned to his headquarters. His officers were apprised of the plan. His new division was confident, ready. The title "Light Division" had already been bestowed, and the spirit of the men and the lightning-like technique of maneuver that were to earn the appellation merely awaited the first test. A. P. Hill was ready for the morning of the 26th. He had every reason to expect that Stonewall Jackson would be likewise.

On June 24 A. P. Hill issued warning orders to his division for the coming operation. Brigade commanders were directed to draw two days' rations, have them issued, cooked, and packed in the light cloth haversacks which each man carried by a strap over his shoulder. Each brigade was to select one of the several batteries of field artillery attached to it, and get it ready to accompany the division. The remaining batteries were to be left in present positions. The division was assured of marching "light" because regiments were forbidden to take with them more than one wagon apiece, and that to be loaded with ammunition. Knapsacks, normally carried on the back, were to be left behind; each man was to carry one blanket slung in a roll over his shoulder, in which an extra shirt might be packed. Units were to be "shaken down" for extra duty and special duty men, all of whom, except for the sick and the necessary camp guards, were to accompany their units.[5]

The movement into the attack position was to take place under cover of darkness. At sunset on the 25th the men were ordered to fall in. They were lined up and given a little talk by their company commanders in which "we were told that fighting would begin tomorrow, and that we must be brave boys and stand firm, be true to our country, etc."

"That was a solemn moment to me," said one of the Georgians, "I will never forget it!"[6]

The brigades then marched to the vicinity of Meadow Bridges, where they bivouacked behind the trees, out of sight of the Federals north of the Chickahominy. Field's Brigade, in whose defensive sector the division was now assembled, outposted the south bank of the stream where the

---

[5] 11, O.R., Pt. 3, p. 616. See also S.H.S.P., Vol. 29, p. 349.
[6] S.H.S.P., Vol. 29, p. 349.

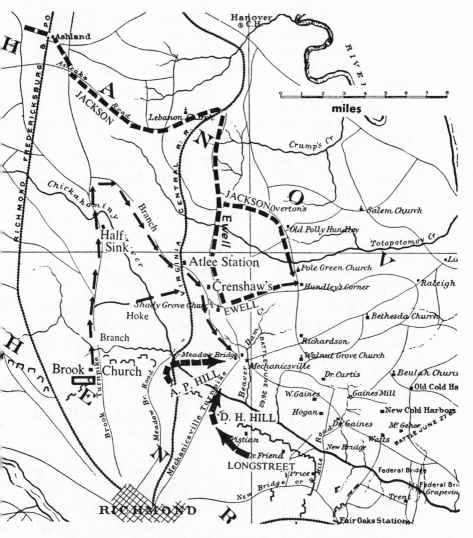

MAP 4. ROUTES OF BRANCH AND JACKSON ON JUNE 26, 1862

Confederates were in contact with a few lonely Federal
pickets on the north bank.

Branch's Brigade marched north on Brook Turnpike that
same evening from its camps near Brook Church, to the
vicinity of Half Sink, just below where the pike crossed
the Chickahominy River.

Branch's orders stated that Jackson, presumably marching

via the Ashcake Road from the vicinity of Ashland, would cross the Virginia Central Railroad at 3 a.m., on Thursday the 26th. Since he was to move abreast of Jackson, keeping in liaison with him, Branch allowed an hour for transmission of a notification from Jackson. Therefore he got his men up at three-thirty, and by five in the morning was in formation in the open fields south of the crossing over the Chickahominy.[7]

Already the sky was beginning to lighten. Soon the sun rose in a cool summer morning, the air clear after several days of rain. As the mists swirled away from the meadows the Confederates knew they were plainly visible to the watching bluecoats opposite. Still no word from Jackson!

At eight o'clock a message came in from General Hill: "Wait for Jackson's notification before you move, unless I send you other orders."

Branch became uneasy lest the enemy report his presence, thus disclosing the entire plan. Hoping to deceive the Yankees, he marched his unit rearward for a half mile and placed them under cover of a wooded hill.[8]

Finally, at 10 a.m., General Branch received a note from Jackson to the effect that the head of his column was crossing the railroad at 9 a.m. Within ten minutes Branch was on his way. His leading elements crossed the river without opposition, turned sharp right, and proceeded down the road leading toward Atlee's Station. He planned to have Lieutenant Colonel R. F. Hoke's regiment, which had been on picket duty at Crenshaw's Bridge, join the rest of the brigade at Crenshaw's farm.

Although Branch had only some seven miles to march, the necessity for clearing enemy cavalry pickets from the way ahead, deploying the leading companies occasionally, then re-forming on the road, consumed so much time that over four hours elapsed before the head of his column

---

[7] 11, *O.R.*, Pt. 2, pp. 881-82.

[8] This didn't fool the Federals. McClellan, or at least Porter, received prompt reports from the cavalry that large bodies of troops, "believed to be part of Jackson's command," were in that area. *Battles and Leaders*, Vol. 2, p. 329.

arrived near Atlee's Station. Although infantry can march at an average rate of two and one-half miles an hour if unopposed, or even faster for short spurts, it is safer to count on a speed of only about one and one-half miles per hour if there is any resistance. In this case the presence of Federal cavalry, with occasional shots from its pickets, and the ever-present danger of deadly ambush in the woods, were sufficient to retard Branch.[9]

As his column passed Atlee's Station they encountered a covering force of Federal cavalry which was well out on McClellan's right and rear. In this particular area the screen consisted of the 8th Illinois Cavalry, commanded by Colonel John F. Farnsworth. They were outposting the road running from Hanover to Mechanicsville, with a company each at Atlee's Station, Mrs. Crenshaw's farm, and Shady Grove Church. When contact was made, brisk fighting took place, with a few casualties on each side. The Federal cavalry fell back slowly, cutting down trees across the road, tearing up bridges, and firing upon the Confederate advance from concealed locations.[10] Hoke, too, was delayed, It was three o'clock before he got over the river at Crenshaw's Bridge and joined Branch.

Jackson, who had started his march from the vicinity of Ashland that morning, was similarly retarded by the Federal cavalry. In addition, Jackson was unfamiliar with the roads, and distrusted his local guide. He also was apprehensive lest his units mistake friendly forces in the woods for the enemy and fire upon them. But by 4 p.m. his leading elements under Ewell, moving parallel to Branch's troops and coming within a quarter of a mile from them near Crenshaw's farm, established liaison with Branch. Branch and Ewell conferred briefly then continued the march, Branch heading southeast toward Mechanicsville and Ewell veering off to the east in the direction of Pole Green Church.

Late in the afternoon Branch reached the Mechanicsville battlefield, having taken some seven hours to accomplish his

[9] *Ibid.*
[10] 11, *O.R.*, Pt. 2, pp. 232-33.

march. Since he had been delayed in getting started, no blame falls on Branch. Jackson, the cause of the delay, marched at an exceedingly slow rate. Part of this was due to the screening activities of the Federal cavalry, which has not been given adequate credit for its contribution to the campaign. On the other hand it does not reflect credit on the Confederate command's computation of time-and-space factors, especially in failing to allow for possible interference from the enemy. There were also additional causes for Jackson's delay, as will be discussed later.

Powell Hill had hoped to be able to attack soon after daylight, or by 8 a.m. at the latest. As the morning wore on, and there was still no word from Jackson or Branch, he became increasingly fidgety. This was his first opportunity to distinguish himself as a division commander, and something was obviously wrong. Were the arrangements for liaison with Jackson faulty? Was Jackson already in place, and was it only that the word had failed to reach him?

Hill is described as being impetuous. He was that. A man with a rapid rate of metabolism, under pressure he came to a boil quickly. By 3 p.m. he could wait no longer. Without first checking with General Lee, who was only two miles away on the high ground south of the Mechanicsville Turnpike Bridge, he gave the word to Field to start the advance. Then, as he sat on his horse beside the road watching his leading regiment pass, the smile returned to Hill's face.

Dr. J. William Jones, at that time a private in one of the Virginia regiments, but who had known Powell in Culpeper before the war, and who later was his chaplain, described him as he saw him at this time:[11]

> He was dressed in a fatigue jacket of gray flannel, his felt hat slouched over his noble brow, sitting his horse with easy grace, glancing his eagle eye along his column as it hurried past him into battle, and yet taking time from his pressing duties to give me a warm grasp of the hand and a cordial greeting as he inquired after the boys of the old Thirtieth.

---

[11] *Confederate Veteran,* Vol. 1, pp. 233-36.

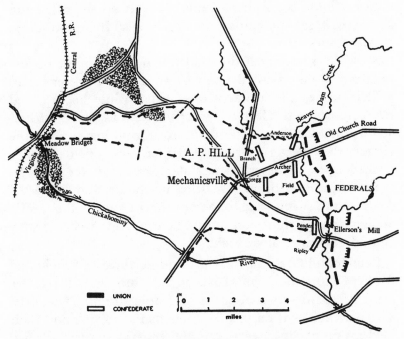

MAP 5. BATTLE OF MECHANICSVILLE

General Field's skirmishers ran across Meadow Bridge,
fanned out in the fields on the north side of the river, and
drove the enemy pickets rapidly toward the northeast. The
brigade, in a column of fours, followed at two hundred
yards, with the brigades of Anderson, Archer, Pender, and
Gregg—in that order—next in column. The first three brigades marched northeast on the Meadow Bridge Road for
a mile, while Pender and Gregg turned sharp right and
headed toward Mechanicsville on a route through the
meadows and fields roughly parallel to that of Field and
Archer.[12]

The ground sloped uphill gradually to the low ridge on
which the crossroads hamlet of Mechanicsville was situated.
The Federals had stationed there a regiment of infantry,
supported by cavalry and artillery, to alert their main line
of defense east of Beaver Dam Creek, and give Porter's main
force time to occupy its fieldworks. A. P. Hill's advancing

[12] 11, O.R., Pt. II, pp. 835 ff.

55

columns could see Federals moving about on the ridge and under the trees and among the dozen or so frame buildings of Mechanicsville.

As Field approached the road junction northwest of Mechanicsville he was fired upon by an enemy detachment in a little grove. There was a brief pause while he deployed two companies to clear the woods. Then, as the Confederates turned east into the main road running toward the village, they began to receive artillery fire. Field at once formed in two lines perpendicular to and on the right of the road. A. P. Hill, quickly sizing up the situation, directed Anderson to swing wide to the northeast to attack the hostile artillery on its right and rear. Then he had Archer deploy and advance in rear of Field.

Pender and Gregg now formed in line abreast of Field and Archer. Thus the Light Division took up the advance toward Mechanicsville, about a half mile distant. The brigades marched as if on parade, their banners flying and their field music playing gay airs.[18] The Federal artillery opened on them as they came in view of the heights east of Beaver Dam Creek. At first the fire was too high to be effective but as the enemy gunners corrected the laying of their pieces, shells began cutting gaps in the Confederate lines. The Southerners maintained their formation as they steadily marched toward the village. They stopped two or three times to fire volleys from the front ranks against the enemy bobbing about among the scattering of houses and trees along the ridge. Two of their accompanying batteries galloped into position in the center and opened up on the enemy. The Federals withdrew swiftly to a position east of Beaver Dam Creek.

It was now four o'clock. The village had been taken by the Light Division. The road running north and south through Mechanicsville had been cleared for the march of

[18] President Davis, General Lee, and a large number of civilian members of the Confederate government were watching the show from the high ground south of the Mechanicsville Bridge. On a hill nearer Richmond many other inhabitants had gathered, too, to see the battle. "Hill was so near us as to be almost in sight. The drums and fifes of his regiments could be easily heard." *Rebel War Clerk's Diary*, J. B. Jones, Vol. 1, p. 137.

D. H. Hill north to join with Jackson. The Light Division had accomplished its initial mission.

But the main enemy position back of Beaver Dam Creek was still intact. The Federals could still pour artillery and rifle fire into the flank of D. H. Hill's Division if it marched across their front. Apparently the enemy were not being forced out by the expected arrival of Jackson on their right and rear. Had Jackson indeed arrived? It seemed doubtful.

A. P. Hill, his shirt torn in several places, was dashing about Mechanicsville, directing his brigades, which had converged on the village, to spread out again and continue the attack toward the main enemy line. Field's Brigade started down the road leading toward Ellerson's Mill. As soon as they debouched from the cover of the town the men began dropping from the rapid fire which was directed upon them. Again Field formed line, obliqued to the left, and aimed at the center of the Federal position. Archer was advancing on Field's left, with his own flank now on the Old Church Road. He, too, was taking heavy losses from increased small-arms and artillery fire. The enemy batteries on both ends of their position and in the center were able to bring their sheaves of fire to a focus between the creek and the town, concentrating on Field and Archer. In a few moments the thinned Confederate lines began to waver, and an increasing number of men started running back up the slope. The commanders had their regiments lie down in such little depressions as the ground afforded.

On the right Pender was driving toward Ellerson's Mill. On the left was Anderson, who hadn't swung out far enough to take the enemy artillery in flank. He had struck the creek almost in front of the Federal battery, had succeeded in getting E. L. Thomas' Georgians across, and was trying to advance the whole brigade over to support Thomas.

The situation appeared to be critical, but not yet desperate.

D. H. Hill, south of the destroyed Mechanicsville Bridge, was also eager to get across and into the fray. His leading brigade, under Brigadier General Roswell Ripley, scooted

57

across the river on improvised footbridges. Some artillery, sandwiched in between Ripley and the following brigade, also attempted to cross but immediately were bogged down. Someone sent for the pioneers, who commenced frantically to repair the crossing for the vehicles. They were interrupted by the arrival of a long cavalcade of horsemen galloping madly across. This was President Davis, General Lee, their aides, and staff; as well as a host of politicos who had come out to see the fun and whose herd-bound horses were now carrying them willy-nilly into the danger zone. When the distinguished party came to the head of Ripley's column, now a half mile north of the crossing, they reined up briefly and someone—perhaps Davis [14]—ordered Ripley to go to the support of Pender, now hard pressed on the right. There was much confusion on the battlefield, too many people giving too many orders.

General Lee, arrived on the high ground near the town, had earlier sent a Lieutenant Sydnor, a native of the area, to find A. P. Hill and tell him that there was quicksand up where Anderson was trying to cross. Hill was to hold up the attack. Hill got this message, but chose to disregard it. Perhaps he felt that his men were too closely engaged to permit breaking off the action at the moment. Or maybe he thought that the order applied only to the north flank. At any rate he directed Pender to hurl his men again at the Ellerson's Mill defenses. The Thirty-fourth North Carolina Regiment again advanced gallantly into the holocaust of fire, which was practically point blank in their faces as they approached the creek. The attack broke down with extremely heavy losses. The surviving men were withdrawn a few yards behind a slight rise in the ground just west of the crossing.

About this time Ripley's two regiments came up on the right and charged over practically the same ground as Pender had done. Apparently Ripley's men caught fire from the fighting spirit of the Light Division. They made a magnificent charge, but were cut to pieces by overwhelming fire.

[14] E. P. Alexander, *Some Memories of a Confederate*, p. 119.

The Forty-fourth Georgia lost 335 out of 514 men. The First North Carolina sustained 142 casualties, including all their field officers and the regimental adjutant.

It was growing dusk. The advance had stopped. Gregg, who had followed Pender into Mechanicsville, was held out of the last assault and placed in reserve on the left. Branch, similarly reporting in with his brigade from the north, was directed to form in line in rear of Archer and Field. The division was now assembled, in place, and ready to resume the attack then or on the following day. Darkness came on slowly, as the firing gradually died away. By nine o'clock the battlefield was quiet except for occasional shots from pickets, and the moans and cries for aid from the wounded scattered about over the field.

The Light Division, in its initial action, had suffered a bloody repulse, but the men, and their leaders, were not beaten, not dismayed. They had demonstrated that they had all the gallantry, courage, and dash required to make a first-rate fighting outfit. The Light Division had proved that it was a reliable weapon.

Toward midnight General Lee held a conference at Mechanicsville for his commanders and staff. Jackson was not present, not having been sent for. This appears somewhat surprising in view of the key part that Jackson was expected to play in the entire operation. Lee critiqued the day's action and discussed plans for the morrow. He very pointedly checked to insure that Hill had received the order sent him through Lieutenant Sydnor,[15] but other than that he made no comment on Hill's failure to comply with the orders. Neither did he question Hill's having attacked at 3 p. m. contrary to plans. But this was Lee's way. Most of his orders were of the mission type, leaving considerable to the discretion of the commander on the ground. He never upbraided a man who, like A. P. Hill, erred on the side of excess zeal. He wanted men who would *fight*, and Powell Hill had demonstrated that he was that kind of man.

---

[15] Freeman, in *Lee's Lieutenants*, 1, pp. 514 and 515, cites this incident from the papers of Jed Hotchkiss, Chief Topographer in Jackson's corps.

At about 5 p. m, Stonewall Jackson's long column of three divisions had closed up in the vicinity of Hundley's Corner. Jackson was disturbed that there was no message from Lee, and that D. H. Hill's Division was not there to join him. He could plainly hear the heavy firing going on to the south, but apparently he did not feel that his orders required him to move in that direction nor to join in the battle unless specifically directed to do so. This, of course, is speculation, but it may be deduced from the wording of Jackson's report[16] and from the fact that he calmly went into bivouac for the night and the next day resumed the march toward Cold Harbor.

Jackson's inadequacy in this, his first battle under Lee's direction, has been the subject of endless speculation. The mystery has been heightened because of Jackson's previous marked success coupled with the brilliant and completely cooperative manner in which he subsequently served Lee. Students of the Civil War have remarked, too, on the fact that Jackson himself never offered any explanation or excuse for his failures during the Seven Days. Lee made no comments on Jackson's shortcomings in this period. Jackson's reports[17] for the campaign do not indicate the slightest awareness that he was remiss. Douglas Southall Freeman in *R. E. Lee* explores this question at length.[18] In considering the numerous reasons which have been advanced for Jackson's conduct at this time, Freeman works out a detailed schedule of Jackson's activities for the period beginning with June 23 and running through the Battle of Gaines's Mill, showing how little sleep Jackson had had. He points out that this was far less than the normal man requires, and was unusually detrimental to Jackson.

There may be some merit to this argument. Officers and men who have been in battle and have had very little sleep often become abnormally lethargic and apathetic. This aptly describes Jackson during the Seven Days. He appeared to see,

---

[16] 11 *O.R.*, Pt. 2, p. 552.
[17] 11 *O.R.*, Pt. 2, pp. 552 ff.
[18] See particularly Vol. 2, App. 2.

to hear, and to react to external stimuli, but actually he may have been in something akin to a stupefied state without himself realizing it. Testimony of his staff appears to bear this out. On the other hand, Jackson's fellow officers seemed to stand up under the physical ordeals of the campaign. Furthermore, Stonewall himself in prior and subsequent rigorous conditions never experienced the same trouble.

Freeman, by way of further explanation of this enigma, also observed that Lee's orders for the attack were not entirely unambiguous. Jackson *could* have interpreted them as being merely march orders, directing him to Cold Harbor, and his report indicated that perhaps he did so regard them. Undoubtedly Jackson knew full well that an attack was to be made, but it is possible that he thought that Lee, being on the ground, would give the word when the attack was to be launched, after the situation had developed to the point where such an attack would enjoy the greatest success. Here was Lee's written order, probably confirming an oral order issued at the conference on June 23:[19]

General Orders)	HDQRS. ARMY
)	OF NORTHERN VIRGINIA
No. 75)	June 24, 1862

I. General Jackson's command will proceed to-morrow from Ashland toward Slash Church and encamp at some convenient point west of the Central Railroad. Branch's Brigade, of A. P. Hill's Division, will also to-morrow evening take position on the Chickahominy near Half-Sink. At 3 o'clock Thursday morning, 26th instant, General Jackson will advance on the road leading to Pole Green Church, communicating his march to General Branch, who will immediately cross the Chickahominy and take the road leading to Mechanicsville. As soon as the movements of these columns are discovered, A. P. Hill, with the rest of his division, will cross the Chickahominy near Meadow Bridge and move directly on Mechanicsville. To aid his advance, the heavy batteries on the Chickahominy will at the proper time open upon the batteries at Mechanicsville. The enemy being driven from Mechanicsville and the passage across

---

[19] 11 *O.R.*, Pt. 2, pp. 498-99.

the bridge opened, General Longstreet, with his division and that of General D. H. Hill, will cross the Chickahominy at or near that point, General D. H. Hill moving to the support of General Jackson and General Longstreet supporting General A. P. Hill. The four divisions, keeping in communication with each other and moving *en echelon* on separate roads, if practicable, the left division in advance, with skirmishers and sharpshooters extending their front, will sweep down the Chickahominy and endeavor to drive the enemy from his position above New Bridge, General Jackson bearing well to his left, turning Beaver Dam Creek and taking the direction toward Cold Harbor. They will then press forward toward the York River Railroad, closing upon the enemy's rear and crippling and arresting his progress.

II. The divisions under Generals Huger and Magruder**

* * * * * * *

By command of General Lee:

R. H. CHILTON,
Assistant Adjutant-General

Apparently all the division commanders except Jackson comprehended the intent of this order. By his failure to ask questions at the conference on June 23, he signified that he understood it too, and unquestionably thought that he did. But his later actions showed that he did not. During the first two days of the action beginning on June 26 he seems to have been preoccupied with carrying out that portion of the order which says "General Jackson, bearing well to his left, turning Beaver Dam Creek and taking the direction toward Cold Harbor. . . ." One must wonder, however, before transferring the blame from Jackson to Lee, why only *one* of the generals involved' failed to grasp the problem.

Despite Jackson's failure to comprehend and to carry out Lee's designs, the plan did succeed at least in part. For McClellan, though he was in a very strong position which "it had long before been determined to hold."[20] had already, even before he was sure of Jackson's approach, decided to

---

[20] 11 *O.R.,* Pt. 2, p. 19.

withdraw. Jackson's arrival in the area hastened his retreat. McClellan's attitude is best described in his own words: "I was satisfied that I had to deal with at least double my own numbers[21] . . . [but] was sure that I could extricate the army from any difficulty in which it might become involved." He had already, in his own mind, abandoned his mission of capturing Richmond, concerning himself solely with the safety of his command.

In the Battle of Mechanicsville A. P. Hill was immediately opposed by McCall's Third Division of the Federal V Corps. In the front line of the main position along Beaver Dam Creek were two brigades of the Pennsylvania Reserves under Brigadier General John F. Reynolds, who was to be killed a year later while commanding a corps at Gettysburg. In reserve in rear of the line was George G. Meade's brigade, also of McCall's division. The other two divisions of Porter's corps were at Gaines' farm, about three miles to the east. McCall's division was supported by six batteries of field artillery.

Early in the afternoon, when the firing commenced, General Porter was joined at the Beaver Dam Creek position by McClellan. Reports kept coming in during the afternoon from the cavalry to the north, who were delaying the advance elements of Jackson's command. McClellan and Porter also claimed afterwards that great columns of dust were plainly visible to the northwest. The two Federal leaders remained on the field until ten o'clock that night, by which time they were satisfied that they had repulsed the Confederate attack. Finally McClellan started back to his own headquarters, telling Porter that as soon as he got there and had evaluated the reports received during the day, he would send orders either to remain in position or withdraw to the Gaines' farm position. At 2 a. m. on Friday the 27th Porter

---

[21] *Battles and Leaders*, Vol. 2, p. 315, gives McClellan's strength as 105,445 as against Lee's 80,000 to 90,000. Livermore's weighted figures show less of a preponderance for McClellan: Federals, 98,032, Confederates 86,748. Livermore was considering "effectives."

received word to retire. The movement started at daylight, with the brigade of Seymour acting as rear guard.[22]

The opposing forces at Mechanicsville were approximately equal in number. Livermore lists 15,631 effectives for Mc-Call's Federal division as against 16,356 for A. P. Hill's Division plus Ripley's Brigade. Hill and Ripley suffered 1,484 killed and wounded, whereas McCall's casualties totaled only 256.[23]

[22] 11 *O.R.*, Pt. 2, pp. 19-21 and 221-24.
[23] Livermore, *op. cit.*, p. 82.

CHAPTER 4

Gaines' Mill

*F*ITZ JOHN PORTER commenced to pull back from his Beaver Dam Creek position at dawn on Friday the 27th. The movement was covered by a rear guard formed in accordance with the best tactical doctrine. It consisted largely of artillery with a thin shell of infantry between it and the Confederates to keep up a show of force until the main body had gotten well out of range. The artillery kept up a brisk fire into A. P. Hill's troops during the early hours before daylight, but a gradual slackening of the fire, together with the light amount of musket fire evidently indicated to Hill that a federal withdrawal was taking place.

Hill had discovered that the water above the dam at Ellerson's Mill was so deep as to constitute an obstacle to a direct advance. He had, therefore, placed Gregg on the right and Anderson on the left, with orders to cross the creek around the respective ends of the Federal position. These two brigades started forward soon after daylight, meeting only a scattering of fire.

Pender had shifted his brigade over slightly to the left to make room for Gregg. Then he rode out in front of his lines, took the stump of a cigar from his mouth and, holding it between thumb and forefinger, delivered a short address. He thanked his men for their good work of the previous day and urged them to keep it up on this new day. About eight o'clock he had them start across the dam and mill race in single file.[1] The other brigades were to his left,

---

[1] *N.C. Regts.*, Vol. 1, pp. 751 ff. See also 11 *O.R.*, Pt. 2, p. 899.

awaiting their turn to move out as soon as an increased volume of fire should indicate a renewal of the engagement.

The enemy fire however, stopped altogether. As Gregg's troops moved down toward the stream they encountered the bodies of many dead and wounded from Pender's and Ripley's unsuccessful assault of the previous evening. These had to be moved to make way for the artillery. The bridge had to be repaired. As a result, it was after eight o'clock before the leading elements got across and up the bank on the far side. Here the men passed through the earthworks and camps of the enemy, where they found piles of knapsacks, boxed rations, arms, and other stores. The temptation to pillage was great, but the command pressed on. Later in the war they would have stopped; but at this time they were not yet in the hungry and ragged condition which became the lot of the Confederate soldier as the war dragged on.

Anderson likewise found the enemy position to be evacuated. He formed up in column of fours, marched down the far side of the stream, and fell in behind Gregg on the road leading east from Ellerson's Mill. The remainder of the division also joined the march eastward. The road ran towards New Cold Harbor and Gaines' Mill. Longstreet was marching on a parallel route to their right, and D. H. Hill, followed, it was hoped, by Jackson, was on a similar route to the north.

After marching about a mile and a half, the advance elements of Gregg's Brigade received artillery fire from the direction of Walnut Grove Church, wounding an officer and a soldier. It was Jackson's column, mistaking them for enemy troops. Jackson had not moved until nearly eight o'clock that morning. His vanguard, furthermore, had not become familiar with either the geographical or tactical situation. They thought, therefore, that they had contacted the enemy when they ran into Gregg's troops. Maxcy Gregg, who had so recently exhorted his troops, was now beside himself in consternation at suffering two casualties as the result of the first shots fired by Jackson in the campaign.

As he put it in his report, Captain W. T. Haskell of his First South Carolina Volunteers prevented further damage by effecting communication with Stonewall's troops, "so as to avoid the risk of further mischief."[2] General A. P. Hill rode forward to confer with Jackson.[3] They talked briefly about the incident, and there is no doubt but that Jackson's later cautious advance was due in part to his apprehension over the danger of attacking friendly troops in the woods. In a few moments General Lee came up on his famous white horse, Traveller. After greeting Jackson in a friendly way, he dismounted and sat on a stump in the churchyard. In a few moments Hill departed, leaving the two noted generals in deep conversation, the gist of which has never been reported. Hill rejoined Gregg and told him to resume the march on the road running toward Dr. Gaines'.

By now Lee was beginning to think that the enemy would be encountered in force along Powhite Creek, which ran south into the Chickahominy from Gaines' Mill. As Gregg approached the Hogan house, Lee's headquarters at the moment, he was stopped along the roadside by General Lee, who told him to put his brigade in battle formation and head toward Powhite Creek. Gregg formed the brigade in two lines abreast of the road and gave orders for the advance. Then he rode into the grounds of the Hogan estate in compliance with a request sent by Longstreet, who had just been told by Lee that Gregg could brief him on the situation. A. P. Hill was there talking to Longstreet, but soon departed. It was noon, and most of those present took the opportunity to eat lunch while discussing plans for the expected battle. An eyewitness described this scene as follows:[4]

> Maxcy Gregg sits his horse in the shade [at Hogan house], conversing with a few about the affair at Ellison's [sic] Mills, and seems a very modest, quiet gentleman of about 50. His hair is grey; he has full whiskers and moustaches and a ruddy complexion; in person he is thickset,

[2] 11 *O.R.*, Pt. 2, p. 853.
[3] *Ibid.*
[4] *Battlefields of the South*, p. 333.

of medium height, and is jocular in his manner. His uniform looked the worse for wear; even the three stars[5] upon his throat being dingy and ragged, while his common black felt hat would not bring a half dollar in peacetime . . . But he is well mounted and armed, and keeps an eye on General Lee, by whom he expects to be called any moment . . . Gregg is called! He leans his head through a window and converses with Lee, but trots away as if dissatisfied. "There goes Gregg," someone remarks, "looking as black as thunder because he is not appointed to the advance."

Lee sat in the south portico, absorbed in thought. He was neatly dressed in a dark blue uniform, buttoned to the throat; his fine calm open countenance and grey hair would have tempted an artist to sketch him in this thoughtful attitude. Longstreet sat in an old garden chair, at the foot of the steps, under shady trees, busily engaged in disposing of a lunch of sandwiches. With his feet thrown against a tree, he presented a true type of the hardy campaigner; his once grey uniform had changed to brown, and many a button was missing; his riding boots were dusty and worn, but his pistols and sabre had a bright polish by his side, while his charger stood near, anxiously looking at him. Though the day was warm, the general's coat was buttoned up, and as he ate and conversed with those about him, it was evident that his sandy beard, moustaches, and half-bald head had latterly but distant dealings with a barber. He is a little above medium height, thickset, inclined to obesity, and has a small inquiring blue eye; though thoughtful and slow of motion he is remarkably industrious.

Gregg, who had resumed the march in column, came upon Federal skirmishers along the west bank of Powhite Creek at Gaines' Mill. It was about one-thirty in the afternoon. Although he had two companies out in front as skirmishers, Gregg decided to clear the road quickly with a show of greater force. He deployed his two leading regiments, who at once chased the Federals across the creek and into the woods along the road leading east to New Cold Harbor. After a short delay during which the bridge below the mill dam was repaired, the brigade filed across and formed in two lines on the opposite bank. Under the eye of A. P. Hill, who

---

[5] The insignia of the Confederate general officer, any grade, was three stars.

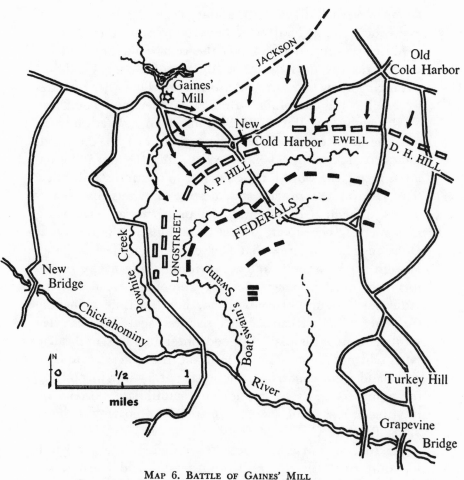

MAP 6. BATTLE OF GAINES' MILL

sat on his horse on a low eminence just below and west of
the mill, Gregg's men charged forward at the double-quick.
They pressed on for a half mile, suffering a few losses from
sharpshooters in the woods. At the crossroads of New Cold
Harbor they encountered an enemy detachment in abandoned Federal campgrounds, where heaps of burned supplies
were still smoking. A short, sharp charge, and they were
through the hamlet and into the open field beyond.

At once Gregg requested permission from Hill to continue the pursuit. Hill withheld permission, though he permitted Gregg to form his whole brigade in line of battle

69

facing toward Turkey Hill, about two miles to the southeast, where the Federals were believed to be in force.

Anderson crossed next, took the right-hand fork and advanced rapidly until he came abreast of Gregg. Field was advancing a few paces in Anderson's rear. The other brigades were following in column—Branch, Archer, and Pender.

Although Powell Hill had admired Gregg's advance in what he later, in his official report, described as "the handsomest charge in line I have seen during the war,"[6] he delayed giving the word for the pursuit to continue. Hill knew that Jackson was nearby and, despite previous disappointments, thought that Stonewall was preparing an enveloping movement to coordinate with a frontal assault by the Light Division. He also knew that Harvey Hill was near at hand. Powell, furthermore, wanted to withhold affirmative orders to Gregg until he received word from Longstreet that the latter was in supporting position. For the time being the Culpeper Cavalier curbed his reckless aggressiveness. He wanted to take his place in good order in Lee's well-calculated scheme. As far as A. P. Hill and the Confederate high command were concerned, the entire army was in position for a united effort to envelop and annihilate Porter's retreating troops which were apparently preparing a stand along Powhite Creek.

Jackson, of course, had been scheduled to follow a parallel route to the left of Hill toward Old Cold Harbor. Because of Stonewall's late start on the 27th, however, D. H. Hill's Division, originally assigned to support Jackson, had moved in ahead of the latter's column. Thus the two Hills now headed the pursuit in parallel columns. Powell, by dint of the vaunted speed of his men and a more direct route, had been the first to make contact with Porter's rear guard. He believed that Longstreet was ready and in support of the Light Division. D. H. Hill and Stonewall Jackson were supposedly approaching on the left. Powell Hill, therefore,

---

[6] At the time Hill wrote this report, 11 *O.R.*, Pt. 2, p. 836, six months later, Gregg had just been killed. Hill possibly wanted to eulogize his brigade commander, although his battle reports almost always reflected his outspoken sincerity.

reasoned that he would not be fighting alone that day. Unfortunately, Stonewall Jackson, upon learning that A. P. Hill had made contact, broke off his advance and halted his own troops. He then ordered the eagerly pressing D. H. Hill to swing to the left and establish the flank of a sort of ambush into which Jackson expressed the "hope" that Hill and Longstreet would "drive" the Federals. Unlike the 4:30 p. m. bivouac of the preceding day, however, Jackson's report contains an "explanation" of his maneuver of the 27th. He wrote:

> Soon after General A. P. Hill became engaged, and being unacquainted with the ground, and apprehensive, from what appeared to me to be the respective positions of the Confederate and Federal forces engaged, that if I then pressed forward our troops would be mistaken for the enemy and be fired into, and hoping that Generals A. P. Hill and Longstreet would soon drive the Federals toward me, I directed General D. H. Hill to move his division to the left of the road so as to leave between him and the wood on the right of the road an open space, across which I hoped the enemy would be driven. Thus arranged, it was in our power to distinguish friend from foe in case the enemy should be driven as expected.[7]

Powell Hill did not have a copy of Jackson's report available at 2:30 p. m. on the 27th of June, 1862, at Gaines' Mill, Virginia. He wasn't much concerned with the direction in which the enemy should be driven. That they were to be driven, however, was the intention not only of its commander but of every man in the Light Division.

At 2:30 p. m. a courier handed Powell Hill the awaited message from Longstreet.[8] In the meantime, since Gregg's initial skirmish, Branch had come up to form on Gregg's right. J. R. Anderson in turn was on Branch's right, with Archer forming the extreme right flank of the Light Division. Field's Brigade connected Anderson and Archer. Pender, who had been clearing the right flank, was now re-

---

[7] 11 O.R., Pt. 2, p. 553.
[8] 11 O.R., Pt. 2, p. 836. Hill's full report on the Gaines' Mill engagement appears on pp. 836-37.

lieved and placed in reserve. Lindsay Walker, Hill's chief artillerist, was not on duty because of illness, so the artillery was being handled principally by the batteries of Captains Crenshaw and Johnson. They were placed on Gregg's right.

Now, at word that Longstreet was ready, Hill ordered the attack. First Gregg engaged furiously. The Union skirmish line[9] broke before the South Carolinians. But, as the latter advanced into the woods, they were met with a murderous volley of rifle fire, immediately followed by the crash of artillery. Gregg had reached a well-concealed, prepared defensive position of unknown strength. He was stopped cold. Branch and Anderson immediately joined the attack in echelon. At the unexpected strength of the defense, Dorsey Pender's reserve brigade was thrown into the fight in support of Branch. Hill, realizing the futility of hurling the entire Light Division at this apparently impregnable line, sent Field and Archer in a flanking movement to turn the Union left. They found, however, that they had to cross an open field before they could assault the enemy now revealed as being entrenched in a triple line on the slope of a long, wooded hill, the crest of which, in Hill's words, was "studded with guns."

Field's and Archer's men twice advanced to within a short distance of the Union works but were checked each time by overwhelming firepower. Gregg, Branch, and Pender, on the original line of battle, pressed savagely forward. On two occasions, Pender's men pierced the Federal lines but superior numbers pushed them back. Not only was the Light Division outmanned, but the cream of the old-line Regular Army under capable Major General George Sykes were among the troops holding the positions on that bloody hill.

Young Captain Willie Pegram's battery, although badly mangled the previous day at Mechanicsville, was now put in some semblance of condition and went into action in a vain attempt to consolidate the penetrations by Branch's and Pender's infantry. It was to no avail. Finally Powell

---

[9] Likely this was an outpost line in advance of the main position.

72

Hill sent out the order to have the men lie down and dig in against a counterattack.

Longstreet, in the meantime, had been unable to get his division into the action. His forces were in a line at right angles to the Light Division. They could not get up to Hill's relief without completely exposing themselves to enfilade fire from McClellan's long-range artillery. Lee, furthermore, wanted to send Longstreet against the Federal left at the same time that Jackson would attack their right. Stonewall, instead of attacking, was waiting with D. H. Hill to bag the enemy after they had been "driven" by Hill and Longstreet. Shortly past four o'clock it became apparent to Powell Hill, after two hours in that holocaust, that his men could not hold on longer without help. The colorful Federal Zouaves and Sykes' Regulars in counterattacks threatened to overrun the gallant, battered Light Division, its lines riddled with casualties and its weapons fouled by protracted fire. Longstreet now came up to relieve the pressure on the right although no word had yet been heard from Jackson.

With Longstreet in the fight, the counterattacking Federals withdrew. The Confederate strategy was now to contain the enemy until Jackson could get into action against the Union right. The primary mission of the Light Division had been accomplished although its fighting was not finished for the day. The retreating foe had been caught, engaged, pushed back to their prepared defensive line, and then held at bay. These things the men of A. P. Hill had achieved without aid from any of the other forces under Lee's command. Actually this was the first engagement of what was now officially known as the Army of Northern Virginia. Its first hours of battle, however, had been fought entirely by some 12,000-odd of the army's total of 56,000 men—the 12,000 under the command of the aggressive, uncompromising, fighting young general from Culpeper.

Those two terrible yet glorious hours near Gaines's Mill on June 27th served to develop the character of the Light Division and its officers. The great figures of the division's history now began to emerge. Dorsey Pender, destined one day to be its commander, showed his high caliber as a fighting leader as, in fact, did all the brigadiers. Then there was Colonel Edward L. Thomas, whose Thirty-fifth Georgia Regiment was one of those that smashed into the Union lines although it could not hold for want of support. Thomas earned his entitlement to the next divisional promotion to the rank of brigadier by his work along Powhite Creek despite being handicapped by a wound suffered the previous day at Beaver Dam. Perhaps the brightest star in the constellation of the Light Division on the 27th was Maxcy Gregg. He proved himself not only a masterful tactician in lining up his brigade for the magnificent charge that opened the battle but he was revealed as a savage combat fighter despite his age [48], and his quiet, cultural background.

They were all good, however, the men and officers of A. P. Hill! Theirs was not the privilege of resting, moreover, even when the reinforcements arrived. Finally, at about four-thirty, Jackson made his presence known on the left. Today, at least, he got into action before it was altogether too late. Now, just as Longstreet reinforced the tattered but still holding right wing of the Light Division, Ewell's men were sent by Jackson to aid Hill's left flank. The fresh troops under Old Baldy did well, but they still could not penetrate the Union line. Finally Jackson himself arrived on the line of battle and rode up to Lee.

"Ah, General," Lee is reported as saying, "I am very glad to see you. I had hoped to be with you before."[10]

Jackson merely nodded. There was no explanation of his delay. In fact, no satisfactory explanation was ever forthcoming. True, there was the "ambush" into which Jackson hoped Hill would "drive" the Federals. There was the story of a guide taking Stonewall's column on the wrong road. There was the story of a crossroad mixup between Jackson's own column and D. H. Hill's Division. Allowing for all these incidents, however, the spectacle of Jackson,

---

[10] Freeman, *Lee's Lieutenants*, Vol. 1, p. 530.

after finally arriving on the Union right flank, standing by while A. P. Hill alone fought the battle, presents as great a mystery as the enigma of the preceding day.

At last Jackson's men were in line. Now, also, D. H. Hill was released from the "ambush" position and was permitted to attack the Union right as he had wanted to do hours earlier. At this point, John Hood's Brigade was ordered by Longstreet to assault the Federal left thus releasing the pressure on the Light Division. Finally, at seven o'clock, with daylight running short, Lee personally told Powell Hill to advance his whole line. Now the divisions of the two Hills and Longstreet, together with Whiting's and Ewell's divisions of Jackson's command and one of Stonewall's own brigades, were in simultaneous action, the first grand-scale battle by the Army of Northern Virginia.

What happened during the final phase of the battle is best described by several of the participants:

> The Federals were posted on a bluff or abrupt ridge, in front of which ran Powhite Creek.[11] The bluff was so steep that the lines of fortification for infantry were so constructed that the rear line could fire over the front without endangering it. The artillery, about 500 pieces, was posted in rear of the infantry. All along the front the trees had been cut down and the trunks so overlapped as to make it exceedingly difficult for us to pass, even without the embarrassment of two lines of hostile infantry. Notwithstanding the superior strength of this position, the divisions of A. P. Hill and Longstreet made two direct assaults upon it without waiting for Jackson, who was to attack on the right and rear, as at Mechanicsville. In both of these assaults they were repulsed with severe loss; but about 5 o'clock in the afternoon the welcome sound of Jackson's cannon on the extreme left was heard, and at the same time Whiting's Division reached Hill's left, when a general charge along the entire line was ordered. The sound of Jackson's guns and the sight of fresh reinforcements infused new life into the tired and almost exhausted troops of Hill and Longstreet. When the charging step was ordered they responded with an alacrity seldom witnessed.

[11] The main Federal position was behind Boatswain's Swamp, not Powhite Creek as here described. *The Military Annals of Tennessee*, p. 227.

The lines moved steadily and straight to the enemy, and never wavered until their double and triple lines were captured. In less than thirty minutes from the last order to advance, every position of the enemy was carried.

Truly this battle will prove the never-fading honor of A. P. Hill. He was everywhere among the men, leading and cheering them on in his quiet and determined manner. He saw the overwhelming numbers with which they had to contend, but calmly planning his designs, he was fiery in execution of them, giving counsel, as if in private life, but mounting his horse and dashing to the front whenever his battalions began to swerve before the masses of the enemy. Discovering their weakest point, he assailed it with fury, and ordering up the whole line, led them into the conquered camps, hat in hand, and never rested a moment until the enemy were driven a mile beyond. Nor was he contented then, for knowing the value of time, he pushed his advance far ahead, and so punished the enemy that they recalled a whole army corps to arrest his ardent progress.[12]

Artillery on both sides now opened with a terrific roar, and, as evening fell, the flash of guns and long lines of musketry fire could be seen in bright relief against the blue and cloudless sky. After a deafening cannonade of half an hour, and while showers of shell were screaming through the air, and lighting up the face of friend and foe when they burst, loud yells from the distant woods assured us our men were advancing to the assault. For a moment a deathlike silence reigned over all; and then again, our approach being seen, the enemy's artillery opened with extraordinary rapidity, until it seemed as if every tree in the forest was cracking and shivering to pieces. Barns, houses, and stacks of hay and straw were in a blaze. By their light our men were plainly visible rushing across the open spaces through the infernal showers of grape, and swarming into the breastworks. The explosion of caissons was frequent, and the constant pattering of musketry within the enemy lines showed our men were there also. In a little while the Federal guns were silent, a loud noise of many voices was heard, and then a long, wild, piercing yell, as of ten thousand demons, and the place was ours![13]

---

[12] *Battlefields of the South*, p, 362.
[13] *Ibid*, p. 324.

76

Porter managed to avoid destruction by withdrawing. Approaching nightfall made pursuit impossible. The field was won by the South, chiefly as the result of the battle by the Light Division while the rest of the Army "awaited developments." The fruits of victory were meager, however, and the costs were high. Alexander estimated the Confederate casualties on the 27th at 8,358 and stated the reported Federal losses to be 6,837, of whom 2,836 were now prisoners of the Army of Northern Virginia.[14] Of the Southern losses, 2,688, practically one third, were in the Light Division. It might be noted that in Jackson's own division there were only 91 casualties. The division suffering the next greatest number of losses was Longstreet's from which Hood led his spectacular and successful but costly onslaught against Porter's left.

The credit for the first break through the Union lines, just before darkness fell on the 27th, seems to have been claimed by all the Confederate commanders except A. P. Hill. The latter was never overly modest with respect to the accomplishments of the Light Division and, in fact, his zeal for its entitlement to deserved credit nearly proved disastrous at a not too distant date. Nevertheless, having made the bulk of the battle, his weary and casualty-riddled troops did not participate in that first breach that sent Porter again on the road to retreat. Longstreet gives the credit in this respect to Anderson, Pickett, and Hood of his own command. Longstreet, however, did not hesitate to attribute the overall victory to the division which made it possible. He wrote:

> The troops of the gallant A. P. Hill, that did as much and effective fighting as any, received little of the credit properly due them. It was their long and steady fight that thinned the Federal ranks and caused them to so foul their guns that they were out of order when the final struggle came.[15]

---

[14] *Alexander,* p. 131.
[15] *Longstreet,* p. 129.

The "long and steady" fight had not only reduced the troop strength of the Light Division by nearly one third, but it had also cost much of the division's artillery. Crenshaw's and Johnson's batteries had been in the thick of the battle and for two hours had been the only guns in action against the entire Union V Corps. They had been, as Hill put it, "pretty well knocked to pieces." Pegram's Battery wasn't much more than a patched-up shell after Beaver Dam Creek, but it had been whipped into a semblance of effectiveness and actively supported the final advance the evening of the 27th. Braxton had been engaged but his battery was not in bad shape. The rest of the division was spent. Notwithstanding its flaming spirit, it was in no shape to carry on without rest and reorganization. Luckily it received a day of rest on June 28.

CHAPTER 5

Frayser's Farm and Malvern Hill

*T*HE REGIMENTS of the Light Division remained on the battlefield of Gaines' Mill during the night of the 27th, all day on the 28th, and the night of the 28th. Saturday, the 28th, was spent in caring for the wounded and in burying the dead. The digging of the graves was so laborious that some of the companies spent the entire day in this sad work. The men were ordered to cook and pack two days' rations, as it was expected that on Sunday the pursuit of McClellan's forces would be resumed.

During this day's interim, General Lee conferred with Powell Hill and the other division commanders. A plan was drawn up to press the pursuit, although the Confederate high command was still unaware of McClellan's strategy and did not know whether the retreat would be down the Peninsula toward Yorktown, or toward the James southeast of Richmond. Lee's general plan, in either case, was to keep contact with the enemy and eventually force a battle in which he could be destroyed by the same type of flank-attack tactics which had failed on the first two days only because of Jackson's slowness and indecision.

A. P. Hill was placed under Longstreet's orders in the new plan and, pursuant thereto, crossed the Chickahominy in support of Old Pete on the morning of Sunday, the 29th. The day's march was not excessively long, only about 15 miles, but the men were still tired and sleepy, the heat and

79

dust were severe. Consequently many of them dropped by the roadside when the order came to halt.

For several days John Bankhead Magruder's Division had been given the assignment of standing between McClellan's main army and Richmond. Now, with the Union forces apparently in retreat, Magruder was in the position of being directly to the enemy's rear. He would be the one to press the new attack in the first instance. It was thought, however, that Magruder would be confronted by the bulk of McClellan's army. For this reason, Jackson, commanding his own division as well as Ewell's, Whiting's, and Harvey Hill's, was ordered by Lee to sweep down the Chickahominy and White Oak Swamp and join Magruder in the assault. Ben Huger was to move up on the right of the Jackson-Magruder front and attack the Union flank from the west. Longstreet and Powell Hill were to attack that same flank to Huger's right. General T. H. Holmes, who had been brought over from the south bank of the James, was instructed to endeavor to cut off McClellan from the river after the others had developed the battle. The actual points of engagement could not be determined beforehand because the Union forces were in movement. Furthermore, since Jackson's command had to cross the Chickahominy and White Oak Swamp, a timetable could not be established for these operations.

The task of bringing the various divisions to a place for coordinated attack was made more difficult by the fact that McClellan had succeeded in evacuating his fortified positions in front of Magruder without the latter's knowledge during the 28th and early on the 29th. With his customary excessive caution, Little Mac overestimated the Confederates, decided he might be outnumbered and, therefore, had better withdraw to the James. This procedure was in progress before Lee knew in which direction his enemy was going. The withdrawal thereby was well under way long before Lee's somewhat complicated plan of attack could be put into effect.

It was anticipated that Jackson could get across the

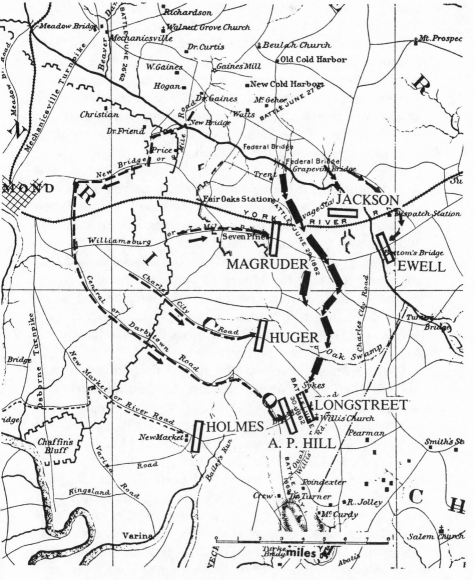

MAP 7. LEE'S PLAN OF PURSUIT, JUNE 30-JULY 1, 1862

Chickahominy by the morning of the 29th. But, as he claims, he had difficulty in repairing Grapevine Bridge on the 28th, and still had not completed the work by the 29th. Grapevine Bridge was about three miles from Savage Sta-

81

tion. Jackson's subsequently tendered excuse lacks validity. The river could have been forded at several places. Also, he could have crossed at New Bridge, nor far distant. This bridge later proved to be in such good shape that it could quickly have been repaired for troop passage. Nevertheless, Jackson put a detachment to work repairing Grapevine Bridge and sent the rest of his troops into bivouac during the entire day of the 29th.[1] The zealously religious Stonewall thereby observed the Sabbath.

Magruder, contacting the enemy at Savage Station that day, obtained an initial advantage which he could not consolidate because of the absence of Jackson's troops. When Jackson and Magruder met at Savage Station early on the 30th, it was too late. In the meantime, to make matters worse, Magruder, receiving no help from Jackson, had sent an emergency call for Huger to come to his aid. Huger started to do this, but, under the original plan had to be recalled to his assignment after Jackson finally joined Magruder. Huger's phase of the plan thus was thrown off schedule by the better part of a day.

While Stonewall Jackson bivouacked that Sunday, brushing off Magruder's urgent request for reinforcements at Savage Station with a note to the effect that he had "other important duty to perform," [2] Longstreet and Powell Hill spent the day marching into their assigned position on the enemy's flank. Contact was made along what was known as the Quaker Road at a place called Frayser's[3] farm. On the morning of the 30th, Longstreet's Division was in line with the Light Division in immediate support. Lee and President Davis were both on the scene congratulating themselves that Longstreet's and Hill's portion of the plan had been so well executed. They did not know how completely the rest of the plan had gone awry. They thought McClellan was at bay. Longstreet was ordered to prepare to advance at the first sound of Jackson's guns. They waited in antici-

[1] Alexander, p. 136, etc. Here and on preceding pages, Alexander describes Jackson's conduct in this phase of the campaign.
[2] *Ibid*, p. 144. That "duty" was apparently Jackson's observance of Sunday.
[3] Also spelled Frazier.

82

pation of a victory that would relieve Richmond and turn the tide of the war. They waited for Jackson's force, now numbering over 25,000, to attack. They waited in vain. Jackson finally crossed the river, but by noon on the 30th he had again halted, this time at White Oak Swamp where he once more settled down to observe an enemy force that in all probability could never have stopped him had he pressed on in accordance with the orders governing his mission of the day.[4]

General Lee was personally reconnoitering the prospective battlefield at Frayser's farm when a Union battery suddenly opened fire on the Confederate lines near where the general sat astride his great horse, Traveller. He sat there motionless although he was in a partially exposed clearing adjacent to the road which appeared to be the prime target of the guns. Jefferson Davis, President of the Confederacy, who had been proceeding down the road, pulled off into a small clearing. He reined his horse in surprise as he came upon Lee.

"Why, General, what are you doing here? You are in too dangerous a position for the commander of the army."[5]

Lee was somewhat taken aback by his civilian commander-in-chief's advice to leave the dangerous position. "I am trying," he replied, "to find out something about the movements and plans of those people." He pointed toward the Federal positions from which the smoke of the artillery now belched. "But you must excuse me, Mr. President." Lee said, "for asking what you are doing here, and for suggesting that this is no proper place for the commander in chief of all our armies."

Davis smiled. "Oh, I am here on the same mission that you are." The President of the Confederacy and the Commander of the Army of Northern Virginia, disregarding the shellfire, now intensified as more Northern guns went into action, then calmly proceeded to conduct an informal council of war.

---

[4] See Jackson's report on White Oak Swamp, 11 *O.R.*, Pt. 2, pp. 556-57.
[5] See 14 *S.H.S.P.*, 451 for this incident and colloquy which followed.

Powell Hill, hovering nearby, had been keeping an eye on Davis. Now he followed the President off the roadway and into the clearing where Lee sat. The commander of the Light Division had to raise his voice to be heard above the guns. "This is no place for either of you," he shouted, "and, as commander of this part of the field, I order you both to the rear."

"We will obey your orders," replied Davis. Lee nodded assent. They withdrew a few yards into the woods. The cannonading increased. Shells burst about the place where they again stopped to talk. Many criticisms have been leveled at Davis, both in the North and in the South. Charges of physical cowardice, however, were never among them. Lee, of course, was the personification of the gallant soldier of the old school. Neither he nor Davis would be the first to move away from the increasing danger. Hill watched them impatiently. He was anxious to devote himself to preparation for battle. He realized, moreover, that the bravery of his two superiors in remaining under fire was now bordering upon stubbornness. Powell Hill never concerned himself with his own safety on the field of battle. He did not hesitate to exercise his authority in the serio-comic situation which was developing as Lee and Davis sat their anxiously pawing horses amidst the increasingly frequent shell bursts.

"Did I not tell you to go away from here?" Hill raised his voice to full pitch. He had difficulty in restraining an oath. "Why," he shouted, "one shell from that battery over yonder may presently deprive the Confederacy of its President and the Army of Northern Virginia of its Commander."

Davis and Lee now withdrew simultaneously. A. P. Hill wheeled back with reckless abandon toward the front from which he had sent his leaders. It was time for battle. The men of the Light Division awaited the presence and word of their general.

During the interim, just before the Battle of Frayser's Farm[6] commenced, Longstreet had left his command post

84

and had given Powell Hill temporary charge of the field. The original disposition of the troops was, therefore, directed by Hill. Longstreet returned, however, to give the order inaugurating the assault against the Federal flank.

Longstreet opened the engagement with artillery fire in reply to the shelling that had come so near to destroying the high command of the Confederacy. He did not order the advance until firing was heard from the Charles City Road down which Huger was supposed to approach. The latter, however, was not engaged in attacking McClellan's main force in accordance with the basic plan. Instead, he had made contact with a Union division under General Henry W. Slocum.[7] Rather than attempt to push by or through this obstacle, Huger fired a few rounds, which were heard by Longstreet. Then he sat down along the Charles City Road in a futile wait for Jackson, not knowing that the latter had halted for the day at White Oak Swamp. In the meantime, Holmes, whose mission was to cut off McClellan's retreat to the James, ran into strong forces of Union Regulars under Sykes and could make no headway.[8] McClellan's abundant caution had caused him to fortify his line of communication with his base at Harrison's Landing on the James against the very maneuver which Holmes was attempting to perform. Still hoping to drive a wedge between McClellan and his river base, Lee now dispatched Magruder to support Holmes. Magruder's troops, however, tired from their forced march from Savage Station, were unable to get up in time to stem the tide in Holmes' losing battle.

Thus, with Jackson's large command still dallying at White Oak Swamp,[9] Huger waiting along the Charles City

---

[6] Also known as Battle of Glendale or Nelson's Farm.
[7] Maurice, p. 108.
[8] *Ibid.* See also A.S. Webb, *The Peninsula*, p. 151.
[9] Most of Jackson's Southern contemporaries unqualifiedly condemn him for his delay at White Oak Swamp. See Maurice, p. 109, et seq. Henderson defends him on the ground that Franklin's Division was in position to prevent his advance. G. F. R. Henderson, *Stonewall Jackson and the American Civil War*, Vol. II, p. 60.

Road, Holmes being unable to make progress along the James, and Magruder off on a wild-goose chase, the only part of the great Army of Northern Virginia to actually fight the Federals on June 30 at Frayser's farm was Longstreet's Division and the battle-weary and badly depleted ranks of the undaunted Light Division. Arrayed directly against them were Kearny's, McCall's, and Hooker's divisions, totalling about 25,000 men and well entrenched. In reserve was Sedgwick, while nearby, observing Huger on the Charles City Road, was Slocum. The total Union strength in these five divisions, all of which got into the battle, exceeded 40,000 men.[10] The Northern generals commanding these divisions, furthermore, were of the best and the troops were well-seasoned Regular Army veterans. The dashing one-armed soldier of fortune, Phil Kearny, was a great combat leader. But for his death at the Second Manassas, he would have been one of the mightiest figures to emerge from the war. Hooker was a first-class division leader whose later tarnished reputation was earned when he was over his head, so to speak, as an army commander. Sedgwick and Slocum, too, were good, hard-bitten general officers who were to see plenty of successful action in the war. McCall, a capable soldier, was captured by A. P. Hill's Divison in the ensuing conflict at Frayser's farm.

Despite the odds, Longstreet opened the battle with a spectacular charge by Jenkins' Brigade at about 4:00 p.m. Jenkins captured the battery which was his objective. Counterattacking Federal infantry, however, pushing Jenkins back and developed a savage battle along the entire front. This time the initial fighting was done by Longstreet's Division with the Light Division in support. Within a short while Hill was called upon to throw his division into the fray, brigade by brigade. First Gregg, then Branch, followed by Field and Pender, went into action. Archer and J. R. Anderson were held in reserve but not for long. The fighting was at such close range that Powell Hill ordered

---

[10] Alexander, p. 153.

resort to the bayonet. Field's men pressed forward with the bayonet so successfully that they broke the Union line and eventually got so far ahead of the general attack that they were cut off until contact was made again by the fiercely advancing brigade of Dorsey Pender.[11]

Field's Virginians were the first troops of the Light Division to engage the enemy at bayonet point during the Frayser's Farm engagement. The 60th Virginia under Colonel William E. Starke broke the Union infantry lines with such ardor that they catapulted through to the supporting artillery. They soon enveloped a battery of Napoleon guns. The Yankee gunners, however, reinforced by some fragments of retreating infantry rallied for a last ditch defense of their pieces. Starke, waving his sword, ordered his men to charge with fixed bayonets in the manner that had been so ferociously pleasing to Powell Hill at Williamsburg. The beleaguered Union soldiers resorted to their own bayonets and a bloody but brief melee ensued. The Virginians soon prevailed and the battery of Napoleons became their prize.

At about the same time, the 55th Virginia under Colonel Francis Mallory, advancing on Starke's flank, seized another Napoleon battery, this time, however, without further opposition from the retreating Union gunners. These two brigades quickly found that their progress was stopped by the Union reserve line, elements of which now pressed in upon both flanks of the Virginians. Dorsey Pender's North Carolinians moved forward to extricate these two furthest advanced of Field's regiments. Gregg, on the left, came under a heavy counterattack that threatened to push back his South Carolina regiments to the extent that both Field and Pender would be exposed to a flank attack. This might prevent their orderly withdrawal to the relatively stabilized front of the rest of the Light Division.

At this point another of Field's regiments took over the stage of action and resolved the immediate dilemma. Robert

---

[11] 11 *O.R.*, Pt. 2, p. 838. Hill's brief report on Frayser's Farm appears here.

Mayo's 47th Virginia, having overrun a Northern battery, turned the guns on the Yankees and permitted Gregg's men to extricate themselves from the predicament. The brigades of Field, Gregg, and Pender were thus permitted to withdraw in good order to a stabilized front, taking their captured guns with them along with a number of Federal prisoners, including Major General McCall, who was taken by Mayo's men. Reorganized, these three brigades of the Light Division again resumed the attack.

Longstreet's Division, on the right flank, now seemed to encounter more difficulty, so Hill sent Archer's Brigade to support that sector of the field. In a typically colorful Light Division action, Archer, leading his men in his shirt sleeves, stabilized the line. Thereupon the entire battle line settled down to bloody, close-range work. As superior Northern numbers began to exert pressure, Powell Hill brought up his last reserve, J. R. Anderson's Georgians. Again the Confederate line rallied and held its own. Just before dark, a final Federal attack was launched. Hill and some of his young staff officers rode along the line searching for one more rallying point. This was found in a group of Wilcox's men from Longstreet's Division. Some of these battle-dazed troops hesitated and then turned toward the rear. Hill feared that the rest might succumb to panic. He seized the unit's standard and roared above the sound of the battle:

"Damn you, if you will not follow me, I'll die alone."

The retreating soldiers stopped in their tracks. The clear voice of one young trooper rang out:

"Lead on, Hill!"

Hill ordered the men to cheer long and loud, as if reinforcements were coming up, and then move to the attack. This they did. The stratagem seems to have succeeded in the semidarkness, for in five minutes the enemy firing ceased and the foe retired.

The Light Division rested upon the battleground that night until relieved at dawn by Magruder's Division which had finally been ordered back from the futile attempt to support Holmes. Powell Hill's men then took stock of their third battle. Their trophies included fourteen pieces of Union artillery and two stand of colors. Their casualties amounted to about 1,700. Longstreet's Division, committed first at Frayser's Farm, lost about 2,600 men.[12]

The battle of the 30th was not a victory for either side. It could have been the greatest Confederate victory of the war because, with only a fraction of the Army of Northern Virginia in action, the Union troops were fought to a standstill. Their retreat was resumed after nightfall. On the other hand, Sumner, the Union commander on the field, thought he could have carried the day if permitted to continue the fight on July 1st instead of withdrawing.[13] Be that as it may, the withdrawal by McClellan toward the James continued. The Confederates attempted to reorganize to press the pursuit.

Lee exercised possibly the greatest restraint of all time in expressing personal feeling when he wrote of the Battle of Frayser's Farm: "Could the other commands have co-operated in this action, the result would have proved most disastrous to the enemy."[14].

Some of the other Confederates were a little more outspoken in their criticism of the man who had cost them victory. Lee's aide-de-camp, Colonel Charles Marshall, un-equivocally stated: "But for Jackson's delay at White Oak Swamp, General Lee would have this day [June 30] inflicted on General McClellan the signal defeat at which his plans aimed."[15]

Wade Hampton, who was with Jackson at White Oak Swamp, flatly states that there was no reason for the delay in crossing and that he so advised Jackson, urging an attack against the comparatively inconsequential opposing forces. Hampton, in a letter to Marshall several years later, said

---

[12] Alexander, p. 155.
[13] Webb, p. 148.
[14] Alexander, p. 155.
[15] Maurice, p. 109.

that Jackson made no reply to his entreaty but merely "sat in silence for some time, then rose and walked off in silence."[16]

E. P. Alexander, who was to prove the best artilleryman in the Confederate Army and later one of the most able analysts of the war, frequently refers to Jackson as being in a "spell" during the entire Seven Days. Alexander characterized Jackson's official report of his conduct at the Swamp as "simply farcical." [17] Jackson's report covering June 30 is as follows:

> About noon we reached White Oak Swamp, and here the enemy made a determined effort to retard our advance and thereby to prevent an immediate junction between General Longstreet and myself. We found the bridge destroyed and the ordinary place of crossing commanded by their batteries on the opposite side, and all approach to it barred by detachments of sharpshooters, concealed in a dense wood close by.
>
> A battery of twenty-eight guns from Hill's and Whiting's artillery was placed by Col. S. Crutchfield in a favorable position for driving off or silencing the opposing artillery. About 2 p.m. it opened suddenly upon the enemy. He fired a few shots in reply and then withdrew from that position, abandoning part of his artillery. Captain Wooding was immediately ordered near the bridge to shell the sharpshooters from the woods, which was accomplished, and Munford's cavalry crossed the creek, but was soon compelled to retire. It was soon seen that the enemy occupied such a position beyond a thick intervening wood on the right of the road as enabled him to command the crossing. Captain Wooding's battery was consequently recalled and our batteries turned in the new direction. The fire so opened on both sides was kept up until dark. We bivouacked that night near the swamp.
>
> A heavy cannonading in front announced the engagement of General Longstreet at Frazier's farm and made me eager to press forward; but the marshy character of the soil, the destruction of the bridge over the marsh and creek, and the strong position of the enemy for defending the passage prevented my advancing until the following

---

[16] *Ibid*, p. 112.
[17] Alexander, p. 147.

90

morning. During the night the Federals retired. The bridge was rapidly repaired by Whiting's division, which soon after crossed over and continued the pursuit, in which it was followed by the remainder of my corps.

Longstreet passed off the incident of Jackson's delay at Grapevine Bridge in his characteristically bitter, dry humor:

> Jackson was long delayed repairing Grapevine Bridge. He probably knew that the river was fordable at that season, but preferred to pass his men over dry-shod.[18]

Even the Union officers, who were observing Jackson's movements during the Seven Days in constant anticipation of attacks which never developed, were amazed at Stonewall's inactivity. General Franklin, commander of the troops opposing Stonewall at the Chickahominy, wrote:

> In fact, it is likely that we should have been defeated that day, had Gen. Jackson done what his great reputation seems to have made it imperative he should have done.[19]

The dawn of July 1 did not give the troops of the Light Division a chance to enjoy retrospective consideration of the previous day. That, in the words of Tennyson's *Charge of the Light Brigade* "someone had blundered" was of no consequence. Their job was to reorganize their decimated ranks, bury their dead, and do what they could for the wounded, many of whom were to die for want of proper care in the filthy abbatoirs characterized in Richmond as emergency hospitals. The enemy had retreated three miles overnight. McClellan had adopted a new fortified position close to the James at a place known as Malvern Hill. Lee's division commanders reported to him during the early hours of the day. New plans were developed. They all continued to be based on one principle—pursue, engage, and destroy McClellan's army. The Confederate generals received their orders and returned to their commands, many, including Powell Hill, impatient to renew the fight despite the toll of the preceding day.

---

[18] Longstreet, p. 131.
[19] *Battles and Leaders,* Vol. II, p. 381.

As always, Hill was solicitous for the needs of his men. He did what he could for their comfort as they rested practically on their arms the night of June 30. As dawn broke, however, nothing concerned Hill but the knowledge that the drive must be continued and that the enemy army, still intact, was only three miles away. So contagious was Hill's eagerness to continue the fight that anticipation rather than dismay ran through the weary ranks of the Light Division, or what was left of it, when word was passed that the pursuit of McClellan would be continued.

History is written in terms of generals, and maneuvers of divisions, corps, and armies rather than in terms of the blood and sweat of enlisted soldiers and their individual movements and squad operations. The soldiers in both armies facing each other at Malvern Hill at dawn on July 1st, however, like all soldiers in all wars, regarded themselves as individuals, not as expendable cogs in great machines. They also regarded their officers and generals as people whom they knew and understood. When that understanding engendered absolute confidence in their leaders, a morale was established that nothing could shake. So it was with the men of the Light Division and their commander. Further, the common bonds between the soldiers of the Union and Confederate armies were so much stronger than those between our troops and all foreign enemies in the history of the Republic that respect for prominent heroes often transcended the lines of hostility. Again, it was A. P. Hill who had captured the imagination of many of McClellan's men far more than any other soldier in gray. Thus, when a Union trooper rolled out of his blanket in the cold dawn at Malvern Hill and looked down the road for the approach of the Light Division, he merely reiterated a common expression as he grunted: "My God, Nellie Marcy, why didn't you marry him?"

Powell Hill, however, probably was not thinking of Nellie or even of his beloved Dolly and their child when he ordered the Light Division to move out on that morning. He wanted to destroy his old room mate, McClellan, but as an enemy in the field, not a suitor for a girl's hand. War was now the business of the Cavalier from Culpeper and the day's battle had become his passion to the exclusion of all else.

It was not destined, however, for the Light Division to participate in the battle at Malvern Hill as it had in the prior phases of the Seven Days. Now, at last, Stonewall Jackson's fresh troops were the first to engage. Lee himself had watched Longstreet's and Hill's men at Frayser's farm and knew that their ranks were so depleted that they could not be effective as frontline divisions even if the spirit of the men would carry them on in spite of the intense fatigue of each individual soldier. The two divisions were, therefore, in reserve. It was, however, a reserve position extremely close to a blazing front. As Hill reported it, "My division was placed in line of battle near the scene of action and under fire, but passive."[20]

Before the day ended, nevertheless, young Pegram's Battery was sent up into action in support of Jackson's bitter but unsuccessful attack against Little Mac's strong position on Malvern Hill. Davidson's Battery, newly arrived from the Light Division's camp near Richmond, was also sent up to bolster the sadly outgunned Conferedate artillery. Both batteries fought with distinction but were badly mauled. Colonel E. L. Thomas had now succeeded to the command of J. R. Anderson's Brigade, the latter having been hurt at Frayser's Farm. This brigade and Branch's were sent to reinforce Magruder. They saw some action but the battle ended that night before they were engaged in the major conflict.

July 1 at Malvern Hill saw the Confederate forces on the Peninsula at full strength for the first time in any battle of the Seven Days—at full strength, that is, except for the casualties of the preceding days, and the weary condition of most of the troops. Even Stuart's cavalry was brought up and was on the main field of battle by the end of the day. Another massed frontal assault with a strong flank

---

[20] 11 *O.R.,* Pt. 2, p. 839.

attack to support it was the order of the day. Jackson had command of the front. Huger, D. H. Hill, and Whiting were on the forward line with Ewell and Jackson's own division in close support. Magruder and Holmes were on the flank opposing the Union left. As already noted, Longstreet and A. P. Hill were in reserve although close at hand. There seems to have been only one tactical misfortune in the preliminaries on this occasion, and that probably was not sufficiently serious to alter the outcome. Magruder became lost for want of sufficient maps and was late in reaching his position on the flank. Holmes, furthermore, was made somewhat ineffective further south on the flank because of a swamp between him and the Union lines. The main battle, however, was scheduled to be directed squarely at the defenses on Malvern Hill. With all of his disappointments of the last five days dismissed for the time being, Lee again hoped for victory now that the Army of Northern Virginia was massed for action.

Unfortunately for the Confederate cause, however, McClellan had also for the first time concentrated his entire strength at one point. Not only did the Union forces overwhelmingly outnumber Lee's troops but McClellan's artillery was set up in an ideal position on Malvern Hill. The lines of guns were banked three deep on the slopes and were arranged in a convex semicircle covering all approaches that were open to Lee, right, front, and left. Behind them was the James and the Federal supply base, so that ammunition was plentiful and there was no danger from a rear attack. The arrangement has been characterized as an artilleryman's dream. Lee first attempted to neutralize the favorable Federal position by an artillery barrage. He hoped thereby to soften up the enemy and then to attack him with a large-scale advance of infantry. This plan was abandoned when it became apparent that the superiority of the Union guns rendered the Confederate artillery virtually ineffective, despite the heroic efforts of such batteries as Pegram's which were sent into action and kept firing until entirely disabled.

94

Next, Lee looked toward the Union flanks to see if they could be assaulted. Again he concluded that they were too strong to risk a charge. Accordingly, about 3:00 p.m. Lee advised Longstreet that there would be no attack that day.[21] Shortly thereafter, however, a skirmish line of Berdan's crack sharpshooters advanced but in such small force that they were repulsed. A detail of Confederates followed them back toward their own lines, driving the skirmishers into a rout. When Lee observed this incident he mistook the retreat of Berdan's men for a general Federal withdrawal. Fearing that the enemy might escape, he ordered Magruder to press a general attack. D. H. Hill then advanced on Magruder's left. The battle thereby was precipitated in a manner that was literally made to order for McClellan. The Confederate infantry was mowed down as it attempted to advance. Confusion broke out as the attacking brigades lost contact with each other in the smoke of battle. Nevertheless, the Army of Northern Virginia pressed so furiously that a severe fright was thrown into the Union forces before withdrawal was ordered by Lee. Porter, for example, at one stage fearing that he might be taken prisoner, destroyed his dispatch book.[22] Porter's anxiety, probably also based on caution, was occasioned, however, more by the fierceness of the attack than by any actual penetration of the Union lines. Webb probably accurately summed up the battle as follows: "The author, as an eye witness, can assert that never for one instant was the Union line broken or their guns in danger."[23]

The unequal battle, winding up the sixth day, ended at nightfall amidst the wreckage of the Army of Northern Virginia. There was no particular scapegoat as far as the Battle of Malvern Hill itself was concerned. Alexander criticized Jackson for not using more initiative in reconnoitering and attacking the Union right flank. It is doubt-

---

[21] Alexander, p. 160. Alexander's full account of the Battle of Malvern Hill appears on pp. 156-174.
[22] *Ibid*, p. 163.
[23] Webb, p. 167.

ful, however, that any maneuver by any portion of Lee's army could have dislodged McClellan's guns. The truth of the matter is that the battle of the sixth day should never have been fought. McClellan should have been outflanked and beaten at Frayser's farm. Even as it was, with ammunition and supplies running low the Federal commander made no attempt to counterattack. That night he completed his withdrawal to Harrison's Landing where he was prepared to embark, if need be.

The seventh day was little more than an epilogue to Malvern Hill. Stuart's cavalry attacked the Union positions along the James but was unable to do much harm. Some high ground known as Evelington Heights, overlooking McClellan's camp, was seized temporarily by Stuart's men, but the Federals soon drove them off. Thus the fighting of seven bloody, heartrending days came to an end on July 2. Lee brought his battered army into position on the 3d in contemplation of one more assault. Jackson, however, still apparently under the "spell," persuaded him that another attack would be futile in the light of the army's condition. As a matter of fact, Stonewall was very likely on sound ground in giving this advice to his commander. The army needed rest and a chance to reorganize. It was heartbreaking for Lee to watch his last chance to destroy McClellan evaporate. The real chances, however, had been lost forever at Beaver Dam Creek, Gaines' Mill and Frayser's Farm.

Thus, as McClellan entrenched himself in his new supply base at Harrison's Landing, the Confederates moved back toward their camps around Richmond. Both armies were damaged but the one hurt worst was the defender and not the invader, as ordinarily should have been the case in a campaign where invasion was repulsed. The losses were as follows:

	Killed	Wounded	Missing	Total
Confederate	3,286	15,909	946	20,141
Federal	1,734	8,062	6,053[24]	15,849

---

[24] Alexander, p. 171. The missing were practically all prisoners of war.

A. P. Hill surveyed the most battered division as he took stock of his men after the Seven Days. His killed and wounded totaled over 4,000.[25] His guns and equipment were smashed. Some of his best officers were lost. The spirit of the men of the Light Division, however, was high. They had proved themselves in one of the bitterest campaigns in history. They were ready for whatever was to follow as long as their leader was Ambrose Powell Hill.

---

[25] Hill's official report places his losses at 4,074, but there are indications that this figure was incomplete. Alexander's computation of Light Division losses during each of its three principal engagements of the Seven Days would indicate a substantially larger figure.

CHAPTER 6

Aftermath of the Seven Days

*L*ONGSTREET was eager to attack the enemy
camp at Harrison's Landing. Jackson thought
that this was too risky. After making a careful personal
reconnaissance, Lee reluctantly decided that a further offensive was not justified. McClellan's position was too strong,
too well defended by artillery and by gunboats in the James
River. This decision marked the end of the campaign.

A few days later Lee also concluded that the necessary
rehabilitation of his army could proceed more smoothly
and with less interference if the men were pulled back
out of range of enemy fire, and to camps less subject to
the illnesses to be incurred in low, swampy ground. On
July 6 he wrote to President Davis:

> The great obstacle to operations here is the presence of
> the enemy's gunboats, which protect our approaches to
> him, and should we even force him from his positions on
> his land front, would prevent us from reaping any of the
> fruits of victory and expose our men to great destruction.
> These considerations induce the opinion that it may be
> better to leave a small, light force with the cavalry here
> and retire the army near Richmond, where it can better
> be refreshed and strengthened, and be prepared for a re-
> newal of the contest, which must take place in some quarter
> soon. I beg that you will take every practicable means to
> re-enforce our ranks, which are much reduced, and which
> will require to be strengthened to their full extent to be
> able to compete with the invigorated force of the enemy.[1]

Accordingly, on July 8 the commands of Jackson and
Longstreet were ordered to make a night march to the rest

---
[1] 11 *O.R.*, Pt. 3, p. 635.

camps which had been selected for them, Jackson on the Mechanicsville Turnpike north of Richmond, and Longstreet (with A. P. Hill's Division attached) to Cornelius Creek between the Central (Darbytown) Road and the James River.

MAP 8. MOVEMENTS OF LIGHT DIVISION, JUNE 30-JULY 8, 1862

A period of some six weeks now intervened before the next campaign. It was supposed to be a time for rest and rehabilitation, and there was some attempt on the part of the high command to effect a better arming of the men, and to supply other items of equipment, such as tentage, which had been in short supply. For the men, however, it turned out to be mostly a period of idleness, discontent, and sickness. The new camp site was an unhealthy one,

100

or so the men thought. Actually the high sick rate, nearly fifty percent, was caused by ignorance on the part of surgeons, commanders, and men of the simplest sanitary precautions and the fact that most of their ailments were due to bacteria transmitted by flies, fingers, and impure food and water. Field sanitation as it is practiced today was virtually unknown in the Civil War, and in fact for years afterwards. Open, unsanitary latrines were used. Water was drawn from polluted streams—even the generals never thought of digging wells.

Bathing was practiced infrequently. Soon the men and their clothing were infested with vermin, including crabs and lice. There is no record that typhus was present, but as usual there was almost universal dysentery, sometimes so severe as to be fatal. There was still considerable typhoid and malaria. The wounded and sick more often died than recovered in the filthy Richmond hospitals. The discovery of antisepsis was still several years away, though chloroform for anesthesia was already in use. Blood poisoning after an "operation" was considered to be a normal prelude to recovery. Amputation was resorted to in the majority of cases of compound fracture or severe laceration from bullets or shell fragments. Inasmuch as gangrene occurred in nearly 100 percent of the cases where amputation was not resorted to, one cannot blame the surgeons for relying so heavily on amputation.

Some individuals shot through the body or pierced by bayonets or swords survived in spite of the treatment afforded them, thus proving the toughness of the human body, if not the medical skill of the era. When arteries were severed, tourniquets were left on so long that gangrene usually followed. Wounds from which the patient would quickly recover today often proved fatal, due to pneumonia if not to infection.[2]

Bacteria were not the only cause of gastro-intestinal complaints. The ration, and its preparation, left much to be

[2] For a full discussion of the medical aspects of the Civil War, see *Doctors in Blue*, by George Worthington Adams. Henry Shuman, New York, 1952.

101

desired. One of the men wrote, "Our rations were good and plentiful—¾ lb of bacon or 1 lb of beef; 1 1/8 lb of flour; salt, molasses, beans."[3] If the men did not all get scurvy from this "bountiful" issue, then it must have been because they were able to obtain berries from the thickets and roasting ears and fruit from nearby farms. An Englishman who served in the Light Division at this time wrote:

> The chief cause of all our sickness has arisen from the lack of good, well-cooked food, regularly changed and diversified. What kind of bread can you expect boys to make who have never seen the process, and are not furnished with proper ingredients or utensils for rendering it wholesome? For several months it was the common practise to make up flour into "slapjacks" or fritters which were nothing more than a thin mixture of flour and water fried in a sea of bacon grease.[4]

There was no provision for unit cooking. Many officers had Negro servants who accompanied them in the field and took care of their needs. But the men either cooked individually or by small groups. There was no instruction in cooking or baking, and no field bakeries were provided. Flour and other components of the ration were issued in bulk. Fresh meat, not often supplied, had to be cooked and eaten at once or it would spoil. Bacon, salt pork, or fat back was more often the meat component, and it could be kept. But it, too, was usually fried. The flour, instead of being baked into wholesome bread, was usually made into a dough and rolled on a stick to be toasted over a fire or in the ashes.

Tentage, even in semipermanent camps, was scanty. At first the men were exposed to inclement weather, as a period of heavy rains which set in about the time of the Battle of Malvern Hill. In their "rest camp the soldiers huddled together, at first wet and miserable, later sweltering in the summer heat along the river bottoms, and wasting with idleness. Dress parades and guard mount were

---

[3] Caldwell, p. 25.
[4] *Battlefields of the South,* p. 307 ff.

102

the only military exercises." Commanders in both armies failed to appreciate that low morale does not result from hard work, but from idleness and boredom. Had they had better instruction themselves they could have devised a reasonable schedule of training in such things as battle maneuvers, the use of the bayonet and rifle, and in field sanitation. Powell Hill and his officers were certainly no worse than the other commanders in those respects. Hill, as a matter of fact, quickly acquired a high reputation as an administrator and trainer of men, so that the Light Division was never quite as bad off as other units.

Prior to the outbreak of the war many of the Southern militia or volunteer regiments had been dressed in fancy gray uniforms which resembled those of West Point and Virginia Military Institute. A board of officers appointed by the Richmond Government designed a uniform, particularly for the officers, which was said to be patterned after the West Point uniform; early photographs of many of the Carolina and Tennessee regiments bear this out. For the most part the men had to supply their own uniforms, though later they were given an inadequate annual allowance of $25 for this purpose. At the time of the opening of the campaign on the Peninsula, many of the units, especially those which had not seen much hard service, were still in these original uniforms. For example, Branch's Brigade, even though it had seen action, in marching down from Atlee's Station toward Mechanicsville on June 26, was described as "coming up in bright uniforms and shining gaiters, battle flags flying."

G. Moxley Sorrel describes the uniform for officers as being a close-fitting, double-breasted gray tunic:

> For generals, staff, and all field officers, dark blue trousers. The arm of the service was shown by collar and cuff— generals and staff officers, buff; cavalry, yellow; artillery, red; infantry, blue; medical department, black. Dark blue trousers had broad gold stripes on the outer seams, except generals, who wore two narrower and slightly apart. Trousers for all line officers under rank of major were

light blue with broad cloth stripe, color of service arm. Rank was shown on collar and sleeve. Generals wore on the collar a gold wreath enclosing three stars on line, the middle slightly larger. On their sleeves was the ornamented Hungarian knot of four 'braids' width. They usually wore their buttons in groups of twos or threes. There was no difference in the uniform or insignia among the several grades of general officers. Colonels wore three stars in line, of the same size; lieutenant colonels, two; and majors, one. The knot on the sleeve was three braids' width for the three grades of field officers. For captains, rank was shown by three bars lateral on the front of the collar, first lieutenant two bars, and second lieutenant one. For headgear the French kepi, color of arm of service, richly embroidered. But the felt hat, black or any color that could be had, speedily pushed it aside.

The intention of the board was to adopt a tunic like the short, close-fitting Austrian garment, but it went by default. The officers would have none of it. They took the familiar cut of frock coat with good length of tail.[5]

Of course, the foregoing was the dress uniform, the one used by officers when they went home on leave, or had their photographs taken. In the field they wore what was called a gray flannel fatigue uniform. One company commander in A. P. Hill's Division describes himself as follows:

> I have my sword, a blanket, haversack, canteen, and a change of underclothing in a light knapsack, and let everything else go; for our wagons are always far off—you never can find what you put in them—and as we are continually moving about, I find my load sufficiently heavy without adding to it. When ordered to march, I am at the head of my company, heavily laden as any; the boy [Negro servant] makes a fire when the halt is sounded, and throwing myself down on my blanket, I share rations with some "mess" or other, and am ready to move or fight at a moment's warning. As for thinking of toilet and appearance, a full supply of pots and pans for cooking, it is all nonsense. Our wagons are scarcely sufficient to carry tents, ammunition, and flour.
>
> Such an army as ours can never be whipped—generals and

---

[5] *Recollections of a Confederate Staff Officer,* by General G. Moxley Sorrel. Neale Publishing Co., New York, 1905. Page 50.

privates are all lean animals, little else but bone and muscle, reduced to proper fighting weight, and all the better for not being encumbered with the baggage of an Xerxes![6]

The men soon wore out the cadet-type uniforms with which they had first been clothed. Their shoes, too, wore out, so that many of them soon were barefoot, replacements for footwear usually being salvaged from enemy dead or prisoners. The need for shoes was always a critical one. In fact the Battle of Gettysburg was brought on by Heth's Division in A. P. Hill's Corps hastening into Gettysburg on the strength of a rumor that shoes were there "for the takin'."

But already, even at the end of the Seven Days, many of the men were beginning to look like the typical "Johnny Reb" described below. By the end of the summer with its strenuous campaigns, all of them would be in the same condition.

A face browned by exposure and heavily bearded, or for some weeks unshaven, begrimed with dust and sweat, and marked here and there with the darker stains of powder— a face whose stolid and even melancholy composure is easily broken into ripples of good humor or quickly flushed in the fervor and abandon of the charge; a frame tough and sinewy, and trained by hardship to surprising powers of endurance; a form, the shapeliness of which is hidden by·its encumberments, suggesting in its careless and un- affected pose a langorous indisposition to exertion, yet a latent, lion-like strength and a terrible energy of action when aroused.

Around the upper part of the face is a fringe of un- kempt hair, and above this an old wool hat worn and weatherbeaten, the flaccid brim of which falls limp upon the shoulders behind, and is folded back in front against the elongated and crumpled crown. Over a soiled shirt, which is unbuttoned at the collar, is a ragged gray jacket that does not reach the hips, with sleeves some inches too short. Below this, trousers of a nondescript color, without form and almost void, are held in place by a leather belt,

[6] *Battlefields of the South*, pp. 307-20.

to which is attached the cartridge box that rests behind the right hip, and the bayonet scabbard that dangles on the left.

Just above the ankles each trouser leg is tied closely; and, beneath, reaches of dirty socks disappear into a pair of badly used and curiously contorted shoes. Between the jacket and the waist band of the trousers, or the supporting belt, there appears a puffy display of cotton shirt which works out further with every hitch made by Johnny in his efforts to keep his trousers in place. Across his body from his left shoulder there is a roll of threadbare blanket, the ends tied together resting on or falling below the right hip. This is Johnny's bed. Within this roll is a shirt, his only extra article of clothing.

In action the blanket roll is thrown further back, and the cartridge box is drawn forward, frequently in front of the body. From the right shoulder, across the body, pass two straps, one cloth the other leather, making a cross with the blanket roll on breast and back. These straps support respectively a greasy cloth haversack and a flannel covered canteen, captured from the Yankees. Added to the haversack strap is a tin cup, while in addition to some other odds and ends of camp trumpery, there hangs over his back a frying pan, an invaluable utensil with which a soldier would be loth to part. His gun is an Enfield rifle, also captured from the enemy and substituted for the old flintlock musket or shotgun with which he was originally armed.

He doesn't care whether anyone likes his looks or not. He is the most independent soldier that ever belonged to an organized army. He has respect for authority, and he submits cheerfully to discipline. He is perfectly tractable if properly officered—but quick to resent an official incivility.[7]

During the first week after the cessation of the Seven Days' campaign A. P. Hill took stock of his division and appraised his subordinate commanders. The losses had been heavy. If one considers that the division entered the Battle of Mechanicsville with less than 14,000 effectives, its total casualties for the Seven Days were over thirty percent. And these were incurred mostly in the first two battles. Another interesting fact to be gleaned from a reading of the casualty

---

[7] *A Typical Confederate Soldier,* by G. H. Baskette. *Confederate Veteran,* Vol. 1, p. 367.

list, summarized below, is the small number of "missing." This indicates that the division lost few prisoners, and that there was a negligible amount of straggling.

Summary of Casualties [8]

Brigade	Killed	Wounded	Missing	Total
Field's	78	500	2	580
Gregg's	152	773	4	929
Anderson's	62	300	2	364
Branch's	105	706	28	839
Archer's	92	443	..	535
Pender's	130	692	..	822
Artillery	12	96	..	108
Division totals ..	631	3510	36	4177

Unfortunately a high proportion of the wounded, perhaps fifty percent, would either die or be permanently incapacitated. Also, there were severe losses among the senior officers. Many accounts of the fighting in the Civil War describe the officers as leading their units in the attack. Actually, as one soldier said, "Charges were not often led by officers. We read often of such things, but they seldom happen. The officers generally remain in rear of their men to keep from being shot by them." [9]

Nevertheless, during these initial engagements, it was common practice for the brigade and regimental commander to be up close to the firing line, if not actually out in front of it. For one thing, the leaders felt that it was necessary for them to set an example to their green troops. It was the "thing to do." Lee and Davis were constantly getting into the thick of the firing. So was A. P. Hill. Consequently, the brigadiers and the regimental commanders, so often under the eyes of their superiors, and always being observed by their men, were where the bullets were flying. As a result, during the Seven Days, Hill lost six colonels and three majors killed, and two generals and eight colonels

---

[8] *Battles and Leaders,* Vol. 2, p. 317.
[9] *N.C. Regts,* Vol. 2, p. 662.

wounded, in addition to a host of officers of lower rank. This seems to have established a pattern. Gregg, Pender, Branch, and Hill were to be killed in action before the war ended, and many other officers of the division were killed or wounded during the war.

Because of casualties, Powell Hill now had to make some readjustments among his senior commanders. In Branch's Brigade, Colonel Forbes took over the Seventh North Carolina, vice Colonel Reuben P. Campbell, killed; and Colonel W. M. Barbour replaced Colonel C. C. Lee, killed, in command of the Thirty-seventh North Carolina. In Archer's Brigade, Colonels T. C. Johnson and J. C. Shackleford, both killed, were replaced, respectively, by Colonels W. W. Boyd and P. Turney. Pender's Brigade lost two battalions, the 2d Arkansas and 22d Virginia, transferred, and three regimental commanders (wounded), Conner, Riddick, and W. J. Hoke, being replaced by R. H. Gray, E. H. Miller, and L. D. Andrews.

One of the brigade commanders, J. R. Anderson, also had to be replaced. We have seen that he became hors de combat at Frayser's Farm during the Seven Days. He returned to a semi-civilian job at the Tredegar Iron Works without ever again leading his Georgian troops in battle. His successor was a hard-hitting regimental commander named Edward L. Thomas.

Thomas had served with Anderson as his senior colonel. His own regiment was the 35th Georgia, which conducted itself with conspicuous success during the Seven Days. Thomas was wounded on the second day of the campaign, but remained in action and took over temporary command of the brigade at Frayser's Farm. Although he was not officially given Anderson's job as commander for some time, he was actually its battlefield leader after Frayser's Farm. Thomas proved himself in combat as an able replacement for Anderson. He was soon promoted to the rank of brigadier general and led the Georgian brigade of the Light Division throughout the remainder of its period under the leadership of A. P. Hill. Thomas' Brigade then carried on

108

under Harry Heth when the reorganization of the army took place ofter Chancellorsville. Thomas was the only one of Hill's brigade commanders to emerge from the Seven Days' battle who would continue in constant action until Appomattox.

On the 25th of June, 1862, as Powell Hill had prepared for the attack that he would lead the next day, Thomas was a comparatively obscure colonel, with whom Hill had had little chance to become acquainted. It was upon the brigadiers, with whom he had closer contact, that Hill had primarily relied. Though they were largely untried in major operations, Hill felt from the outset that he could trust Branch, Gregg, Pender, Archer, Anderson, and Field in battle. As a result of the fighting during the Seven Days, Hill was assured that his confidence had not been misplaced. During the days ahead he was to find that Thomas was a worthy addition to his cherished group of brigadiers.

The weeks following Malvern Hill were a period in which retrospect was inevitable, providing an evaluation of what might have been. In Hill's mind, as in that of Longstreet, Lee, and others, was surprise and disappointment that Stonewall Jackson had performed so poorly. Lee never publicly commented on this, although Longstreet was quite vocal. A. P. Hill has left no record of his views on the failure of Jackson at Mechanicsville, Gaines' Mill, and White Oak Swamp. Nevertheless, he pondered at length upon the reasons advanced for Stonewall's deficiencies during this campaign. No more than any of his contemporaries nor hundreds of historians, could Powell Hill solve the problem.

To many casual readers of the history of the war, the inference that Stonewall Jackson might ever have been tardy in bringing his command to an important military rendezvous may be surprising or even "lese majesty." To Jackson's champions, from Henderson down the line, such inference would probably either be shocking or lead to an argument. The impartial analyst, however, must conclude that tardy he was, not only at the outset of the Seven Days, but at virtually every crucial point during that campaign. It would seem fair to say that the whole course of the war might have been changed had McClellan's great army been badly smashed during the Peninsular campaign. It would be idle conjecture to assess the blame for the campaign's failure, from the Confederate viewpoint, to any one incident or any one man. It remains an historic fact, however, that McClellan, despite his withdrawal, was able to preserve his army virtually intact, and it suffered far fewer casualties than the Confederates.[10] It is a further historic fact that Jackson's command, although relied upon as the key to the whole Confederate plan of battle throughout the Seven Days, never really got into action until the very end. Why Jackson let this happen is a question for the ages. Historians have not solved it.

The story of A. P. Hill necessarily involves a critique of Jackson's conduct on the field and of his personality. Hill's battlefield activities were very closely related to Jackson's. To ascertain the cause of the two men being constantly at loggerheads, as they were soon to become, requires at least cursory study of their respective characters.

It has been suggested by some close students of the war that there was nothing noteworthy, or even surprising, in anybody's failure to get along with Jackson. Only Lee seemed to understand him and to make allowances for his eccentricities. No other officer ever was taken into Stonewall's confidence. None who served with him were immune to the whiplash of his tongue or castigation in his reports. Courts-martial of subordinates were frequent, even among the ranking generals who were under his orders. In Jackson's favor, however, it must be pointed out that the red-haired Hill was unduly sensitive and had a quick temper. Stonewall was not the only general with whom Hill clashed. In Hill's favor, in this respect, it might be noted that his quarrel with Longstreet, once terminated by the interces-

---

[10] Livermore, p. 86, gives 19,739 killed and wounded for the Confederates, and only 9,796 for the Federals. The latter, however, reported 6,053 missing as against only 875 for the Confederates.

sion of Lee, became a dead issue never to be revived. Hill had no other open animosities. Jackson's quarrels were endless, although none quite reached the depths of vindictiveness engendered by the almost constant turbulence in which he found himself embroiled with the otherwise generally sociable and amiable gentleman from Culpeper.

At West Point, Hill and his friends did not actually express dislike for Jackson. They merely ignored him. The escapades as cadets shared by Hill with his cronies McClellan, Burnside, and Heth represented conduct foreign to Jackson's nature. Even Jackson's slouch-shouldered, awkward appearance kept him apart from the others. There was no common ground for them beyond the fact that they all attended the Military Academy and later went on to Army careers. Hill's Cavalier background, handsome features, and erect, military bearing created in him a scorn for the unusual, extremely unimposing type that Jackson represented in his cadet days. Hill was an extrovert, described by his contemporaries as having a magnetic personality. Jackson was dour, austere, introspective, and unsociable. The vague feeling of animosity toward Jackson which developed in Powell Hill at West Point was in itself enough to create, during the war, deep resentment at what he thought was unjust treatment of himself, his officers, and his troops. This state of mind on Hill's part, coupled with Jackson's smouldering disdain for anybody he felt was crossing him, regardless of rank, set the stage for the months of bickering that were to follow, which at times caused Robert E. Lee as much concern as impending action by the enemy.

Things might have gone more smoothly if the two men had ever become associated in a campaign other that the Seven Days. Hill had tremendous respect for men who could prove themselves on the field. He knew of Jackson's early reputation for his campaign in the Shenandoah Valley and was prepared for a further brilliant demonstration. He secretly wondered how the one-time awkward and unpromising cadet had blossomed into such an outstanding soldier who had earned the war's most honored sobriquet, "Stone-

111

wall." He would have been happy to put aside the old dis-like of Jackson if he had been afforded reason to do so. Instead, he found Jackson to be a disappointment as the campaign opened, and a total failure until Malvern Hill, the last of the Seven Days.

It was not merely the old story of the chasm between the well-to-do, handsome, popular youth and his poor, awkward, self-retiring counterpart. That might have been the way it started. But such differences are generally obliterated between men who become comrades in arms on the field of battle. Unfortunately, the Seven Days' campaign only served to fortify Hill's old prejudice. He felt during that critical week that Jackson was fouling up the whole campaign scheme and causing unnecessary loss among the men of the Light Division. He found himself inquiring as to what else one could expect from a fellow like Jackson.

Such an attitude on Hill's part was manifestly unfair to the hero of the Valey campaigns, the "Stonewall" of the First Manassas, the genius whose unprecedented flanking movement was to confound Pope in the second Battle of Manassas and who was to shine as the wizard of Chancellorsville. It can never be denied, however, that severe criticism was properly leveled at the Jackson of the Peninsular campaign during the seven days of bloody fighting around Richmond.

Douglas Southall Freeman, the great analyst of the war and the portrayer of the men who fought for the Confederacy, concludes that Jackson was in a "spell." It might have been that exhaustion, caused by the hurried movement east, following the hard-riding Valley campaign, placed Jackson in a state from which he could not drive himself to further activity.

Longstreet was one of those who suggested that "Jackson was a very skillful man against such men as Shields, Banks, and Fremont, but when pitted against the best of the Federal commanders he did not appear so well." [11] This argu-

---

[11] *Battles and Leaders,* Vol. 2, p. 405.

ment loses substance when it is noted that Jackson fared very well against the best Union generals in subsequent campaigns.

Whatever the reason, Jackson's inadequacy on the Peninsula was not conducive to instilling confidence or respect in the mind of a fellow commander such as A. P. Hill who, throughout an entire campaign, constantly found himself out on a limb. Where was Jackson on the 26th of June? His absence caused Hill to make the assault at Beaver Dam Creek alone. Tremendous losses were sustained by the Light Division, Porter's lines were not smashed, and this first and vital stage of Lee's plan of attack failed, because Jackson neglected to make a simultaneous attack on the Union right. Yet Stonewall could have done so. He had 18,000 men in bivouac at nearby Hundley's Corner a good part of the afternoon. Though they were there during the crisis of the day's fighting, they never fired a shot.[12] Powell Hill's opinion of Jackson was certainly not enhanced on that first day of the campaign.

Again, what caused Jackson to delay his start on the 27th and then to mistake Gregg's men for the enemy and fire upon them? An eight o'clock departure in the midst of a campaign seemed much too leisurely to Hill and all others concerned, especially to the Confederate casualties who were shot down accidentally by their tardy and ill-informed brothers in arms. Hill's opinion of Jackson was not raised by the incident.

Later that same afternoon, why did Jackson delay in making the attack on the left at Gaines' Mill? He wrote in his report that he "hoped the enemy would be driven" by Hill and Longstreet into a sort of trap that he and D. H. Hill improvised. Once more, however, A. P. Hill, was left to do the "driving" without Jackson's anticipated support. Bearing the brunt of the action, his division suffered heavy and needless casualties. A coordinated attack by Jackson might have achieved a substantial victory. It certainly would

---

[12] See chapters 3, 4, and 5 supra, for references from the *Official Records* and other sources on Jackson's activities during the Seven Days.

have avoided a great percentage of the losses sustained by the Light Division that day. Hill's appraisal of Jackson was now lower that ever. Even Lee had to dip into his self-restraint when he expressed to Jackson, after his tardy arrival, that he "had hoped to be with you before."

The next question posed by study of Jackson's movements during the Seven Days revolves around his delay at Grapevine Bridge on the 28th and 29th. Why did he take nearly two days to cross the Chickahominy at Grapevine Bridge? That seems to be partially answered by the fact that the 29th was Sunday, on which Jackson had religious "duties" to perform. In any event, Jackson remained in bivouac that day while Magruder, desperately engaged at Savage Station, vainly called for help from Stonewall's command. The delay on the 29th again destroyed Lee's timetable for the campaign, and eventually forced Hill and Longstreet to once more engage the Federal force at Frayser's Farm without aid. What sort of dilatory character was this man Jackson? Hill wanted to know.

Finally, to top it all off, what prompted Jackson to "sit down" at White Oak Swamp within sound of the fighting at Frayser's Farm and, as on the first of the Seven Days, do absolutely nothing? Even with the delays of the 28th and 29th, Jackson still could have gotten up before it was too late. Again, however, Longstreet and Hill had to go it alone against over 40,000 Union troops, most of them Regulars under the command of five of the best Northern divisional commanders, Kearny, Hooker, Sedgwick, Slocum, and McCall. How could Hill, by this time, have any respect for the reputation that was built upon victories over the likes of Fremont and Banks?

Henderson weakly defends his champion's wait on the north side of White Oak Swamp by pointing out that Jackson's path was blocked by a Union division commanded by Franklin. The Northern troops concededly were outnumbered several times by Jackson's force. Franklin himself dispels this excuse by bluntly admitting that "We should have been defeated that day had Gen. Jackson done what

. . . he should have done." Jackson's own report, which General E. P. Alexander termed "farcical," fails of any sort of sound explanation for the delay at White Oak Swamp. Similarly, his other reports during the Seven Days do not suggest a reason or an excuse for Jackson's repeated delays and the frightful cost to the Confederacy which they occasioned.

There had been, of course, very little personal contact between Jackson and Hill during the campaign. Although there was nothing upon which Hill could base any new respect for Jackson as a soldier, he still bore him no active personal animosity. There were, Hill realized, good generals and bad. It was better to fight side by side with a good one, but personalities had no place on the battlefield.

The subsequent trouble between Jackson and Hill might have had a background, at least on Hill's part, in the Seven Days, but the act that was to trigger the outward hostility between them was yet to occur. When Hill first joined Jackson's command, a short while later, he did so with a reasonably open mind and a sincere hope that the next campaign would go better. The Culpeper cavalier, moreover, had enough cockiness to believe that his presence would make Jackson a better general. This, incidentally, was a surmise that the events of the next few months would substantiate.

CHAPTER 7

Personalities Clash

*A*BOUT THE MIDDLE of July Powell Hill became involved in a clash of personalities with General James Longstreet. This was the more unfortunate because up to this time the fine personal relationship and coordination of effort between Hill and Longstreet had emerged as one of the most noteworthy items on the credit side of the Confederate ledger as stock was taken of the Seven Days. That highly desirable harmony between the two generals was sharply and permanently shattered.

The trouble started when a vain and dogmatic, although able newspaperman named John M. Daniel accompanied Powell Hill's division during the Seven Days on behalf of the newspaper of which he was editor, the *Richmond Examiner*. Daniel went about the business of "field duty" in the grand manner. He wore specially tailored uniforms and was accompanied by servants. He regarded himself as important in every sense of the word. Somewhat paradoxically, in view of the man's conceit, he actually was important because he was the most widely read war correspondent in the South. At Gaines' Mill he received his crowning glory, a slight wound in the arm which permitted him to return to Richmond as something of a disabled hero. His writings now received more attention that ever. It suited his fancy to memorialize the occasion of his becoming a war casualty by eulogizing the Light Division and its commander.

Unfortunately, Daniel's laudation of Hill was accompanied by snide disparagement of other divisions and other generals. This hit home as far as Longstreet was concerned because he and Hill had teamed together during much of

117

the fighting. Old Pete became justifiably rankled at repeated articles giving all the credit to the Light Division in battles where his own troops had also fought with honor, distinction, and success. The camel's back was broken finally when Daniel wrote a summary of A. P. Hill's achievements which included credit for the latter's handling on June 30 not only of his own division but also of "one of Longstreet's two divisions." This account went on to snipe at Longstreet by inferring that he was not present at the start of the battle and that an inexcusably unwarranted burden had been thrown on Hill. His troops having been belittled and his own character assailed, Old Pete now entered into the newspaper arena.

He had his adjutant, Major G. Moxley Sorrel, write a reply to Daniel's stories about Hill. Sorrel's article was printed in the *Richmond Whig*. Sorrel went a little too far in the opposite direction with respect to giving credit to the Light Division. Now it was Hill's turn to become angered. After all, he had nothing to do with Daniel's stories and did not feel any responsibility for them, although his fierce pride in the Light Division unquestionably gave him a glow as he read the somewhat exaggerated accounts of its exploits. Powell felt, therefore, that Longstreet had no business interjecting himself into a situation that had developed through no fault of anybody officially connected with the army. Hill immediately (July 12) wrote through channels to Lee, requesting relief from command of Longstreet. The latter forwarded this letter with the indorsement: "I see no particular reason why Maj. Gen. A. P. Hill's request should not be gratified."[1] Lee then sat on the communication for a while, hoping that the disagreement would be ironed out by the passage of time. In the interim Longstreet had occasion to request, through his adjutant, Major Sorrel, a report from Hill on some routine matter. Hill indorsed this back with the statement that he "declined to hold further communication with Major Sorrel." [2]

---

[1] 11 *O.R.*, Pt. 2, p. 640.

118

This action by Hill took the affair from the category of a newspaper squabble, involving bragging and name calling, into the status of military insubordination. With all his famed impetuosity, Hill was a good soldier, ready to obey any order, and undoubtedly would not have acted as he did had he not felt that the honor of the Light Division had been impugned. Longstreet had probably had enough of the original dispute by then, but he could not afford to gloss over Hill's insubordination. He directed Sorrel to place Hill under arrest. This was done. Hill, in cold silence, accepted the order placing him under arrest and restricting him to camp limits. Then, apparently with time on his hands, Hill took up his pen and wrote a scathing letter to Longstreet in which he, in effect, supported Daniel's assertion that Longstreet had been derelict in his duty on the 30th. Longstreet, rather foolishly, it would seem, replied with vituperation. Hill responded in the only manner available to a Virginia Cavalier of that day. He challenged Longstreet to a duel. Longstreet accepted. Seconds were making "arrangements" when word got back to Lee. The commander of the Army of Northern Virginia was beside himself. His hands were full mapping strategy for the conduct of the war, and now he had to take time out to prevent one of his two best generals from killing the other.

Lee first appealed to the patriotism of the antagonists and pointed out that military necessity absolutely forbade the course which they were pursuing. He then took more tangible action. He had already sent Jackson to Gordonsville to watch Pope. He had intended to reinforce Stonewall before long in any event. Therefore he seized upon the instant situation and ordered the Light Division to join Jackson at Gordonsville forthwith. The orders pointed out that Hill was under arrest but Lee also advised Jackson that Hill's senior brigadier, Anderson (still with the divi-

---

[2] Entire incident related by Sorrel in *Recollections of a Confederate Staff Officer*, pp. 84-89.

sion), was not of sufficient experience to be entrusted with the command. The inference was that Hill's arrest would soon be over. The necessary steps were taken and on July 26, with A. P. Hill restored to command, the Light Division left to serve with the Hero of the Valley and enigma of the Peninsula, Thomas J. Jackson.

The friction between Longstreet and Hill never again flared into the open but all cordiality between them was ended.

As far as congenial relations with his immediate superiors were concerned, it was out of the frying pan into the fire for Hill. A long series of incidents was soon to mar his service with Jackson. Those incidents, however, were not in any way to interfere with the fighting efficiency of the Light Division nor with the well coordinated teamwork between Jackson and Hill which, for the next few months and through several hard campaigns, was to write a memorable page in the history of the Confederacy.

Sorrel feared that he had incurred the hatred of the fiery Powell Hill because of his part in the affair. Hill, however, had an abiding sense of fairness and justice. He realized that Sorrel had acted under orders from Longstreet. Sorrel thought Hill's manner later was somewhat menacing but conceded after the war that this was his imagination. Powell was always ready to give credit where due and, during the final year of the war, recommended Sorrel for promotion to brigadier general. Moxley served with distinction under Hill as a brigade commander during the last days before Appomattox.

Sorrel was later to see the letter which Hill sent to the War Department requesting his services to fill a vacancy calling for a brigadier general. Sorrel was only a lieutenant colonel, but Hill's request was so strong that it was approved by Lee and passed on to the President, who endorsed thereupon with his characteristic scrawl, "Make the appointment. J.D."[3] Writing later of the incident in his *Recollections*, Moxley Sorrel said:

---

[3] Sorrel, p. 89.

It is not necessary to say how much I appreciated [Hill's] action toward myself. It proved him magnanimous and free of petty spite in that affair, and such was his nature. When I reported to him no one could have been more warmly welcomed, and thence-forward I had nothing but kindness and the most valuable support and help while with his corps.

That Sorrel was regarded as quite a soldier in his own right is indicated by Longstreet's order relieving him from his headquarters duty with the First Corps on November 4, 1864, and assigning him to Hill's Third Corps with promotion to the rank of brigadier general. Longstreet's order stated:

The loss of this officer to the First Corps with which he has been so permanently connected since its organization, will be severely felt. Distinguished alike for gallantry in the field and for energy and skill in the administration of his department, his value cannot be over-estimated. He will carry with him to his new command, so richly won, a sure promise of success in the record of the past.[4]

Sorrel was among the few high ranking officers to serve under Longstreet and A. P. Hill. He was apparently the only subordinate officer to have close personal relations with each of them. The fact that he deeply admired them both and heaped equally lavish praise on each in his postwar writings speaks for itself. Sorrel was a Georgia bank teller, with absolutely no military experience, when the war broke out. His rise in rank and his distinguished record stamp him as well out of the ordinary run of civilian soldiers. His intelligent appraisal of Hill and Longstreet, based upon personal observation, serves to place a common denominator under the two men. It points up the many respects in which they were similar to each other. Above all, however, it establishes the fact that each was what is termed a "soldier's soldier," because after he left the Central Railroad Bank in Savannah in 1861, Moxley Sorrel stopped being a civilian and became a soldier in the truest sense of the word. No

---
[4] *Ibid,* p. 296.

greater compliment could be paid Hill or Longstreet, even by Lee, than the expressions of esteem that Sorrel wrote many years later.

Although it was unfortunate that Hill and Longstreet never became real friends after the newspaper incident, that fact was less significant to their common cause than the never-ending friction between Powell and Stonewall Jackson. Hill and Longstreet were never teamed together as division commanders after the Seven Days. As corps commanders, they subsequently operated somewhat independently of each other and always under the constant control of Lee. They never again ran afoul of each other and the Confederate war effort never suffered as a result of their lack of cordiality, as it certainly did, at least indirectly, because of the Jackson-Hill feud. The unnecessary nervous tension engendered in both Hill and Jackson, as well as the time consumed in planning their charges and countercharges, to say nothing of the added burden placed upon Lee by his efforts to placate them, surely hampered the Confederate cause, even though the two headstrong protagonists of the drama always buried their differences in actual battle.

Even if Longstreet and Hill had been compelled to serve together, once the heat of the Daniel affair had cooled, their natures were such that they would have gotten along without difficulty. There were not the fundamental differences between them that created the chasm between Hill and Jackson. They might have fought a duel over real or fancied insults to their troops, but they would have seen eye to eye in problems of command, methods of handling their men, and even in their respective outlooks on life generally. The Sorrel incident exemplifies this.

We have seen that Old Pete was quick to praise Hill's work as a regimental commander at Williamsburg. He also praised the Light Division at Gaines' Mill where he described Hill as "[pressing] his battle with great zeal and courage." [5] Then, even after the altercation about each of

---

[5] Longstreet, p. 126.

their respective division's press credits, Longstreet applauded Hill at Sharpsburg, where he described the collapse of Burnside's advance as caused by his being "outflanked and staggered by the gallant attack of A. P. Hill's brigades." [6] Finally, there was Old Pete's laudation of the Culpeper Cavalier after Hill was killed in action near Petersburg, when he referred to him as a "sword made bright by brave work upon many heavy fields." [7]

Hill never lived to write a book about the war, so he never had a chance to reciprocate the good things Longstreet wrote about him. He always regarded Longstreet highly as a soldier, nevertheless, and though there was a distinct coolness in their personal relations after the newspaper episode, there was never any bitterness between them or anything but respect in their appraisal of each other as men and soldiers.

Longstreet represented a somewhat different aspect of the Southern soldier than the Virginian, Hill, the North Carolinian, Pender, or the South Carolinian, Gregg. Longstreet was born in South Carolina, raised in Georgia, and lived for a while as a youth in Alabama, from which state he received his West Point designation. His Southern heritage was tempered by the fact that his father had been a native of New Jersey. The cumulative effect of this background made Longstreet suspicious of those who gloried in their native states as much or more than in the Confederacy itself. This, of course, was especially true of Virginians. It accounts to some extent for Longstreet's flareup at Hill over the Daniel newspaper articles. There were many officers who would have laughed off the incident. More significantly, it accounts for Longstreet's frequent disagreements with Robert E. Lee, for Longstreet always felt, and history would seem to bear him out, that Lee's whole strategy was designed to protect Virginia at the expense of the Confederate States of America. This critical attitude led in turn to serious breaches between Lee and Longstreet, such as that which

---

[6] *Ibid,* p. 261.
[7] *Ibid,* p. 605.

existed on the field of Gettysburg. One must wonder what might have happened if there had been neither a Jackson-Hill feud nor basic differences between Lee and Longstreet. The combined military talents of the four men, even lacking harmony, outshone anything of corresponding nature on the Union side. What might they have accomplished if there had been existing among them perfect harmony and tranquillity in battle plans, and the execution thereof?

The weeks immediately following the Seven Days were utilized by many Confederate commanders, even by General Lee, to take leave to visit their homes, or to meet their families in Richmond.

Powell Hill, for one, welcomed the cessation of hostilities after the Seven Days' Battle as a cherished opportunity to rejoin his wife and baby. His first child, baby Henrietta, had by then suffered the frequent fate of infants in the war-torn South. She had fallen ill and died, probably for want of little more than routine medical care which was simply not available to civilians at the time. A second daughter, Francis Russell Hill, had been born in late 1861. Mother and child were then visiting members of the Hill family near Richmond. Culpeper, being in the line of fire, so to speak, had been evacuated early in the War by many of the residents. As a matter of fact, a strong Union force under General Pope had moved into the vicinity of Culpeper within a few days of the end of the fighting on the Peninsula.

Powell Hill, apparently more than most professional soldiers, needed his wife's companionship even in the heat of campaigns. As the war progressed he managed to keep Dolly near at hand. He was criticized for this by some of his contemporaries who found it a nuisance to have to include in campaign plans arrangements to care for the Hill family. Lee, however, did not object. Perhaps he felt that all reasonable steps should be taken to provide for the happiness of the man whose work on the Peninsula had stamped him as the Army's best fighting general.

The smashing cannonade and the wild bayonet charges are easily chronicled by the historian of the "big picture" of the War Between the States. The mechanical chronicle of a battle, however, cannot begin to tell the story. The story is that of the men who fought and bled. Dorsey Pender did not regard himself as a mere figure in a "big picture" even though, as a brigadier general, his was a larger and more formidable place on the canvas of history than those of the soldiers in the ranks who unhesitatingly followed his command. In turn he would be a relative pigmy when compared to his immediate commander, A. P. Hill. Then, Hill would be dwarfed by Lee, Jackson, and Longstreet who in history's final grand view of the war would be cast as the stars of the play.

Each, however, from Lee to the lowest ranking private in the Light Division, went through the day, whatever their respective duties might have been, as men. They had the fears, hopes, thoughts, and sentiments of men. In the heat of battle, they experienced fear. In the success of the moment they found elation. And so it was with Dorsey Pender. But when the evening halted the hostilities for a few hours, he exemplified the feeling of all of the troops, North and South, as his thoughts turned to Fanny. He wrote to her almost daily. He was faithful to his custom even as the smoke of battle lifted toward the stars over Virginia.

> My Dear Little Girl: I will avail myself of the chance to let my dear wife know that she is not forgotten.*** I have told you often enough that I thought you pretty and you know, as you have often said, you can do anything with me. Darling, I love you more than you can know and how much superior you are to any of the ladies around you. I have a good wife. Oh! how good; intelligence, youth and beauty; what more could I ask? If I was not satisfied I would indeed be difficult to please.[8]

This probably expressed the thoughts of hundreds of men at night after battle more articulately than they could have done themselves, but Dorsey Pender's letters to Fanny ex-

---

[8] These and following excerpts from *Pender Papers*.

pressed something that was common to all soldiers. It was an expression of loneliness and longing, but nevertheless of hope and confidence that all would soon again be well and normal. The strength that enabled Dorsey Pender to write love letters from the bloodiest battlefields, rather than to wail in despair was attributable to three things. First, he was a soldier in the true sense of the word. Second, he was a man who would exhibit courage under any circumstances of war or peace. Third, he had completely immersed himself in Christian religion. He carried his Bible at all times. Even in darkest moments of personal danger he turned to it to discuss its teaching with his wife hundreds of miles away. He wrote briefly of the battle and somewhat more at length about his men: "One cannot imagine the degree of confidence and high spirits displayed by our men. The men seem to think that I am fond of fighting. They say I give them 'hell' out of the fight and the same in it."

He was proud of the tribute and would not deny to Fanny that he was "fond of fighting." Nor did he hesitate to quote the word "hell," although he never used profanity. This was as characteristic of Pender as his refusal to ever question or even experience annoyance at Powell Hill's frequent and violent oaths. Nevertheless, after duly reporting on the events of the day and the state of his command, he would proceed to devote the bulk of his letters to affairs much closer to Fanny and far remote from the field of action. Having learned that she suspected pregnancy, he turned to that subject and based his text upon the Bible.

Now my dear let me write about you a little. I wrote asking you to send me word of your symptoms and I suppose you would not comply because you felt that there was no longer any doubt. I was reading the Bible the other night. It stated that children were such a blessing, and given as an evidence of favor in God's sight. Ought we to complain so at what is evidently His Divine Will— for did we not try to oppose it? and with what effect? Let us look upon the bright side of it and be cheerful. I do wish you could go through with it without being so sick.

126

You will not, poor thing, be able to enjoy this spring and summer any.

My love to all. Tell Turner never mind if no one will write to papa for him, that he can spite them some of these days. My dearest little wife, accept of my entire devotion and believe that you are ever in my heart. May God bless you,

Your devoted husband.

Powell Hill's thoughts of Dolly were equally tender. He could not, however, bring himself to such flowing expression of what his heart felt. Perhaps it was partly that it was not fitting for a Cavalier to become oversentimental. The constant necessity to keep driving himself until he had accounted for every detail concerning the plans of battle and the welfare of his troops also tended to make love letters, such as Pender's, difficult for him to write. Finally, the dislike of public demonstrations of religion forced him to keep such things to himself, at least when Dolly was not there. He couldn't find the solace in writing of love and the Bible that eased the evenings for Dorsey Pender after the violence of the day.

One wonders about the effect of repression of emotions upon his health. True, he would explode in great bursts of temper if occasion warranted. His tender personal emotions were, however, never openly expressed, especially once he passed to high command. His love for Dolly was as passionate as Pender's for Fanny. Like many personal feelings, however, he confined it to his inner thoughts. Profanity in the heat of battle; outbursts when military detail became confused; these were part of his life as a soldier. His inner self he felt belonged to no one else.

The carefree, almost playboy type of life that had been Hill's at West Point, in Mexico with the senoritas, and in whirlwind courtships at Washington and other urban points of his military service was gone. In its place there was now little except the vibrant activity of impersonal duty during the day and lonely introspection at night. Perhaps Pender's open exercise of religious beliefs and feelings would have been palliative to the attacks of illness that were becoming more common to A. P. Hill as the months on the battle line went by. It is true that Jackson, deeply and outwardly religious, seemed much like Hill. Jackson's activity in the line of duty often led to displays of temper, frequently climaxed by tantrums. In Jackson's life, as in Hill's, such days were followed by nights of solitude and deep thought. Jackson, however, had always been temperamental and moody. For Hill, it was something new.

Just what his illness was, Hill didn't know. His refusal to take doctors from what he felt was their more important work of aiding and rehabilitating wounded troops kept him from getting the medical attention he often needed. He was, however, aware that something was very much wrong. It has been inferred by some that Hill's sickness was to some degree psychosomatic, possibly because his mother had been something of a hypochondriac. The sickness that struck him down at critical points of his career, however, was definitely not a mere product of his mind. He hated to be deterred from his duties on the field by frailty of the flesh. He probably didn't help matters any when he wracked his brain as to the cause of what seemed to be increasing periods of partial disability. Attempts at analysis and failure of solution made things even more difficult. The doctors, on the few occasions that he asked for physical examinations, passed him without question. They had no means, such as the modern X-ray or blood analysis, for diagnosing abdominal disorders. The doctors' ignorance of the cause of Hill's illness made him remember that he had been found physically qualified for West Point only to be stricken with the ailment that the Academy doctors couldn't name. That had meant an extra year for him at the Point and had delayed the start of his military career to the extent that some of his contemporaries, Jackson included, had acquired a jump on him in the Mexican War. It had always irked him that he had never overcome this handicap from the promotion standpoint, while he and his contemporaries wore the blue of the United States Army.

128

He had contracted yellow fever in the swamps during the Indian campaigns. The aftermath of that disease certainly did not bolster his health, but he knew that it was something deeper and more mysterious than that. The feeling of weakness, developing practically into helplessness, that hit him at the Military Academy came back in the war years. He often felt effects of the strange sickness as night fell, and it forced him to withdraw even further than usual into the shell that would have been abhorrent to the prewar dazzling Cavalier of Washington drawing rooms and the ballrooms of Virginia society. The pallor and the sunken cheeks revealed in his last pictures indicate that his health was growing progressively worse. This began to be reflected in the appearance of the commander of the Light Division as the stress of constant months on the battle line took its toll. It was to be increasingly evident when he later assumed the heavy responsibilities of a corps commander and, at the very end, of chief field advisor to Robert E. Lee.

Though the cause of his illness was never known to Powell Hill, its physical effect on his features distressed him long before the disease brought on temporary disability during the war. As a cadet at West Point, and later as a young officer, he had been cleanshaven. He had been a devil-may-care redhead who had no trouble in making acquaintances with the ladies. He felt a moustache to be in order when he grew older and served—socially, as well as with respect to his duties—in Washington just before the war. It was not long after that when he noticed a slight hollowing under his cheek bones. He first hazarded a small chin beard to offset what seemed to him, if not his female acquaintances, this blemish upon his handsome features. The next step was a full beard.[9] Dolly didn't disapprove. She thought it made him look more mature or perhaps a bit more the subject of envy among the less fortunate girls. In any event, the beard did serve to cover to some extent the effects, real or fancied, of his chronic poor health upon his features. Once the war had commenced, of course, Hill

[9] See the photo taken before the war.

129

cherished his red beard as a mark of seniority and distinction.

Pender's robust health might have been a good tonic for Hill if his own ailment had been merely psychosomatic, a word, incidentally, that was not known in the 1860's and today is often used loosely when illness cannot be better diagnosed. When Hill felt poorly, especially in the aftermath of strenuous forced marches or a hard battle, he found comfort in Pender's attempts at spiritual ministrations, as well as in Dorsey's apparent boisterous, healthy well-being. At such times, he welcomed visits by Dorsey and the soft-spoken attorney from South Carolina, Maxcy Gregg. Gregg would join him in a glass of bourbon on occasions when it was available and the troops were comfortably bedded down. Hill would never indulge in the luxury of relaxation, let alone liquor, unless the men were as well off as he. When the occasion was right, however, and singing echoed from the camp fires, Hill and Gregg would sip a drink and Pender would join in a pipe of good tobacco.

"General Pender," Hill would say, "this is good tobacco, Virginia tobacco."

"You are right, General," Dorsey would reply, "this is good tobacco, but perhaps it comes from the fields of Carolina, where the best is grown."

"*South* Carolina, down around Columbia," Gregg would interject in his deep drawl.

At other times Pender turned his thoughts for a few moments toward home and Fanny.

Hill's chores were endless. He had no time to think of wife and family. He had no time to worry about the nauseous weakness to which he would not permit himself to yield. It never occurred to him to seek solace in Bible, contemplation, or prayer. He was the commander of a division consisting of 14,000 men, all dependent on him for their safety and well-being.

130

CHAPTER 8

Cromwell and the Cavalier

ABRAHAM LINCOLN wanted a Union general who would show more aggressiveness than McClellan had exhibited on the Peninsula. In June, 1862 he brought Major General John Pope from the West, where Pope had enjoyed some success, and appointed him to the command of a newly formed "Army of Virginia." This force, containing 38,000 infantry and artillery and 5,000 cavalry, comprised the divisions of Fremont, McDowell, and Banks. Fremont, objecting to being under the command of his junior in rank, was replaced by Franz Sigel. On assuming command, Pope ordered the concentration of his scattered divisions, with the mission of moving on Gordonsville and Charlottesville in order to take some of the pressure off McClellan.[1]

General Lee was unable to devote much attention to Pope until after the Seven Days' battles. By that time, Pope was moving against the loop of the Virginia Central Railroad, connecting Richmond with Gordonsville. This action, threatening the Confederacy's important granary in the Shenandoah Valley, could not be ignored. Lee was in a quandary. Was it safe to divide his numerically inferior force in the face of the threat still posed by the Army of the Potomac, and send part of it west to resist Pope? In answering this question, he had to consider the delicate situation presented by the fact that Jefferson Davis, sensitive to the danger to the capital, was almost daily peering over his shoulder. Nevertheless, Lee did not hesitate. He decided

---

[1] Major General John Pope, "The Second Battle of Bull Run," *Battles and Leaders of the Civil War*, Century Co., New York, Vol. 2, pp. 449 ff.

to detach Jackson and send him to Gordonsville. This decision was made easier by Lee's growing dislike of Pope. The latter, by his bombastic pronouncements and ill-advised threats to shoot hostages, aroused the ordinarily mild Lee into regarding Pope as little better than a vermin which ought to be suppressed.[2] On July 13 Lee ordered Jackson with his own and Ewell's divisions to proceed to Louisa Court House and, if practicable, to Gordonsville, there to oppose the reported advance of the enemy from the direction of Orange Court House.

Realizing that Jackson had only about 18,000 troops, Lee was naturally somewhat worried over the situation. On July 25 he wrote to Jackson, in part, as follows:

> I wrote you on the subject of sending you re-enforcements and the difficulty. I am extremely anxious to re-enforce you, and would send General A. P. Hill's division, but he is now in arrest. General D. H. Hill I have been obliged to send south of James River to take Holmes' place . . . Although feeling weak, uncertain which side of the James River the enemy will advance, and being obliged to watch both, I could send you a force to suppress Pope could I see a chance of your hitting him which did not involve its too long absence . . . If Pope goes far enough, could you swoop down north of the Rappahannock, suddenly uniting with Stuart, and clear the left bank opposite Fredericksburg?

By now the Army of Northern Virginia had been organized into two "commands." Under the existing laws of the Confederate States of America no provision was made for military organizations larger than divisions. This, of course, made it extremely difficult for Lee to maintain coherent control of the army. The situation became worse when the army was divided, one part at Gordonsville, the other remaining around Richmond. The practical solution, therefore, was the establishment of two informal "commands," one under Jackson, the other under Longstreet. They were soon to be formalized into corps by legis-

---

[2] Freeman, *Lee*, Vol. 2, p. 264. See also 12 *O.R.*, Pt. 3, p. 917 and 919.

lation. For all practical purposes, the framework of the army was by mid-July built in the form in which it was to exist until Jackson's death the following spring.

There were two divisions now under Stonewall: his own original division, now under hard-bitten Charles S. Winder, with John R. Jones, William B. Taliaferro, (pronounced "Tolliver"), and A. R. Lawton as brigadiers; and Ewell's Division, which included brigades commanded by Jubal Early and Isaac Trimble, together with "Dick" Taylor's old Louisiana Brigade, now under Harry Hayes.

Serving under Longstreet were his own division and those of D. R. Jones, Lafayette McLaws, Henry A. Wise, A. P. Hill, and R. H. Anderson. D. H. Hill, Magruder, and Huger had been relieved of their commands and assigned to other duties.[3] Whiting's Division was kept under Lee's direct control as a sort of headquarters unit. The army's cavalry, under the command of Jeb Stuart, was divided into two brigades, one commanded by Wade Hampton, who had previously been with Jackson, the other by Fitzhugh Lee, nephew of R. E. Lee. There was still no separate artillery organization. Each brigade had its own battery, subject only to the orders of the division commander, although in effect, Longstreet and Jackson, respectively, had the ultimate control of all the batteries in their commands.

On July 27 Lee made his decision to augment Jackson's command. The following order was published:

> The Second Brigade, Louisiana troops, is temporarily attached to the division of Maj. Gen. A. P. Hill.
> Maj. Gen. Hill, with his division, will proceed by railroad with the least practicable delay to join Maj. Gen. T. J. Jackson at Gordonsville, Va.

The Light Division was now by far the largest in the entire Confederate Army. The brigades that had emerged from the Seven Days had been refilled to make up for the casualties they had sustained. They continued to be com-

---

[3] Magruder and Huger were relieved because of inefficient work on the Peninsula. D. H. Hill was reassigned to the comparatively important command of troops south of the James.

manded by the same brigadiers who had reported to A. P. Hill when the division was organized in late May, with the single exception, as we have seen, that Colonel E. L. Thomas now headed Anderson's Georgians.

The attached Louisiana Brigade was under Colonel Leroy A. Stafford.

Powell Hill was proud of his command, pleased with his officers, and happy at the recognition shown him by the War Department in adding a brigade to his division as the new campaign was about to begin.

Hill entered upon his new assignment by disregarding if not technically disobeying Lee's orders. Lee had directed him in writing that if he was to take his own wagon trains, he should cut this transportation down to the lowest limit. He was informed that Jackson would furnish him wagons when he got to Gordonsville, and that the troops remaining near Richmond would need all available transportation to haul provisions. Now Hill, who was always very close to Lee and completely responsive to his commander's desires, in this case probably regarded the order as a routine directive from the Quartermaster. Very likely he had little confidence that Jackson would share any transportation with him, and, like all enterprising commanders, he was resolved to see to it that his own command was properly provided for. Consequently, instead of loading on the flatcars only the "lowest limit of transportation," he took an excess. Lee didn't discover this until too late to require Hill to disgorge the extra wagons, so he simply wrote to Jackson to retain them for use with future additional troops which Lee hoped to send him.[4]

The Light Division moved out quietly on July 27 or 28, arriving in Gordonsville on the 29th. This movement was soon detected by the Federals, however. On August 2 Brigadier General S. W. Crawford of Bank's division re-

---

[4] There was nothing unique in Hill's action. A close study of the records of subsequent wars will disclose that commanders habitually acquire and retain as much transportation as they are able to "get away with" despite repeated orders to turn in excess and captured vehicles.

ported that "A. P. Hill arrived yesterday with 10,000 infantry."[5]

"Little Powell," happy enough to get away from Old Pete, experienced no special misgivings at serving under the man whom he felt had let him down so badly during the last campaign. His first contact with Jackson, however, proved distasteful. When he arrived at Jackson's Gordonsville headquarters, ready for action, he found that his new commander was engrossed in the court-martial of one of his more able brigadiers, "Dick" Garnett. Garnett was extremely popular with his men and fellow officers. It is difficult to believe that he could have committed a dereliction of duty meriting court-martial. It might be noted that Garnett was subsequently removed from Jackson's command to Longstreet's—the converse of the disposition adopted by Lee to stem the conflict between Hill and Longstreet. Garnett was destined to die a hero's death in Pickett's charge at Gettysburg. On July 29 at Gordonsville, however, he was just a defendant before a court-martial. That this sort of thing was going on bothered Hill. He learned, furthermore, that courts-martial of high ranking officers were frequently resorted to by Jackson. One proposed victim of charges by Jackson was Major General W. W. Loring. Another was Colonel William Gillam, who had been on the faculty at V.M.I. with Jackson. Neither rank nor previous friendship meant anything to Stonewall where enforcement of his concept of discipline was concerned.

Jackson, on his part, was indifferent to the quarrel between Longstreet and Powell Hill. His only reaction to the affair was gratification at having his command increased by the arrival of the Light Division on July 29 at Gordonsville. As a matter of fact, Jackson rarely read the newspapers at all. For one thing, if he had any spare time for reading it was devoted to Holy Writ. Besides, he didn't want to submit his "Christian humility" to the strain of the praise that the press continued to heap upon him despite his failures on

[5] 12 *O.R.*, Pt. 3, p. 525.

the Peninsula. There was, however, one document that he did read in connection with Hill's arrival.

It was a letter from Lee which contained the following:

> A. P. Hill you will, I think, find a good officer with whom you can consult, and by advising with your division commanders as to their movements much trouble can be saved you in arranging details, as they can act more intelligently. I wish to save you trouble from increasing your command.[6]

It can be readily seen, therefore, that Lee was a bit apprehensive of Jackson's "lone wolf" attitude and his recalcitrance at coordinating his actions into any sphere of common endeavor in which views of others might be at variance with his own. Lee knew that Hill would take orders like a good soldier. He also knew that if treated in an unfair manner his spirit might rebel as it had against Longstreet and that thereby the effectiveness of the army's best division might be impaired. Although Lee's letter to Jackson was well intentioned, the Confederacy's cause might have been better served if it had never been written. Jackson never attempted to follow the suggestions therein and he resented the rather elementary advice which it contained. This resentment seems to have been, albeit perhaps unconsciously, transferred to Powell Hill in Jackson's gloomy, introspective mind.

Hill was eager for action and glad to start out in a new command with a clean slate. He observed at the outset, however, certain things about Jackson's command which were entirely foreign to the Light Division. Hill noted that discipline throughout Jackson's forces, especially in Winder's Division, was maintained by punishment bordering on brutality, rather than being based upon esprit de corps as in the case of his own men. Desertions were numerous among Jackson's troops. Imposition of the death penalty, unheard of in the Light Division, was common. Even this early in the war, Winder's men were wont almost openly to observe that "Winder's next fight would be his last."

---

[6] 12 *O.R.*, Pt. 3, p. 919.

Jackson was personally less unpopular than Winder but probably only because he was held in more awe. He was respected as a general by his men but the respect was not born of admiration as in the case of A. P. Hill. Jackson was a martinet and has been likened to Oliver Cromwell. It is little wonder that the Cavalier from Culpeper often looked askance at the conduct of his superior with respect to his troops.

The testimony at Garnett's trial was favoring the defendant when Jackson received word that Pope had divided his command and was maneuvering in the vicinity of Culpeper. Some have said that Jackson was anxious for an excuse to break off the apparently ill-advised court-martial. This was probably true, but above and beyond that, Stonewall had been withholding battle only until he received reinforcements and was given a propitious opportunity to move to the attack. Now A. P. Hill was with him, and reports indicated that Pope's command was divided and vulnerable. Without preliminaries, Jackson on August 7 walked out of Garnett's court-martial and issued orders putting his entire command on the road toward Orange Court House, which was only twenty miles below Culpeper. This was the place at which it was anticipated contact with the enemy would be made.

Jackson's orders called for the three divisions of his command to march at dawn. The order of march was to be: first, Ewell, then, Hill, with Jackson's own division under Winder closing the rear.[7] At this point occurred the first friction between Jackson and Hill. Almost immediately after issuing the original orders of march, Jackson revised his plans and decided to send Ewell by another route under orders to reunite with the rest of the column near Barnett's Ford on the Orange-Culpeper Road. This move was tactically sound as it would relieve congestion on the main route and serve to confuse Pope who would be unaware of Ewell's ultimate destination. Unfortunately, however, Jack-

---

[7] 12 *O.R.*, Pt. 2, p. 214.

son neglected to tell Hill of the change in plans. At dawn, therefore, Hill was ready at the head of his leading brigade waiting for Ewell to pass by so that the Light Division could swing into place behind him.

Sometime after sunrise the impatient Powell Hill observed troops proceeding down the road in the appointed direction and assumed they were Ewell's men. They were, however, elements of Jackson's Division which, under the revised plan that had never been disclosed to Hill, were intended by Jackson to follow the Light Division. A brigade passed before Hill realized this was Jackson's Division. Jackson from his headquarters was watching the confusion sometimes attendant upon breaking camp of a large body of troops. At first he failed to realize that anything was amiss. Finally, it was called to his attention that men of A. P. Hill's Division were merely standing around, aimlessly waiting.

Jackson angrily rode to Hill and unceremoniously asked why his division was not marching. Hill's reply that he was waiting for Jackson's Division to pass might have been a bit abrupt and not couched in the best prescribed terms to indicate deference to a superior. The fact remains, however, that the mixup was entirely occasioned by Jackson in not taking Hill into his confidence as directed by Lee, and Powell was justifiably piqued at being taken to task.

Jackson's infantry under Winder continued to pass Hill's waiting column. Jackson in his haste and unwarranted anger now made another mistake. He rode to the head of what appeared to be the next brigade coming up the road and ordered the commander to move on with full speed. It so happened that the troops which Jackson thought constituted the head of a brigade were only the vanguard of his wagon trains. The officer in charge, however, being under Stonewall's direct orders, started the trains in motion without permitting Hill to fall in line behind Winder as he had intended to do. The now seething Hill thus had to wait until all of the wagons had passed before he could put the Light Division on the road. By this time it was afternoon. The vaunted speed of the Light Division had been utterly wasted. Nevertheless, Hill rode out past the slow-moving columns to see if anything could be done to hasten things. After all, he was now in country that he knew like a book. Roads and fords between the position of the column and Culpeper were the familiar scenes of his boyhood.

At the head of the column, however, he found things in even worse state. Ewell's Division had reached the rendezvous at Barnett's Ford on the Rapidan simultaneously with Winder's arrival. Lacking orders as to precedence here, Ewell had gone on first, taking his full accouterment of baggage with him, while Winder's troops waited. Further progress for the Light Division that day was out of the question although it had moved little more than a mile. Hill reports that he then received verbal orders from Jackson to go back to Orange Court House and encamp for the night.[8] He thereupon ordered his men to bivouac where they were. He asked Jackson for orders for the following day, and offered to lead the Light Division over a different route to Culpeper through the country with which he was so familiar and thereby relieve the congestion on the main highway. Jackson sent back word to continue on the original route, adding that the baggage trains would be moved off the road to expedite passage of the fighting troops the following morning.

Thus ended the hot, futile day of August 7, 1862. Jackson had intended to engage Pope that day near Culpeper and to precipitate a battle if the Northern general had been caught off balance as Stonewall hoped. The day ended with the Confederates far from Culpeper and with Pope having been given ample time to organize for an engagement.

Everything had gone wrong. Jackson did not hesitate to attempt to fix the blame for the debacle, the obvious selection for a scapegoat being Powell Hill. Jackson endorsed upon Hill's report a series of statements charging the day's failures to lack of compliance with orders upon

_____
[8] *Ibid.*

139

Hill's part.[9] Most of Jackson's arguments in this rather unusual document were labored and failed to establish any disobedience in his subordinate's actions. He did, in effect, however, accuse Hill of being a liar in that Jackson denied categorically ordering him to bivouac at Orange Court House that evening as reported by Hill. These amounted to "fighting words." Jackson's report, however, was not written until some time later and Hill probably did not at the time understand the full import of the accusation. In any event, there was a war in progress, and the commander of the Light Division was now on his "home grounds" and anxious to fight for his cause rather than with his cantankerous chief. The Light Division was prepared for battle the following day.

Analysis of what transpired on August 7 shows clearly that Jackson was at fault. Why did he almost seem to hasten to create trouble with Hill? Why could he never take a subordinate general into his confidence? Despite his many successes, how much more could he have achieved if he had worked *with* his colleagues, instead of regarding them as automatons who must anticipate and perform his wishes, or be pushed aside and subjected to humiliation and punishment!

A. P. Hill was the type of soldier who could and did put himself in the right place at the right time. As a result, he worked well with Jackson, at times when they were scarcely speaking to each other, or even when charges and countercharges flew between them to Lee's great consternation.

Hill was far from being blameless for the extent to which the bitterness grew. It was the Cromwellian attitude of Jackson, however, that kindled the fire and goaded the quick-tempered redhead into the angry retorts to his superior that placed the matter eventually far beyond the power of Robert E. Lee to mediate.

Jackson resembled Oliver Cromwell in more than one

---

[9] 12 *O.R.*, Pt. 2, p. 216.

respect. They were both able and extremely successful soldiers. They were both martinets with respect to their troops and their officers, regardless of rank. They both eschewed panoply in their own military dress and pomp and ceremony in those they commanded. They were both devoutly religious men to whom God symbolized the cause for which they fought. Neither could understand the "cavalier" viewpoint. Jackson probably never was conscious that there was a "cavalier" viewpoint in the Army of Northern Virginia. He honored and respected the cavalier Lee, who was his superior. He disdained the cavalier A. P. Hill, personally, but readily availed himself of the latter's services as a first-class field commander. He probably never used the word, "cavalier" with respect to either Lee or Hill, or, for that matter, any other officer with whom he was associated.

On the other hand Hill, who had studied Cromwell, recognized him in Jackson. It was a matter that might have amused the carefree junior officer of a few years before. Now there was no time for amusement in his wartime relations with Thomas J. Jackson. Hill had no more desire than Jackson to fight again the old British war between Cromwell and the royal family, among whose retainers Hill's ancestors were found. The basic disparity in the respective makeups of the two men was, nevertheless, generations old. The contradiction in pattern between their attitudes, not only toward the war, but toward life in general, constantly rubbed the sores of their personal differences.

Jackson could never understand the state of mind that led Cadets Burnside, Hill, McClellan, Heth, and others to risk expulsion from the Military Academy for a few hours of fun, a few drinks, and the transient attentions of young ladies. Hill could never comprehend how a fighting man could risk a campaign to conduct a service in his capacity of elder in the Presbyterian Church in which he personally administered the sacrament to all members of his command who desired it.

141

Strangely, however, the two men were so able to complement each other in battle that their differences melted in the heat of the moment. Within ten days of their first personality clash, Jackson called upon Hill to extricate the whole command from a bad situation at Slaughter's Mountain. Hill responded with distinction. At the Second Manassas, Jackson assigned to Hill the key job of holding the critical left of the line. Hill succeeded in what appeared a hopeless task. At Harpers Ferry, Jackson, at the last moment, released Hill from a state of arrest in which he had placed him, after one of their more violent quarrels, and put him in a position of authority. This set the stage for the famous forced march of the Light Division to Sharpsburg, arriving just in time to save the entire Army from possible annihilation.

And so it went, Cromwell and Cavalier, always putting aside personal differences when the crisis came. The paradox of this incongruous fighting team continued until the Battle of Chancellorsville. Here Hill held Jackson in his arms while waiting for the surgeon who vainly treated Stonewall's fatal wound. A few days later the Culpeper Cavalier succeeded the deceased Cromwell of the South as a corps commander in the cause for which they both gave their lives.

They never reconciled their divergent views on life, religion, and almost everything else, except their common devotion to their cause and their concepts of duty.

The fighting, aggressive mood of the Confederacy in the summer of 1862 as exemplified by A. P. Hill and the Light Division, found an interesting contrast in the North. We have already seen that McClellan's Peninsula campaign failed largely as the result of McDowell, and the 40,000 troops under his command, being withheld, because of the Federal Government's constant fear of a surprise attack on Washington. The deception employed in moving Jackson's forces from the Valley to the Peninsula partially accounted for the Northern apprehension. A jittery U.S. War Department had feared, until the last moment preceding the Seven

142

Days, that Jackson was still in the Valley and that he had designs upon Washington. Fear for the safety of the Capital continued to control the Northern thinking that summer. The Union war effort in Virginia was now further hamstrung by a congressional "investigation" of the conduct of the war, prompted by public uneasiness. This was coupled with another handicap in the form of an unfortunate selection of a new commanding general for the forces in central and northern Virginia. Thus, while Powell Hill and his troops, together with other units of Jackson's command, were well primed for an offensive campaign, the Northern leadership had adopted a defensive attitude, with an uncertain strategic policy bordering on chaos, and with inept John Pope in the field against Lee.

The hearings of the Congressional Committee on the Conduct of the War[10] afforded a sounding board for Northern alarmists and military amateurs. Lincoln and the War Department, for obvious political reasons, were compelled to listen to this new interference with the cohesive conduct of the war, although they were aware of the probable unsoundness of whatever plan the committee might produce. Lincoln, the Secretary of War, and the chief of military operations, General H. W. Halleck, then proceeded to join the committee in being impressed by Pope's statements to the effect that, if he had McClellan's army added to the force already under his command near Washington, he could not only dissipate all danger to the Capital, but could march to New Orleans if necessary, to end the rebellion."[11]

Pope testified to that effect before the Congressional Committee at the Capitol. He then traveled to the White House to repeat his boasts. The Congressmen were interested in any plan that would assure ample protection to Washington. Their attitude was primarily defensive, but they would gladly support an offensive strategy if it was fool-proof from the viewpoint of the capital's safety. The Pope plan appeared sound to them. Lincoln and his advisors had nothing

---

[10] A. L. Long *Memoirs of Robert E. Lee*, p. 182.
[11] *Ibid*, p. 183.

better to offer after McClellan's failure on the Peninsula. So it was that John Pope took the field as the new battle leader to oppose the Army of Northern Virginia. The offensive portion of the plan, however, could not be put into full effect by that first week of August, 1862, because McClellan's army was not yet reorganized and ready to be turned over to Pope to complete the grand army that he proposed to lead to New Orleans if need be.

Pope did have a large force on the field in northern Virginia at the time, but not one that he or the War Department wanted to risk in large-scale offensive action. Pope, nevertheless, had probed as far south as Culpeper in an attempt to learn what Lee might be planning. Banks commanded the forward unit of the probing force. Although Pope was keeping an eye on the Washington defenses and was not at all ready to precipitate a battle, the man (Banks) who previously had been Jackson's victim in the Valley, being as courageous as he was inept, was not averse to getting another crack at Stonewall.

The Northern strategy on August 7, therefore, was to deploy cautiously around Culpeper, keep Lee where he could be watched, and try to maintain the status quo until Pope was sufficiently reinforced to begin a great campaign that would end the war. Aside from the personal feelings of General Banks, the Northern attitude was by no means aggressive that day.

On the Confederate side, many of Powell Hill's men were only a few miles from their homes. They were stung by the thought of the Yankee occupation. They had proven themselves in battle, had confidence in their commander, and were proud of their division. They felt that they were on the march to drive the enemy back north. Theirs was a definitely aggressive point of view. There was no time to await reinforcements. Just as the spirit of the Union troops was not at fever pitch, because they knew that the big advance would not take place until another army was ready to join them, the Confederates were grimly determined, because they knew there would be no reinforcements for them. They realized that if their homes were to be retaken, they would have to do it themselves.

Pope had proclaimed that his headquarters were "in the saddle," and that it would be the business of his army "to seek the adversary, and to beat him when found."[12] This dramatic statement was given considerable notice in the Press on both sides, but lost much of its desired effect when some Confederate wag wrote that "Pope's headquarters were where his hindquarters ought to be."

Jackson and A. P. Hill, for their part, made no such proclamations as they rode north from Gordonsville. They were, nevertheless, about to demonstrate the efficacy of actual "headquarters in the saddle." They were, furthermore, seeking their adversary, not running from him. The next day they would find and beat the impetuous General Banks.

---

[12] *Ibid*, p. 184.

CHAPTER 9

Battle of Slaughter's Mountain

*C*OMPARED to the battles of the Seven Days and some of the subsequent fighting, the affair at Slaughter's Mountain[1] was a minor engagement. It did have certain significance, however, in the overall picture of the war. In the first place, it definitely eliminated any question of McClellan's remaining on the Peninsula for a renewed campaign against Richmond. One of Lee's major purposes in sending Jackson on the campaign was to arouse the consternation in Washington which always followed any movement by Confederate troops in the general direction of the Northern capital.

Major General H. W. Halleck, an undistinguished soldier, who had been lucky in the west and who was known as "Old Brains"—a misnomer if ever there was one—had recently been brought to Washington and placed in charge of all Union military operations, with the title of General in Chief. Upon observing Confederate movements around Gordonsville Halleck hastened the recall of McClellan from Harrison's Landing despite the latter's request for reinforcements and permission to continue the fight on the Richmond front.[2] By quitting his position on the James, McClellan now surrendered without firing a shot the very objective which Grant was to attain some two years later after a long and bitter campaign involving appalling Union casualties.

---

[1] Also known as the Battle of Cedar Mountain or Cedar Run. Local inhabitants, however, have generally referred to this hill as Slaughter's Mountain after the locally prominent Slaughter family.
[2] Marshall, p. 122.

The Slaughter's Mountain engagement also precipitated the important Second Battle of Manassas. In fact it might almost be called the first stage of that battle. The clash of August 9th was further noteworthy in that it marked the end of Jackson's "spell" of inactivity, although it indicated that Stonewall was rather inept in the handling of a diversified command including several divisions. Finally, Slaughter's Mountain had significance in that there, for the first time, A. P. Hill went into action as part of Jackson's command and demonstrated that he could function brilliantly in that capacity despite personal differences. The Light Division saved the day on the 9th and it was not the last time that it performed this feat.

Jackson's and Ewell's Divisions had been reduced to considerably less than full strength before they were sent to Gordonsville after the Seven Days. They did not total much over 12,000 men between them. The Light Division was at effective fighting strength of 12,000.[3] It might also be noted that, despite recruiting difficulties, the Confederates had an intelligent policy of handling what manpower was available to the Richmond government. They sent recruiting parties out to secure replacements in the areas where the regiments had been raised originally, thus maintaining continuity of unit lineage and esprit. Recruits were interspersed among seasoned troops so that completely green troop units were not constantly being added to the army as was the case in the North. The result was that a reinforced division such as Hill's was well balanced even though it contained many inexperienced men. The Union's inexplicable policy, on the other hand, was to keep veteran and rookie outfits entirely separate. There were in Pope's command, as a result, several extremely green and ill-trained regiments. In addition, Pope, somewhat less than a military genius himself, was assisted by a group of corps and division commanders of considerably poorer quality than those who had been fighting under McClellan on the Peninsula.

---

[3] Alexander, p. 180.

They included Banks, Jackson's victim on more than one occasion in the Valley; Franz Sigel, a German soldier of fortune; Milroy, still the commander of an independent brigade despite his unfortunate experiences at the hands of Stonewall; and Irwin McDowell, a good officer whose only combat experience to date had been the debacle at Manassas. Banks, Sigel, and McDowell commanded the I, II, and III Union Corps, respectively. The Federal cavalry was under the capable John Buford. By now, Pope's entire force aggregated 49,500.[4]

As Jackson's command hurried along the dusty road toward Culpeper in the wake of the confusion of the preceding day, the emphasis was upon haste at the expense of caution. Jackson's inadequate reconnaissance failed to reveal either the position or the strength of the enemy until contact was made without warning early in the afternoon about halfway between Orange Court House and Culpeper on the slopes of a hill which the local citizenry called Slaughter's Mountain. This hill lay west of the Orange and Alexandria Railroad. Jackson did not know what troops were before him. He feared that he might have run into a superior force because he knew that Pope's overall strength outnumbered his own command by two to one. Actually, however, the Union force with which contact had been made consisted of only a portion of Banks corps which numbered not over 8,000.[5] Hill's Division was not yet up but Jackson had on the line Winder's entire division and all of Ewell's except Lawton's Brigade which, along with Gregg's Brigade of the Light Division, had been detailed to guard the wagon trains in the rear. The contact with the enemy was so sudden, however, that Winder and Ewell could not readily break their divisions out of their marching column formation into array for battle. Guns were brought up and artillery fire was used to screen the maneuvering of the troops into combat position. Almost in the first reply from Banks' guns, Winder, who was engaged

[4] John C. Ropes, *The Army Under Pope*, p. 4.
[5] *Ibid*, p. 19.

in getting his division in line so as to constitute the Confederate left flank, was hit by a shell. He died on the field very shortly thereafter. The prophecy that "his next battle would be his last" was fulfilled. His, however, was a hero's death. His men were responding to his orders without thought of mutinous murder when Winder was hit.

Winder's command now fell upon his senior brigadier, William B. Taliaferro. Taliaferro was to develop into a brilliant leader of troops. At the moment of Winder's death, however, he was in a most difficult predicament. The field was still in a confused state, his predecessor not having had opportunity to complete deployment of the division. The Union positions and strength were still unknown quantities and, worst of all, nobody had confided in Taliaferro the plan of action which Jackson had decided to adopt. That plan called for the right of the Confederate line to be established by Ewell who was to cross over the shoulder of the "mountain." Taliaferro's command at that time had an exposed left flank and was not in contact with Ewell on the right. The latter was still engaged, as Winder had been, in transforming his division from a marching column into a battle line. As Taliaferro desperately attempted to rise to the situation for which, through no fault of his own, he was so ill prepared, the Federals hit his exposed left.

Banks was under orders to do no more than feel out Jackson with skirmishers and not to precipitate a battle without sending to headquarters at Culpeper for reinforcements.[6] Limited though his command ability might have been, however, Banks was a brave and impetuous man. He thought he saw a golden opportunity in the obvious Confederate confusion to even old scores with his tormentor of the Valley. In disregard of orders, therefore, he moved to the attack, concentrating upon turning the Southern left, a logical maneuver even though Banks was unaware of the added advantage he had in that sector of the field as a result of Winder's death.

[6] *Ibid*, p. 20.

Hill was not "up" when the fighting started. He was not far behind, however, having determinedly pushed the Light Division throughout the day to close the gap between it and the leading divisions of Winder and Ewell. Powell was smarting from Jackson's comments of the previous day but he did not sulk. On the contrary, he wanted the Light Division to so distinguish itself that Jackson would have to eat humble pie.

The latter event was something that would never transpire during the short life span that lay before Stonewall Jackson. As far as the Southern Cromwell was concerned, the criticism of yesterday would never be expunged by the exploits of today. Despite the unpleasant personal situation that had arisen, however, it was extremely fortunate that the Confederate reserve element on August 9th was the strong Light Division. Much of its effectiveness probably would have been lost if it had been the first to arrive on the confused field of Slaughter's Mountain in accordance with the plans which of necessity had been revised by the comedy of errors of the preceding day.

Hill was as unaware of Jackson's plans as was Taliaferro. He had the advantage, however, of being in a position to estimate the situation before committing his troops. The division's order of march as it approached the sound of battle near Slaughter's Mountain was: Thomas, Branch, Archer, Pender, Stafford, and Field.[7] Gregg had been assigned to guard the trains. Jackson rode up to Hill as the van of the Light Division hurried along the dusty road to the west of the "mountain." He requested a brigade to support Taliaferro's faltering division. Thomas was dispatched upon this duty. Then, quickly reconnoitering the line of battle, Hill observed the gap between the left wing and Ewell on the right. He immediately ordered Lindsay Walker, his artillery chief, to rush guns into the breach. Walker found the road so clogged with ambulances and wagons, however, that he could bring up only two bat-

---

[7] This and other details of the battle appear in Hill's report. See 12 *O.R.*, Pt. 2, pp. 214-216.

teries. Fortunately those were the two whose commanders were the most persistent and drove the hardest. It goes without saying that one of them was led by the irrepressible Captain Willie Pegram. The other was Fleet's Battery under the temporary command of Lieutenant W. B. Hardy. Thrown into an exposed position, these batteries were nearly surrounded by advancing Federals as they were brought into action without infantry support. Jube Early, however, got over the shoulder of the hill at the critical time and, leading a savage charge, rescued the guns and gunners.

In the meantime, the fight on the left was going badly for the Confederates. Taliaferro's troops, including men of Jackson's prized Stonewall Brigade, broke as the Federals enveloped their flank. Thomas' Georgians from the Light Division were holding fast but everything else in that sector of the field was crumbling. Jackson now rode into the thick of the melee, waving his sword and exhorting the troops of his old division to rally and follow him. He roared exhortations like a preacher of the Gospel on horseback. He succeeded in restoring some semblance of order among the retreating men. The line continued to be forced back, however, until Powell Hill, alertly grasping the situation, was able to get Branch's Brigade in formation to establish a new left flank. Then Archer and Pender brought their brigades into play. Hill now threw his coat aside, drew his sword, and rode among the men of the Light Division. The veterans of the Seven Days quickly reversed the rout of Taliaferro's troops and savagely counterattacked, their cheers for their general echoing across the slopes of the mountain so that they might almost be heard in his native Culpeper. A member of Powell's staff, J. William Jones, recalls that

> I saw him [Hill] at the crisis, with coat off and saber drawn, throwing out skirmishers to stop stragglers, tearing off the bars of a lieutenant who was skulking to the rear, and giving his clear, crisp orders as he hurried his veterans

152

into the fight and hurled back the blue lines who were advancing flushed with victory.

Now as the three brigades of Powell Hill's Division, Branch in the van, Archer and Pender in support, drove

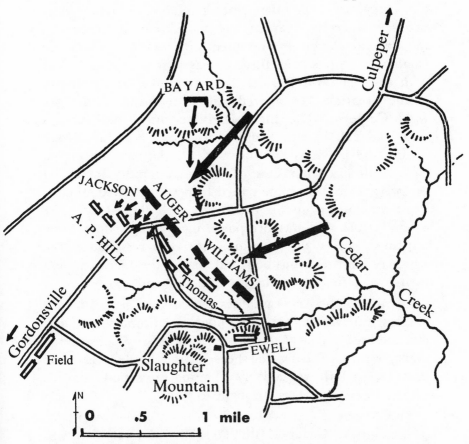

MAP 9. BATTLE OF SLAUGHTER'S MOUNTAIN

Jackson, marching from Gordonsville toward Culpeper, encountered two Federal divisions on the high ground beyond Cedar Creek. He deployed his own division, then under Winder, astride the Culpeper Road, and sent Ewell's Division to the right, over the shoulder of Slaughter's Mountain. An artilley duel ensued for two or three hours, during which Winder was killed and succeeded by Taliaferro. About 5 p.m. the Federals attacked, driving part of Taliaferro's division back in disorder (indicated by small arrows) on A. P. Hill who was just coming up. Hill sent Thomas to the right to support Early, and deployed Branch to the left of the road. Pender and Archer were thrown in successively to Branch's left. These three brigades stopped the Federals, inflicting heavy loss. Toward the close of the day Bayard's cavalry made a charge which swerved across the front of Hill, but accomplished nothing. Field and Stafford did not get into action.

153

the Federals back on the Confederate left, Thomas was switched over to aid on the right flank in support of Early's Brigade. At this point, Banks appears to have received at least some reinforcements because he sent out a brisk cavalry charge to cover his retreating infantry. It is not clear precisely where this cavalry had come from. In any event, the Federal charge was repulsed with heavy loss and the Confederate press continued. It was now nearly dark, but with the field won Jackson wanted to take full advantage of the situation. He ordered Hill to lead the advance toward Culpeper. The Light Division pushed on about a mile and a half with Stafford, who had been in reserve during the previous fighting, now in the van. By eleven o'clock, in pitch darkness, Hill sensed rapidly increasing resistance before him. He halted to permit the redoubtable Pegram to bring up his battery to shell the enemy. The enemy return fire was overpowering. Jackson, upon coming up to survey the situation, ordered a cessation of the advance. The victorious but tired men of the Light Division then bivouacked upon the ground they had won.

In addition to the casualties which they had inflicted, the Light Division took a number of prisoners that day. Not the least among them was the Union brigadier general, Henry Prince. During the heat of the battle, while the shirt-sleeved Hill was actively directing the action from his saddle, Prince had been brought to him.

The Northern general bowed with old school regard for the amenities. "General Hill," he said, "the fortunes of war have thrown me in your hands."

"Damn the fortunes of war, General," shouted Hill, "get to the rear; you are in danger here!" [8] Then, after watching his captured adversary being taken to a safer place, Powell Hill went about his business of directing his troops, heedless of the bursting shells which had already that day struck down one Confederate general.

Despite the rout of Banks' troops and the trophies of

---

[8] 19 *S.H.S.P.*, p. 182.

war that had been won, the affair at Slaughter's Mountain was a somewhat hollow victory for Jackson's command. William E. "Grumble" Jones, who had been in charge of cavalry reconnaissance to the west, rode in from Madison Court House to report the approach of General Sigel's corps.[9] Jackson also knew that Pope's command contained a third corps, McDowell's, as well as 5,000 cavalrymen under Buford. He knew the position on the Culpeper Road could not be held. He also knew that the impetuous Banks was subject to attractive lures that often led him to go off half-cocked. Stonewall, therefore, elected to make a strategic withdrawal toward Gordonsville. On the evening of the 10th, after a day given to burial of the dead and removal of the wounded, the retreat commenced.[10] Jackson's stratagem nearly worked, as Pope himself started in pursuit with a force which the Confederates might have ambushed had it continued beyond the Rapidan. At the river, however, the Union general began to become apprehensive at the ease with which he was permitted to follow his enemy. This, coupled with a rapidly rising river, compelled him to turn back. The fighting between these forces was not to be renewed for a fortnight. Manassas was to be the next battlefield.

Jackson paid tribute to Branch's Brigade during the battle for having stemmed the attack through Taliaferro's position, then overrunning the Federals and inflicting heavy losses. Stonewall, in the flush of the battle, rode behind the advancing lines and doffed his cap in admiration.[11] In his official report, however, Jackson gave no more than brief acknowledgment to Branch and even less to the other Light Division brigades that had been actively and brilliantly engaged—Archer's, Pender's, and Thomas'. A. P. Hill, and all of his brigadiers and troops, nevertheless knew that they had won the day and they knew that without them Jackson's other divisions would have been engulfed and

---

[9] 12 *O.R.*, Pt. 2, p. 239.
[10] Almost a year later many of the dead were noticed lying on the hillside by Averell who passed that way during the Chancellorsville campaign.
[11] 12 *O.R.*, Pt. 2, p. 223.

destroyed by Banks' wild and impetuous attack. Branch exulted in the occurrences of the day as he wrote in his journal:

> I had not gone 100 yards through the woods before we met the celebrated Stonewall Brigade, utterly routed and fleeing as fast as they could.[12]

It must be said for Stonewall, himself, however, that he was at last back in the aggressive mood which characterized his campaigns in the Valley. His courageous appearances on the battle line also enhanced his popularity with the troops. On the other hand, it was apparent that he had great difficulty in handling three divisions in a single action. The entire initiative for the successful operation by Branch, supported by Pender and Archer, was Hill's. Jackson did no more than watch Branch's charge and offer congratulations. The gap in the original battle line, which Hill temporarily plugged with artillery, was also the result of faulty reconnaissance and generalship. Jackson reported a "victory" to Lee. All in all, however, it was a much more satisfactory day for Powell Hill.

Although the battle cannot be classified by history as a major Confederate victory in the true sense of the word, it brought some satisfaction to the South in that the Union casualties far exceeded those of Jackson's command. The Federal losses aggregated 2,381. The Confederate casualties totaled 1,307.[13] This reversal of the casualty trend on the Peninsula heartened both Lee's headquarters and the Richmond press. Powell Hill was even more pleased at the favorable ratio of losses between his brigades and the portions of Banks' corps against which they were pitted. The Light Division sustained the comparatively low total of 394 casualties[14] despite the fact that the Union's heaviest losses that day were inflicted by the men of Branch, Pender, and Archer. For example, the Tenth Maine Regiment lost 173 of 461 officers and men in attempting to stem the tide

---

[12] *Ibid.*
[13] Alexander, p. 183.
[14] 12 *O.R.*, Pt. 2, p. 216.

of Branch's onslaught.[15] Battle statistics such as these have resulted in the characterization of the little mountain south of Culpeper as the most appropriately named battle site of the war.

---

[15] Ropes, p. 28.

CHAPTER 10

Holding the Line at Manassas

*L*EE NOW SENT Longstreet to join Jackson
at Gordonsville. It was apparent that Mc-
Clellan was committed to a withdrawal from the Peninsula.
Accordingly, the only divisions left along the James were
those of D. H. Hill and McLaws.[1] The rest of the Army
of Northern Virginia was concentrated for what Lee hoped
would be a devastating blow at Pope. The Commanding
General himself established headquarters at Gordonsville
on August 15th.

The Light Division at its augmented strength of seven
brigades was a bit cumbersome for the easy maneuverability
which Powell Hill desired. To correct this situation,
Stafford's Brigade was transferred to Jackson's Division.[2]
Hill now had his original command of six brigades. He
anticipated a campaign of fast flanking maneuvers and hard
fighting. Powell Hill wanted the Light Division again to
play the major role. He was not disappointed.

The campaign of the next few days which culminated
at Second Manassas, or Bull Run as the field of action is
better known in the North, was nearly disastrous for the
Union cause. As has been stated, this narrative is confined
generally to the activities of A. P. Hill and the Light Division, together with incidents bearing directly upon their
participation in the campaigns of the Army of Northern
Virginia. Nevertheless, one of the preliminary phases of
the Second Battle of Manassas should be commented upon
here. Upon his arrival at Gordonsville, Lee immediately

[1] Marshall, p. 124.
[2] 12 *O.R.,* Pt. 2, p. 668.

perceived that Pope was in a precarious position between the Rapidan and the Rappahannock. The Confederate leader also realized that he commanded a superior force but that his superiority would be overcome when McClellan got back to the Potomac, thus enabling Washington to send reinforcements to Pope. Lee therefore determined upon a maneuver which would employ his entire army in an attempt to cut off Pope's force completely and annihilate it. To accomplish this, Jackson and Longstreet were ordered to cross the Rapidan, after which Jackson was to take up a position to engage Pope's front while Longstreet was to swing around and face the enemy's right flank. In the meantime Stuart's cavalry was also to cross the Rapidan and get around Pope's left so as to be in the rear of the Union lines. Jeb was then to commence an attack in that sector at the same time as Jackson and Longstreet hit the Union front and flank.[3]

The timetable called for movement by the cavalry on August 18th. Unfortunately for the Southern cause, however, Stuart's cavalry had been divided into two parts. These had to be united if a force were to be placed on the field sufficient to make effective the attack on the Northern rear. Fitz Lee was at Fredericksburg with the missing cavalry, so Jeb Stuart immediately sent him orders to rejoin the main army on the 17th. For reasons that are still the subject of lively debate, Fitz Lee did not return in time, as a result of which the whole plan had to be abandoned. The best explanation seems to be that Fitz did not understand the importance of his returning on the specified date. Apparently the staff and command functions of the Army of Northern Virginia were still so inefficient that it was necessary to specify the importance of missions directed in orders and to advise whether or not it was really necessary to comply in all respects! The loose manner in which orders were obeyed, almost at the whim of the subordinate, seriously hurt the Confederates throughout the war. The

---

[3] Marshall, p. 124 ff., summarizes this plan and the reason for the failure of its execution.

160

cavalry commanders were the chief offenders. In this case, an additional disaster nearly resulted from Fitz Lee's failure to comply with Stuart's instructions. Jeb, alarmed when Lee did not appear, set off with a small staff to find the latter. Failing to locate any trace of the missing cavalry, Stuart and his group stopped for the night at a place called Verdiersville (Map 1). At dawn the next morning a Federal cavalry scouting party came upon them. Jeb fled in such a hurry that he lost his famed plumed hat. He and his staff escaped only by a sensational exhibition of horsemanship in leaping a high fence.[4]

The hat was later regained by Stuart. The opportunity to fight Pope under such favorable circumstances, however, was forever lost. The eventual success of the South at the Second Battle of Manassas a few days later, even after Pope had been tremendously reinforced, indicates that but for the cavalry fiasco the Union forces would probably have been crushed along the Rapidan. By the 20th, however, Pope realized the precariousness of his situation and hastily withdrew. Washington was bustling to get fresh troops on the field between Lee and the Potomac.

Lee shunted aside his disappointment. His genius as a strategist now asserted itself. This genius, coupled with Jackson's ability to perform unbelievable flanking maneuvers by forced marches, was soon again to put the reinforced Union army in a most serious predicament, one nearly as bad as that which it faced between the Rapidan and the Rappahannock.

Stonewall was himself again. The Second Manassas may be regarded as one of his two greatest battles, the other being Chancellorsville. It is interesting to note, however, that although Jackson magnificently executed the flanking maneuver assigned to his wing of the army, the plan itself was that of Robert E. Lee. It will further be noted that much of the brunt of the actual bloody fighting on the Manassas battlefield, credited, and properly so, to Jackson

---

[4] 12 *O.R.,* Pt. 2, p. 726.

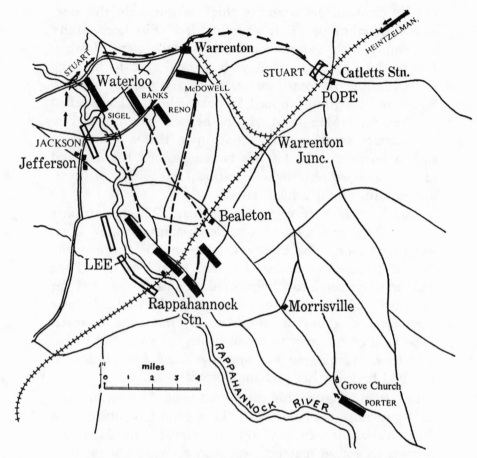

MAP 10. CAMPAIGN OF SECOND MANASSAS GETS UNDER WAY

This shows the situation on August 22, after Lee had crossed the Rapidan and confronted Pope at Rappahannock Station. A. P. Hill, as a part of Jackson's Corps, is upstream covering the crossing near Sulphur Springs. This night Stuart makes his raid on Pope's headquarters at Catlett's Station, capturing papers which confirm that it is too late for Lee to crush Pope before the latter can be reinforced by Heintzelman and Porter, both of whom are moving by rail and marching toward Warrenton Junction. Pope, sensing that Lee is sideslipping toward Waterloo Bridge, is moving McDowell, Sigel, Banks, and Reno from the Rappahannock Station area to Warrenton and Waterloo, as shown.

as the wing commander, was performed by the men of the Light Division under the personal, on-the-firing-line direction of A. P. Hill.

Lee has been criticized for dividing his command just prior to the Battle of Manassas. Actually he did not intend to engage the Union forces in a major battle at this time.[5] He planned a series of maneuvers that were designed to make Washington apprehensive to the point of recalling Pope to the defenses of the capital. It was the early stages of this campaign of swift feints and flanking movements that Jackson carried out so well. The success of these maneuvers and the ease with which they baffled the enemy precipitated the actual battle. In the final analysis, both wings of the army were brought into concerted action. The result was a Confederate victory. The aforesaid criticism of Lee must be tempered accordingly.

On Sunday afternoon, the 24th of August, Lee issued the orders sending Jackson's wing on the famous march that brought it around Pope's right, through Thoroughfare Gap, and eventually squarely behind Pope's army. For several days prior to the 24th, Jackson had faced the enemy along the Rappahannock. Now Longstreet took over this position, his troops quietly relieving Jackson's men at night so that the enemy was unaware of the move.

On the afternoon of the 24th, A. P. Hill's batteries under Lindsay Walker, had engaged in duel with Northern guns across the river.[6] The Light Division gunners, however, were relieved by Hood of Longstreet's Corps so quietly that the enemy apparently never realized that on the following day they were confronting the artillery of a different division. As a result, the entire Light Division, artillery and all, was ready for one of the fastest extended marches of the War, 54 miles in two days.[7] The order of march issued by Jackson provided for Ewell's Division to lead, followed by A. P. Hill, with Taliaferro bringing up the rear.

The placing of the Light Division behind Ewell was a deliberate gesture by Jackson to reflect displeasure provoked by another clash between himself and Powell Hill. This incident occurred on August 20th. Preparations were then being made to cross the Rapidan and take up the posi-

---

[5] Marshall, p. 130.
[6] 12 *O.R.*, Pt. 2, p. 670.
[7] *Ibid.*

tions which were occupied on the 24th when the flank march to Manassas started. Jackson had apparently received personal directions from Lee to move out at the "rising of the moon." Lee's official orders, however, which presumably were transmitted to A. P. Hill, called for the movement to begin at "dawn of day." Therefore some time after moonrise but before dawn, Jackson visited Hill's bivouac. He was enraged when he found the division had not started to move. Jackson angrily ordered Hill's leading brigade on the road. Hill, of course, was justified in not getting on the road earlier, in the light of Lee's written orders to the army. Here, as on so many occasions, Jackson's failure to take his subordinates into his confidence had caused the trouble. Again he blamed the subordinate. Jackson entered the incident in his "black book" as the basis for subsequent court-martial charges against Hill along with the incident of August 8 at Orange Court House.

Jackson had also far from endeared himself to the men of the Light Division by arresting General Maxcy Gregg and all his regimental commanders because of an extremely minor violation by a few of Gregg's men of one of Jackson's standing orders against destruction of private property. On the night of August 21, near the Rappahannock, while the great forced march to the field of Second Manassas was being organized, a number of the soldiers in Gregg's Brigade burned some fence palings to make a bonfire. Jackson, perhaps overwrought from working on the details for the fabulous march around Pope, flew into a rage when he learned of the incident. He promptly ordered Gregg and all five of his regimental commanders arrested.[8]

Nothing came of the case, as the Light Division moved out under Jackson's orders shortly thereafter. The troops forgot about it in the excitement and pleasure of plundering the big Union supply depot at Manassas Junction a few days later. Gregg, however, extremely conscientious and dedicated to his still comparatively new occupation of soldiering,

---

[8] 14 *S.H.S.P.*, p. 209.

was deeply hurt. Despite his personal innocence, he felt responsible. His reaction was to take steps to make sure that such a thing would not happen again among his men. Jackson's order was in line with Lee's policy, but it was impossible of enforcement when applied to troops in the field on the eve of a campaign. Nevertheless, the courtly South Carolinian wanted nothing to happen on his own part or in his command that could conceivably displease his superior.

Powell Hill knew that Gregg's desire in this respect could never be fulfilled. There was no officer in the army whose conduct could always escape Jackson's ire. There was certainly no subordinate commander whose troops could fail, sooner or later, to break one or more of Stonewall's rules. Hill snorted when he heard of the arrests. When Gregg and his officers were soon released, he merely slapped Maxcy's back and told him to forget it. More coal, however, had been heaped on Hill's smoldering feud with Jackson.

Gregg and the other "offenders" were released and permitted to go upon the Manassas march only after the farmer whose fence had been destroyed had been compensated by them.

Nevertheless, the march of the 25th and 26th was undertaken in good spirit. Jackson, moreover, tirelessly riding up and down the column keeping the ranks closed and encouraging the men, soon won their admiration. On the night of the 25th as they marched into their bivouac near Salem the men started to cheer Jackson as he stood by the road watching them pass. Stonewall expressed pleasure but immediately sent out word that there could be no cheering, as it might alert the enemy. This was probably a sound precaution because Pope had not the slightest idea that Jackson had three divisions near Salem opposite his right flank. He thought the whole Confederate army was still along the Rappahannock 25 miles away. Lee's plan called for Jackson to take his three divisions up a little valley formed by the Blue Ridge Mountains on the west and a low range, little more than foothills, called the Bull Run Mountains, on the east. There was a pass known as Thoroughfare Gap through

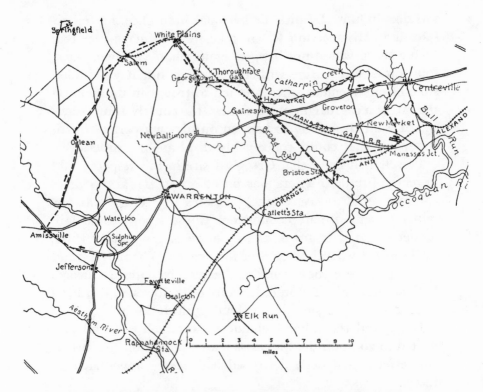

MAP 11. MOVEMENTS OF LIGHT DIVISION, AUGUST 24-28, 1862

Jackson's march around Pope commenced at dawn on the 25th, with
Ewell leading, followed by Hill and Taliaferro. That night the divisions
bivouacked near Salem. The next day they completed a march of 54 miles,
reaching Bristoe Station. On the morning of the 27th they moved up the
railroad to Manassas Junction where they enjoyed some looting of Federal
stores, and Hill crushed Taylor's New Jersey recruits. Then Hill headed
toward Centreville, near which he spent the night. The next day he
marched west toward the Stone Bridge and joined Jackson near Sudley
Springs, in the area where the Second Battle of Manassas was to be fought.

the Bull Run Mountains. Jackson was to go through that
gap and proceed to a position directly to Pope's rear. On
the 26th, the column arrived at the gap.

They found the pass wholly unguarded. The Federal army
had been completely fooled. Jackson continued to press on.
The initiative was now Stonewall's because Lee's plan could
not have anticipated the point at which resistance might be
encountered. Jackson, however, had been told to keep an
avenue of retreat open so that, if necessary, he could pull

166

back into the Shenandoah Valley where he could be reunited with Longstreet.

The occasion by night of the 26th was more propitious for continued advance, now directly toward Washington, than it was for thoughts of retreat. Stuart's cavalry now joined the column, having overtaken the infantrymen after following by the same route north and then east through Thoroughfare Gap. Jeb was restored to good spirits having avenged the loss of his plumed hat by capturing Pope's hat and cloak, as well as personal papers, in a raid from which the Federal commander was as lucky to have escaped as Stuart had been at Verdiersville. He was already in the process of negotiating the exchange of Pope's cloak for his hat.

Ewell's Division, constituting the head of the raiding column, hit the Orange and Alexandria Railroad at Bristoe Station. Capturing two trains and cutting the tracks there, the Confederates for the first time revealed their presence to the amazed Union command. Manassas Junction with its large Federal Army stores was also taken on the night of the 26th.

As a raid Jackson's march had been successful. Halleck at Washington and Pope, however, now knew what the situation was. The surprise element was gone from the campaign. It is true that Jackson was only 27 miles from Washington and was between Pope and the capital. However, he had only about 24,000 men including the cavalry.[9] Pope's reinforced command amounted to about 80,000 in addition to which there was a strong force around Washington which was constantly being augmented as elements of McClellan's army arrived daily from the Peninsula.

Lee still wanted to avoid a major conflict. Obviously, neither half of his divided force could long stand up to Pope's army. Lee therefore prepared to reunite Longstreet's and Jackson's wings, probably in the Shenandoah Valley, depending upon developments.

In the meantime, of course, Jackson had stirred up a hornet's nest. Taliaferro and A. P. Hill were at Manassas

---

[9] Alexander, p. 190.

Junction. Ewell remained at nearby Bristoe Station.

Maneuver and flanking operations were the order of the day. Nevertheless, a certain amount of contact with the enemy became inevitable. It was, therefore, quite natural that Stonewall looked to the men of the fighting Light Division, as the first Federal counterattack developed at Manassas Junction on the morning of the 27th.

Powell Hill's troops, in common with all the men brought by Jackson on that 54-mile march, were a tired and footsore lot as dawn broke on the 27th. One of the officers of Gregg's Brigade wrote on August 26, "We were in wretched plight. Many men were barefoot, many more without a decent garment to their backs, more still ill with diarrhea and dysentery, and all half famished . . . I paid an old woman 25 cents for a mouldy, half-done hoe cake that had laid on the cabin floor."[10]

Food, shoes, and supplies of all kinds, however, were now in abundance from the U.S. Government stores and sutler's supplies at Manassas. The ragged, shoeless and half-starved Confederates had a field day. Even champagne and such tidbits as imported sardines were available for the taking.

Hill's men, however, had the chore of disposing of the initial Union counterattack from the Washington area before they were free to fully enjoy the spoils. Branch's Brigade, on outpost duty, first had a skirmish with the 12th Pennsylvania Cavalry. Next came a New Jersey brigade under the command of Brigadier General George Taylor. Apparently they were unaware of the Confederate force at Manassas Junction. Hill deployed Field, Pender, Archer, and Thomas on a line constituting the Confederate right. Taylor led his inexperienced troops into this formidable array. They were overwhelmed, some being cut down while still disembarking from the cars which had brought them from Alexandria. Taylor himself was killed, 135 of his men were killed or wounded, and 204 captured.[11] The entire

<hr>

[10] Caldwell, op. cit., p. 30.

[11] A. P. Hill's report of this incident, followed by the rest of the Second Battle of Manassas, appears at 12 O.R., Pt. 2, pp. 670-673. That report constitutes the source of the battle details related here unless otherwise annotated.

168

brigade would probably have been taken if the Confederates had not been overeager to engage them and return to the feasting at the Junction. As it was, most of the Jerseyites escaped in a disorderly rout. Hill's men then joined the other Confederates in gorging themselves. Jackson ordered the liquor destroyed but it was a manifest impossibility to keep all of it from the exulting men. The result was a wild celebration culminating in the destruction at midnight in a great roaring fire of all the depot buildings and stores together with two miles of loaded freight cars. At one in the morning Hill moved the Light Division to Centreville.

In the meantime, Ewell's Division awaited developments at Bristoe Station a few miles to the south. Hooker with 5,500 men, still unaware that Jackson's whole corps was in the vicinity, attacked Ewell the afternoon of the 27th. Still under orders to avoid major engagements, Ewell withdrew and rejoined Hill and Taliaferro at Manassas.

Hooker for the first time realized the proportions of Jackson's "raid." He sent word back to Pope but did not attempt to follow Ewell's superior force.[12] Pope now directed his attention to surrounding and overwhelming Jackson. He sent McDowell's and Sigel's corps with Reynolds' division, a total of 40,000 men, to Gainesville, thus cutting off Jackson from Thoroughfare Gap by the route which he had taken to Manassas. He sent Heintzelman in support of the foregoing force to Greenwich, and he sent Porter to join Hooker at Bristoe Station. These movements put Jackson in a pocket. He had no open route now to get back to the rest of Lee's army. Pope, however, made the mistake of forgetting that Longstreet might not "stay put" while he bagged Jackson. On the afternoon of the 26th Lee sent Longstreet, in execution of his basic plan, to effect a union with Jackson wherever developments would permit.

Jackson now adopted the strategy, that was to prove so successful, of hiding his entire command from Pope's observation until Longstreet could join him. First he sent Talia-

---

[12] Alexander, p. 195.

ferro to the woods above Groveton. Then he ordered Ewell to join him there, leaving Hill temporarily at Centreville to deceive the enemy. At 10 a. m. on the 28th Hill received orders from Jackson stating that the enemy were retreating and that he should intercept them and cut them off from the fords and bridges of Bull Run. Powell Hill's alert pickets, however, had captured two separate couriers bearing messages from Pope to McDowell ordering formation of a battle line on Manassas Plains. Hill immediately realized the error of Stonewall's estimate of the situation and, on his own initiative, pushed on to join Jackson. This was one occasion on which Jackson did not criticize Hill for disobeying orders. His movement was so swift, moreover, that Pope could not keep him under observation. As a result the Union commander came upon a burned and deserted Manassas Junction and a deserted Centreville. He was completely ignorant as to the location of a Confederate force of 25,000 men, hidden in the woods within seven miles of the ruined stores at Manassas.

At this point Rufus King's division of Burnsides' corps was apparently ordered by Pope from Gainesville to Manassas. Then its march seems to have been reversed when the evacuation of the latter place was discovered by the Union commander. In any event, King marched right in front of Jackson's hiding place. Stonewall determined to attack although the enemy would probably have passed without noticing the presence of the Confederates. It was necessary, however, to leave open an avenue of escape to the northwest. The road to Aldie at the north end of the Bull Run Mountains was decided upon for this purpose. Powell Hill was assigned the job of holding this road open while Ewell and Taliaferro moved to the attack on King. In the execution of this mission the Light Division was about to engage in some of the most savage and bloody fighting of the war.

The attack on King's column had the inevitable effect of precipitating the general engagement which Lee desired to avoid and which, in any event, prudence dictated should be delayed at least until Longstreet arrived on the scene. The

170

initial result of the fight with King could be termed a Confederate success except that Ewell and Taliaferro were both seriously wounded, Ewell losing a leg. As the general battle developed on the 29th, however, the Union strategy resolved itself into an attempt to turn the Confederate left and thus overwhelm Jackson. The Light Division, in its position to protect the road to Aldie, constituted the Confederate left flank. It was against the men of A. P. Hill's Division that the most furious onslaught by the Northern forces was now made. If the Light Division were to break, the day, the campaign, and perhaps the war would be lost. Powell Hill's men were equal to the task. With their commander, sword drawn, riding among them in personal charge of the field, they held the line.

Pope, of course, had a force vastly superior to that commanded by Jackson. But he was still so bewildered by the turn of events, that he never properly massed his troops. Instead he put them piecemeal into the fray. This gave Powell Hill a chance to take on the Union divisions one or two at a time. It made possible a stand that would have been impossible, despite the gallantry of his troops, if the enemy had made better organized and massed attacks. The position of the Light Division was in wooded, hilly country that made the use of artillery nearly impossible though it afforded good cover to infantry so that the opposing forces could close on each other without being observed. As a result, the fighting of Friday the 29th was often at extremely close range. The division's front line from left to right consisted of Gregg, Thomas, and Field. Branch, Pender, and Archer were in support. Maxcy Gregg's Brigade, constituting the extreme left of Jackson's entire line, was the primary Federal objective. During the morning the scholarly lawyer from South Carolina handled the situation so skillfully that a successful counter-attack was made and the enemy were driven well back. Thomas also advanced. By afternoon, however, the Federal pressure became intense. The whole left flank was put on the defensive.

There was a railroad cut in front of an interval of about

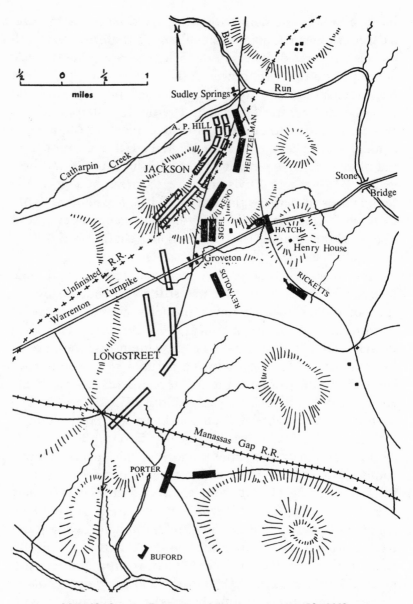

MAP 12. SECOND BATTLE OF MANASSAS, AUGUST 29, 1862

A. P. Hill's Division is on the left flank of Jackson's Corps. His brigades
are in position in two lines, Field, Thomas, and Gregg, from right to left,
in front; and Branch, Pender, and Archer in support. It was from his
position on a rocky knoll that Gregg offered to fight the enemy with the
bayonet and rocks when his ammunition was exhausted. Toward the end
of the day's engagement parts of Early's and Lawton's brigades come up
in rear to stave off a threatened breakthrough between Thomas and Gregg.

125 yards between Gregg's and Thomas' Brigades.[13] A large number of Federal soldiers slipped into this cut. They broke out with a surprise attack in the very heart of the Light Division's forward wall, attempting to overwhelm Gregg's and Thomas' men.

Gregg was not caught napping. He had held Colonel Samuel McGowan's Fourteenth South Carolina Regiment in reserve. McGowan was brought up with such a fierce charge that the line was stabilized. The Federals nevertheless hung on tenaciously, as the firing roared at the point-blank range of ten paces.[14] Powell Hill, riding along the line, observed McGowan's desperate struggle, on which hinged the chances of Jackson's entire corps' escaping annihilation. Hill sent a message to Gregg to inquire if he could hold out.

"Tell General Hill," replied Gregg, "that our ammunition is exhausted, but rocks are plentiful, and we will hold our position with them until we can get ammunition."

Hill rounded up his staff and the messengers who always clustered about a field headquarters. He had them fill all their pockets and haversacks with cartridges. Then he hustled them off to distribute the ammunition to Gregg's men. After telling his ordnance officer to get a wagonload of ammunition up quickly, he galloped to where the South Carolina brigade was fighting and shouted, "Good for you, boys! Give them the rocks and the bayonet. Hold your position and I will soon have ammunition and reinforcements for you!"

This excited the wildest and most vocal enthusiasm from Gregg's regiment.[15]

Hill committed all of his reserves to stem the ever-increasing blue tide. Phil Kearney was commanding the Federal attacking forces.[16] Kearny, a great combat leader now fighting his final battle, sensed that the Light Division could not hold on much longer. He pressed forward with every-

---

[13] 12 *O.R.*, Pt. 2, p. 680.
[14] *Ibid.*
[15] Confederate Veteran, Vol. 1, pp. 233-6.
[16] Roper, *op. cit.*, p. 106.

thing he could muster. Caldwell, the historian of Gregg's Brigade, describes the situation in part, as follows:[17]

About three o'clock the enemy gathered up their whole force for a final spring. The woods swarmed with them. They closed in upon us from front and right and left, pressing up with an energy never before witnessed by us, and certainly not surpassed since. They plied their great advantage over us most skilfully; for line after line of theirs was hurled upon our single one, which was already fearfully thinned by nearly a whole day's fighting and almost ready to faint from fatigue and heat. And, in addition to all this, they had a crossfire on our salient angle. The firing was incessant. They seemed determined not to abandon the undertaking; we were resolved never to yield. There was a perfect death storm all around. All the sounds of Babel roared about us; the trees and the earth were raked by balls. Standing, kneeling, lying, we fought them, so close that men picked out their marks, and on some occasions saved their lives by anticipating the fire of some one on the other side. Officers used their pistols with effect.

The pressure was particularly heavy on the Rifle Regiment. The enemy drove forward into the corner of the field, on the left, where they were posted. Yet this regiment, after a terrible contest, forced them back to their cover. It is these hand to hand fights that make war the devil's work; for it is they which excite all the bloodthirsty passions and utterly silence every sentiment of humanity. One may fight at long range as a patriot and a Christian, but I believe that no man can engage in one of these close struggles, where he can look into the eyes of his adversary and see his blood, but he becomes for the time, at least, a mere beast of prey.

By half past four the pressure of the attack, the sixth such of the day, became terrible. Losses on both sides were ghastly. Hill learned at this point that the brigades of Lawton and Early were nearby and could be spared to come to his assistance. He immediately ordered them up and pushed them to the front in a counter-attack against Kearny's men. Gregg then rallied the tattered remnants of his brigade. He ordered them to lie down and let the reinforcements pass

[17] Caldwell, *op. cit.*, p. 35.

over them. Then he told them to hold fast and "if our friends are overpowered and have to fall back over us to wait until the enemy are very near, then rise and drive them back at the point of the bayonet."[18]

Such a desperate contingency did not occur. The comparatively fresh Confederate troops pushed Kearney back. In the meantime the right sector of the Light Division's line had been reinforced by Hay's Louisiana Brigade, commanded by Colonel Forno. Thus assisted, at about six o'-clock, Hill's beleaguered men under the urging of their leader made one final mighty heave forward; whereupon the Union attack broke. They had had enough. So had the Confederates. The ranks were depleted, men were exhausted, and the ammunition was almost gone. But the line had been held!

Powell Hill sent the following message to Jackson: "General Hill presents his compliments and says the attack of the enemy was repulsed."

"Old Jack" is reported to have exhibited one of his few smiles as he replied: "Tell him I knew he would do it."[19]

Night fell upon the battlefield that 29th of August while the men of the Light Division refilled cartridge boxes, did what they could for the wounded, and tried to ready themselves for another day.

The Second Battle of Manassas was far from finished. There was, however, a deep feeling of confidence throughout the Confederate ranks as the sun went down that evening. Longstreet had arrived! Old Pete had pushed through Thoroughfare Gap without resistance and his divisions during the late afternoon had fallen into the battle line alongside Jackson's wildly welcoming men. Pope had failed to beat half of Lee's army on the 29th. He must face the whole army on the 30th.

---

[18] 12 *O.R.*, Pt. 2, p. 681.
[19] Henry Kyd Douglas, *I Rode With Stonewall*, p. 138.

CHAPTER 11

Victory at Heavy Cost

A. P. HILL'S field headquarters was a grim place that night. The commander's gray flannel battle uniform was soiled from sweat and the dust and smoke of battle. His soft hat was battered out of shape. Never a model of parade-ground pomp and ceremony, the command post of the Light Division now bore an air of extreme informality. There was, however, no chaos or purposeless movement. Powell Hill, at the center of the scene, displayed no emotion as he received the reports of his brigadiers and took stock of the day. It was not that he did not experience emotion of searing depth. The casualties had been the heaviest of any single day's fighting during the war. Hill reciprocated the respect and affection that his troops had for him. The tragedy of war is forgotten in the heat of battle. Its full realization comes in the quiet of the night bivouac. No commander in either army drove his troops harder in battle than Powell Hill. Few, if any, suffered more while studying the casualty reports that came in as darkness shrouded the field of action.

Now the line soldiers tried to rest in preparation for the renewal of the carnage that dawn would bring, but there was very little rest for the commanding general. The formation of the Light Division had to be reorganized. Troop units and officers must be regrouped and reassigned to reflect the losses of the day as well as the plans for the morrow. There was one brigade commander who did not report to Hill that night. Charles Field, seriously wounded, was lost for the balance of the campaign. In his report of the battle, Hill's laudation of Field well expresses the standards of a brigade commander in the Light Division:

> His gallant bearing and soldierly qualities gave him
> unbounded influence over his men and they were ever
> ready to follow where he led.[1]

Henry Forno, who had commanded Hays' Louisianians
so brilliantly that afternoon, was also a casualty. The Louisiana Brigade remained assigned to Hill during the campaign and was now commanded by Colonel H. B. Strong.
Field's command was taken over by Colonel J. M. Brockenbrough of the Fortieth Virginia. The redoubtable Dorsey
Pender had been knocked down by a shell but refused to
leave the field. Archer's horse had been killed under him.
These officers were present with the others that night of
August 29th as Hill announced the battle assignments for
the next day.

Gregg had lost over 600 men and officers, including Colonel Sam McGowan who had been wounded. He still held
the critical left flank of the entire army, however, and it
was tactically not feasible to relieve him. Gregg's battered
brigade, patched up with a few reinforcements, was still
holding the left of the line on the morning of the 30th. To
Gregg's right the front of the Light Division consisted of
Archer's and Thomas' Brigades. Branch, Pender, Brockenbrough, and Strong were in reserve.

Although Longstreet had arrived on the field during the
afternoon of the 29th with about 30,000 men he had not
entered into the general engagement. Hood's and Evans'
Brigades on a reconnaissance mission had collided with
King's Division but had withdrawn after a sharp fight.
Aside from that affair, Longstreet's men assumed their position in line without incident. They had not even been compelled to fight their way through Thoroughfare Gap. A single Union division, that of Ricketts, had been at the Gap.
King had been in support of Ricketts at Gainesville, but, as
already noted, he had been ordered to move east and had engaged Jackson to start the fight on the 29th. Ricketts had

---

[1] 12 *O.R.*, Pt. 2, p. 671.

been advised by the Federal cavalry leader, John Buford, of the strength of the force that was marching through the Gap. He thereupon proceeded to pull out with little more than rear guard action, leaving Longstreet free to contact Jackson and establish his line at leisure.

Lee, who accompanied Longstreet's march, now took charge of the deployment of his united army. Counting Stuart's 2,500 cavalry, the Army of Northern Virginia numbered about 50,000 as it prepared for battle on the 30th. Pope had about 65,000 on the field with 42,000 more at Alexandria 25 miles away preparing to move up.[2] Pope, therefore, still had numerical superiority but, for the moment at least, in no way approximating his advantage of the previous day before Longstreet's arrival. Lee determined upon the establishment of a strong defensive position in the anticipation that Pope would attack. He had Jackson pull back slightly from the line which had been held at such cost on the 29th. Then he placed Longstreet's line at an angle to Jackson rather than in prolongation of the latter's front. Jackson's line now ran generally east and west with Longstreet extending southwest to form an angle of about 30 degrees with Jackson's right. Pope massed his troops inside this angle apparently without comprehending the nature of the Confederate position. On the afternoon of the 29th, the Union commander exhibited his utter lack of knowledge of the situation by ordering Porter with 10,000 men to turn Jackson's right while Kearny assaulted the left. Longstreet, however, had already arrived in front of Porter so that the latter could not possibly obey his orders and get at Jackson's right. It was principally upon the basis of this episode that the infamous court-martial charges were brought against Porter by Pope, resulting in his dismissal from the service and touching off a controversy that raged for years until the able Union general was exonerated by a Congressional Board of Inquiry in 1886.[3]

---

[2] Alexander, p. 211.
[3] See Otto Eisenschiml, *The Celebrated Case of Fitz John Porter.*

179

Pope seemed to devote more attention to finding unwarranted fault with his generals than he did to apprising himself of the current situation. He proceeded to mistake the slight withdrawal of Jackson's divisions for a general retreat and he still didn't really believe that Longstreet was in front of him with 30,000 troops. He unwittingly prepared for the battle of the 30th in the very jaws of the viselike formation set up by Lee.

An ominous silence hung over the field during the hot, sultry morning of the 30th. Powell Hill restlessly rode along his front line. The Union battle line was short and strong. There were 20,000 Federals along the front with over 40,000 in reserve ready to be hurled against any spot in the Confederate line which might indicate vulnerability. The left, still anchored by Maxcy Gregg, had been the chief target on the 29th. Hill reasoned that today it might again be the focal point. He wanted to be ready. His restless movements as he went among his troops were not such as might inculcate nervousness in the men. A. P. Hill had the air of a man who knew what he was doing and merely wanted to make sure that things were as they should be. The blow came at two o'clock as the heat of the day reached its peak.

The Federal attack was general along Jackson's entire line but again there was special emphasis against the left. Once more the Light Division was put on its mettle in savage close-range fighting. For a moment the line faltered. The pressure of the enemy and the intense heat combined to make a living hell of the position along the old abandoned railroad line held by Gregg, Thomas, and Archer. Hill was prepared, however. He had his reserves alerted and poised to fill any breach that might develop. He now called upon the brigades of Dorsey Pender and Brockenbrough. They responded brilliantly. The attack was repulsed and the left side of the Confederate line was stabilized.

Further down the line the situation took a turn for the worse. Pope was concentrating his entire attack against Jackson's position. Whether through stubborn refusal to believe that Longstreet had really arrived with a great force, or for

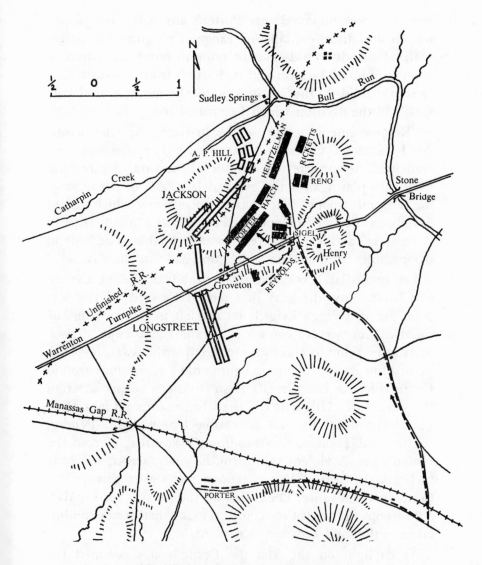

MAP 13. LAST DAY OF SECOND MANASSAS

some unfathomable concept of strategy, the Union commander still ignored Longstreet's Corps which now over-
lapped the Northern left flank. Jackson called upon Lee to
send support from Old Pete's sector of the line. Porter's
corps seriously threatened a breakthrough. Lee sent word to
Longstreet to rush a division to Jackson's aid. Longstreet,

181

however, now observed that Porter's advancing troops had moved into direct enfilade fire range of his guns. Longstreet realized that it would take an hour to move a division in place to support Jackson against Porter's frontal assault. The artillery could do the job in a matter of minutes. Old Pete withheld the division which Lee called for.

"Reinforcements might not be in time," he later wrote, "so I called for my nearest batteries."[4] The effect was immediate. The carnage was terrible as the Confederate guns went into play against the exposed left flank of the advancing Federal troops. The massed formations which might have been effective in frontal assault offered a broad target to Longstreet's artillery. The result was inevitable. The Federal troops broke into chaotic rout. Pope had lost the day.

Lee immediately ordered a general advance along the entire front. Now the gray line moved forward all the way from Maxcy Gregg's Brigade on the left to the flanking element of Longstreet's command on the right. Pope, desperately attempting to make an organized withdrawal, fell back upon a line hastily drawn up behind old fortifications around Centreville. As Longstreet's fresh divisions swung in from the west, A. P. Hill sent the tired but exulting Light Division forward against the retreating Union right. Pender, Archer, and Thomas, spearheading the advance, pierced the Union lines. A violent rainstorm, however, served not only to break the heat of late afternoon but also to disrupt the Confederate advance. Lee called off the pursuit for the day. The troops did what they could to make themselves comfortable in the mud and rain that night.

At daylight on the 31st the Confederates resumed the relentless attack with renewed vigor. It was still raining. Bull Run, a swollen torrent, afforded a protective curtain to Pope's men who had fallen behind the stream during the night and early morning and had destroyed most of the bridges, including famed Stone Bridge.[5] Lee thereupon

---

[4] Longstreet, *From Manassas to Appomattox* p. 187.
[5] Now reconstructed, Stone Bridge is a landmark of the Manassas Battlefield Park.

ordered Jackson to swing around to the left, crossing Bull Run where a bridge was still available. He was then to come down what was known as the Little River Turnpike through Chantilly toward Fairfax Court House. There it was hoped that Pope's flank might be subject to a surprise attack before the retreating Federals had reached the safety of the Washington defenses.

Jackson ordered the Light Division to lead the flanking march. Previously he had found fault with A. P. Hill for marching too slowly. Now he criticized him for moving too fast causing stragglers to drop from the column. Contention that there were any substantial number of stragglers from the Light Division, however, finds no support in the *Official Records* or any other recognized authority. It was probably just a case of cantankerousness on the part of the keyed-up but extremely fatigued Stonewall. Hill and his men were equally tired but they drove on, camping for the night of the 31st at Pleasant Valley and pushing down the pike toward Chantilly the next day.[6]

The enemy was encountered the afternoon of September 1st at a place called Ox Hill. They were not, however, taken by surprise. An attack against a ready and waiting foe was the lot which confronted the battle-fatigued and march-weary Confederates. The Light Division was ordered to the attack while Ewell's and Jackson's own divisions were being brought up from marching column formation. As Powell Hill commenced to deploy his men for the fight, a blinding rainstorm broke in the faces of the troops.[7]

Despite the elements, Hill pressed the attack, sending Branch and Brockenbrough forward. Branch pushed ahead into the Union lines but Brockenbrough was stopped. Branch thus was caught in a pocket without support on his flank. He was subjected to terrific rifle fire in front and flank but fought back savagely. Finally Branch, finding his ammunition almost gone, sent word to Hill of his plight. To Hill there was no alternative to the answer he sent back.

[6] 12 *O.R.*, Pt. 2, p. 682.
[7] Hill's brief account of Ox Hill appears at 12 *O.R.*, Pt. 2, p. 672.

Branch simply had to hold on until the reserves could be brought up.

"Hold your position," he told Branch. "At bayonet point if necessary!"

Gregg, Pender, Thomas, and Archer were then successively thrown into the battle. Now the entire Light Division was engaged. Hill, sword drawn, rode from brigade to brigade urging the men forward. The Federal troops, however, resisted stubbornly.

In the driving rain the battle became a stalemate as evening approached. Early's and Jackson's Divisions, in the meantime, had become involved. They were unable to provide the necessary reinforcements that might have turned the battle of Ox Hill into a rout. The Northern forces finally gave ground in front of the Light Division when both of their field commanders were shot down by Thomas' men. General I. I. Stevens was badly wounded and, worse news to the Union cause, Phil Kearny was killed. Kearny was rallying his troops in the rain and semi-darkness when he rode into the Confederate lines. He was ordered to surrender but elected to lie flat on his horse and attempt to escape. His body was brought to Powell Hill.

"Poor Kearny," said the commander of the Light Division softly, "he deserved a better death than that."[8] The irony of this comment is notable when one considers how remarkably similar were the circumstances surrounding A. P. Hill's own untimely death less than three years later.

As the Federals grudgingly withdrew, they did so without further molestation from the Confederates. Jackson's entire command was exhausted. Longstreet had been unable to press the pursuit over the route taken by Pope's retreat. There was nothing to prevent Pope's battered army from falling into the safety of the great defensive line around the capital. The South had won the battle and the campaign, but the Northern army was still intact.

At Ox Hill, the Union losses had been about 1,000; the Confederate about 500, of which 306 were from the Light

---

[8] *Battles and Leaders*, Vol. 2, p. 538.

Division. The losses for the entire Manassas campaign were:

Confederates (cavalry not included): killed 1,468; wounded 7,563; missing, 81; total, 9,112.

Federal: killed, 1,747; wounded, 8,452; missing, 4,263; total, 14,462.[9]

Most of the missing were prisoners.

The Federal losses from the command standpoint were even more disproportionate. One of the Union's best fighters, Kearny, was killed. Stevens was an eminent strategist, growing constantly in stature, and probably would have succeeded Pope in command if he had not been shot.[10] Then, in one of the most grotesque acts of stupidity in any war, the Northern cause was deprived of its best corps commander when court-martial proceedings were instituted against Fitz John Porter.

The campaign had cost the Light Division 1,854 officers and men. If Hill had lamented Kearny how must he have felt as he studied the casualty lists covering the period August 24th through September 1st. The division had earned more glory, however, and the high spirits of the men who had been such a major factor in driving the Federals from the Rappahannock to the outskirts of Washington comforted their commander in the quiet lonely hours of the aftermath to battle.

---

[9] *Alexander,* p. 219.
[10] *Ibid,* p. 218.

CHAPTER 12

Saving the Army At Sharpsburg

LEE HAD WON a victory at Second Manassas but found himself in something of a dilemma as to which course to pursue next. He had three choices. He could remain where he was and assume a threatening attitude toward Washington. He could withdraw toward Richmond and reestablish defenses along the Rappahannock or some other such natural line. Or he could invade Maryland, thus carrying the war to the North. The difficulty of supply problems and the strength of the Union defenses made the first alternative unfeasible. Withdrawal would be bad for Southern morale, both military and civilian, and would be an invitation to a renewed Federal campaign against Richmond. The third choice was risky because of supply difficulties and the danger of being cut off from avenues of retreat. Nevertheless, the program of invasion would have the advantage of diverting the Union command from thoughts of Richmond as well as emphasizing to the Northern people that the war was not going well and that they were as vulnerable to attack as the residents of Virginia and the other Confederate states.

Lee adopted the latter course. McLaws' and D. H. Hill's divisions arrived from Richmond on September 2. The army was, therefore, at full strength on September 4 when crossing of the Potomac was commenced near Leesburg.

On this day there occurred another mild clash between Gregg and Jackson, resulting in a situation which provoked the placid Gregg into an outburst of temper that would have been more characteristic of Hill. It happened at dawn, just as the advance to the river crossing was to start.

Jackson had ordered each division to march at a specified time. The Light Division had failed to move on schedule. Stonewall could not locate A. P. Hill, so he approached the first brigadier he could find. It happened to be Maxcy Gregg. Gregg's men had been through a terrific ordeal at Manassas, a few days earlier. Their commander was trying to give them as much respite as possible before the next anticipated clash with the rapidly reorganizing Union forces. At the moment, Gregg was watching his men fill their canteens. They should have been on the road according to Jackson's orders, but those orders had apparently never been relayed to Gregg. Whether or not they had been received by Hill is not altogether clear. In any event, if there was fault, it was either Jackson's for not properly issuing the orders, or Hill's for not passing them on. Gregg, however, became the innocent victim. Jackson stormed at him. Gregg, thinking only of the recent heroic action by his tired men, snapped back that the troops were filling their canteens.

Jackson sat silently, glowering, while this work was being finished and then curtly ordered Gregg to the road. Gregg never forgot Jackson's appearance or manner that morning. Before his death, however, not many months later, he not only forgave Jackson for what he thought was unfairness to gallant troops but he begged Stonewall's pardon for his own temperamental display, two things which Powell Hill never did.

The crossing of the Potomac was completed, and the army marched north to a point near Frederick, Maryland, arriving on September 8.[1] Lee's plan called for the capture of Harpers Ferry, Federal strong point at the head of the Valley where the Potomac and Shenandoah Rivers converge. This phase of the plan was vital to keep supply lines open and leave open an avenue for escape to the Valley if the situation should become critical. The balance of Lee's plan called for maneuvers that would keep the Northern army off balance

---

[1] Marshall, p. 149.

trying to guess where the next blow might fall. This would relieve McClellan's pressure on Richmond and might stir up apprehension among many Northerners, some of whom were not too enthusiastic about the war in any event. Lee never intended to engage in a major battle in the course of this campaign unless he should be forced west of the Blue Ridge Mountains and followed by the enemy. In that event he would be as well off from a supply and communications aspect as his adversary. A battle in a strong defensive position upon that basis would be desirable. Otherwise, major conflict should be avoided.

The Harpers Ferry phase of the operation was carried out successfully. The rest of the plan, however, collapsed under a culmination of circumstances which Lee could not foresee. Lee has been criticized for fighting the Battle of Sharpsburg (or the Antietam as it is also known). He probably should have taken steps to avoid it. As it was, the Confederates emerged from the battle with what might be called a draw. Although Lee's losses were appalling, he was able to withdraw safely to Virginia. At no time in the entire war did the Army of Northern Virginia come so close to utter annihilation. One general and part of one division, by dint of a spectacular march, coupled with a fortuitous time of arrival on the battlefield, saved the day. Sharpsburg was one of the bloodiest fields of the war. Practically every unit of Lee's army engaged in desperate conflict along the Antietam that memorable September day. It was, however, the destiny of A. P. Hill to perform the miraculous and literally preserve the very existence of the Army of Northern Virginia, permitting it to fight on for nearly three more long years.

Powell Hill did not get a chance to visit his family after the Second Manassas. There was no respite between campaigns as there had been after the Peninsula. Events moved so rapidly for the Light Division that Hill had little time to think of Dolly and the baby.

While the army was near Frederick, Jackson was given the assignment of taking Harper's Ferry and, despite increasing personal differences, Stonewall selected A. P. Hill to carry the brunt of the action. Prior to the move on Harper's Ferry there had been another and even more serious flare-up between Jackson and Hill. The incident is ignored in the official reports of both officers, and the descriptions thereof from various unauthenticated sources are conflicting. In general, it would seem that the trouble started on September 4th when Jackson that morning berated Maxcy Gregg for not getting his brigade moving early enough.

Stonewall next seems to have taken it upon himself to check up on the rest of the Light Division. He concluded that A. P. Hill was leading his column at too brisk a pace, resulting in straggling at the rear. Therefore he ordered the leading element, Thomas' Brigade, to halt for a rest and to permit the files to be closed. Hill rode quickly back and demanded to know who had ordered the halt. Thomas indicated Jackson, who was still sitting on his horse nearby.

Powell Hill was furious. No one seems to know exactly what was said. Versions of the colloquy vary from a comparatively mild statement by Hill to the effect that if Jackson gave the orders to the Light Division there was no need for a division commander, to a charge that Jackson was not "fit to be a general."[2] In any event, Hill unbuckled his sword and gave it to Jackson. Stonewall told him to keep the sword but advised Hill that he was under arrest. Branch was put in command of the division.[3]

Immediately after Lee assembled the army around Frederick, following the Leesburg fording operation, he sent Jackson against Harpers Ferry. Stonewall started on the morning of the 10th with all three of his divisions under comparatively inexperienced brigadiers. Ewell and Taliaferro were still hors de combat. Hill, riding along behind his division, was under arrest. Jackson led the column on a circuitous route to the west with the intention of crossing back into Virginia at Williamsport and then swooping down upon Martinsburg and Harpers Ferry, surprising the gar-

[2] Freeman, *Lee's Lieutenants*, p. 148 n.
[3] 20 *S.H.S.P.* 385.

190

risons there. Stonewall realized that there was nothing he could do about Ewell's or Taliaferro's absence, but that the services of A. P. Hill could be had by merely giving an order. Old Jack never could forget a grievance but he could put personalities aside where military necessity or the good of the service dictated. He accordingly restored Powell Hill to command of the Light Division before Martinsburg was reached.

In sending Jackson on this expedition Lee had again divided his army. McClellan who had succeeded Pope, immediately set out after Lee with a force numbering 97,000 men.[4] Jackson's mission, therefore, had to be executed quickly and deftly so that the two wings of the Army of Northern Virginia, which included less than 55,000 men at full strength, could be reunited.

Jackson's flanking approach to the objective met with success. On September 12th, 3,000 Federal troops at Martinsburg were surprised and forced to fall back upon Harpers Ferry. Jackson then put the Light Division in the van of the column. Powell Hill, two days previously in arrest, was now leading the Confederate forces in a maneuver that required the ultimate in generalship if a prompt and decisive conclusion was to be reached. Harpers Ferry, well fortified. was garrisoned by over 12,000 men. The Confederates, nevertheless, outnumbered their enemy by a considerable margin. The divisions of McLaws, R. H. Anderson, and John Walker had also been sent by Lee against Harpers Ferry via more direct routes under his plan to completely cut the place off and prevent the Union garrison from escaping. There was, however, no time for a siege or tactical maneuvering by which the superior force might eventually bring about capitulation by the defenders.

McLaws with his own and Dick Anderson's Division was near Harpers Ferry when Jackson arrived on the 14th but was being harassed by Franklin's corps of McClellan's army.

---

[4] Alexander, p. 227. McClellan had never been relieved of the command of the Army of the Potomac, only that of all the armies in the field in Virginia. He was now restored to the combined command of his own army plus that formerly commanded by Pope.

Walker, too, had to be deployed against the enemy's slow advance from the east. The reduction of Harpers Ferry thus rested upon Jackson. He did not hesitate to delegate most of the operation to A. P. Hill. It should not be inferred that McLaws and Walker did not play their parts well at Harpers Ferry. It was simply that they were compelled by Franklin's presence to divert their attention in his direction. McLaws' guns did fire into the town but the artillery could not be moved close enough to be of much effect. Hill, however, experienced very little difficulty in obtaining command of the heights overlooking the Federal positions and the town.

The beleaguered defenders gave up without much of a fight. In executing the relatively bloodless maneuver that sealed the fate of Harpers Ferry, Hill employed Branch and Gregg as flanking units while Pender, Archer, and Brockenbrough executed a swift frontal assault that easily overran the surprised Federals.[5] The high ground so taken is known as Bolivar Heights. Hill then had Colonel Lindsay Walker bring up his artillery during the night. At dawn Walker bombarded the enemy in and around the town below until the Federals raised the white flag after about an hour of futile counterfire.

Harpers Ferry fell to Hill early on the morning of September 14th. His losses were 3 killed and 66 wounded. The Federals only lost 217 killed or wounded, but over 11,000 men surrendered with 12,000 stand of arms, 70 pieces of artillery, many horses and quantities of commissary, quartermaster's, and ordnance stores.[6]

Jackson signified his approval of the Light Division's work by directing Hill to receive the surrender and arrange the terms. The Union commander at Harpers Ferry was Colonel Dixon Miles. He had been mortally wounded, however. The surrender was made by the senior officer present, General White, who had joined the Harpers Ferry garrison following the retreat from Martinsburg. White was dressed in his finest uniform for the surrender ceremonies. This

---

[5] 19 *O.R.*, Pt. 1, p. 980.

[6] *Ibid*, p. 981.

was, of course, much in contrast to the dusty, soiled appearance of both Jackson and Hill. In fact, General White became somewhat apologetic to Hill and mumbled something about having expected to meet "high Confederate officers."[7] One of the Confederates wrote afterwards, "The ragged, forlorn appearance of our men excited the combined merriment and admiration of our prisoners."[8]

The terms of surrender were most generous. All prisoners were paroled and were permitted to take much of their equipment with them. Hill even permitted Union officers to "borrow" a few wagons and horses to carry private baggage. The fact that the horses and wagons had been U. S. Government property until that morning did not assuage Powell's later anger that they were not promptly returned. The wagons and horses apparently were sent back to the Confederates only after a delay of a couple of months. There appear to have been a few violations of the paroles of some officers and troops but there was little else that could be done with such a large number of prisoners.[9] The great majority continued to observe their parole until the end of the war or until they were exchanged. The Culpeper Cavalier in this last war of knighthood and chivalry, never questioned but that the enemy's word was as good as his own. He processed each parole meticulously and then assumed that the prisoners who went on their way, armed with passes from him, were as completely out of action as if they were behind the bars of grim Libbey Prison in Richmond.

Hill was short tempered with those who tried subterfuge to avoid parole, however. One man came to him for a pass saying that he was a noncombatant, although he wore a Federal uniform. He said he'd bought the uniform from surplus Army stores. Hill looked the man over carefully. Then he decided the fellow was a liar. He jumped to his feet, grabbed the man by his shoulders, threw him through the doorway and literally kicked him downstairs, shouting "Get

---

[7] 19 *S.H.S.P.*, p. 182.
[8] Caldwell, p. 43.
[9] Alexander, pp. 238-9.

out of here you damned scoundrel!"[10] Stonewall would have disapproved of the language.

While Hill was performing the paperwork incidental to such a large-scale surrender, the men of the Light Division were having a celebration of some proportions. The supplies which they had seized included great varieties of delicacies as had been the case at Manassas Junction. The hungry men now gorged themselves with everything from candy to lobster. More important, shoes, blankets, and even Federal uniforms were distributed among the men. The other two divisions of Jackson's wing shared in the spoils, they too having been up in position when White capitulated although most of what little fighting took place was by the Light Division. The troops of McLaws and Walker, however, did not get a chance at the booty. There was much grumbling in that corner.

Grumbling or not at Harpers Ferry, there was pressing business back along the Antietam Creek near Sharpsburg. All of the troops that had converegd on Harpers Ferry, except A. P. Hill's Division, were ordered back to join Lee's main force, although the command assembled under Jackson at the Ferry was larger than that with which Lee and Longstreet now confronted McClellan. Jackson had the whole force, except McLaws and Hill, back with Lee by the morning of the 16th. McLaws got started back that evening. Hill remained to complete the details of the surrender.[11]

Lee was still anxious to avoid combat with Little Mac's superior force. An untoward incident, however, had given McClellan information as to Lee's plans and the location of his troops. Before the Confederate commander realized the full extent of McClellan's knowledge of the situation, he found himself being pressed and his flanks threatened. The story of the "lost order" involves a General Hill other than the subject of this book. It has been told many times in various forms. Suffice it to say that General D. H. Hill was

---

[10] 19 *S.H.S.P.* 180.
[11] Alexander, pp. 241-2.

194

given one copy of Lee's orders for the Maryland campaign by army headquarters and another copy by Jackson to whom his division was to be attached.[12] Harvey Hill carefully preserved the copy from Lee but either overlooked the one from Jackson or did not realize its significance. In any event, the second copy was found by Union soldiers as they entered Frederick. It had been carefully wrapped around three cigars which apparently had been dropped by an officer of Harvey Hill's staff. McClellan therefore knew what Lee was doing and did not have to rely on his customary careful reconnaissance and probing which had slowed him so much on the Peninsula. Lee, now finding himself pressed beyond expectation by his ordinarily overcautious adversary, took up a defensive position on the banks of Antietam Creek and rushed orders to Jackson to return posthaste.

The battle lines of the opposing forces took shape along the Antietam on September 15 and 16. Jackson's Corps, with the exception of the Light Division, had taken up position as the Confederate left flank by dawn of the 17th. It was here that the battle opened in earnest. "Fighting Joe" Hooker's Corps, following a savage artillery bombardment, attacked Jackson's position shortly after six o'clock that morning. The attack was repulsed with heavy losses on both sides. This was the type of fighting that would be carried on all day. The battle raged all along the line throughout the morning and into the afternoon. The blood of thousands under both flags stained the fields surrounding Sharpsburg that day. Such landmarks of the war as "bloody lane," the "corn field," and "Burnside's Bridge" became part of history as the day wore on. No attempt will be made here to detail the story of the battle. It is sufficient to say that Lee, Longstreet, Jackson and the men under them fought and held on gallantly, but toward mid-afternoon they were slowly but surely being enveloped on the flanks while being pulverized in the center.

McClellan's plan was to turn both Confederate flanks by overwhelming numerical superiority while neutralizing the

[12] Longstreet, p. 213.

center by artillery fire supported by sufficient infantry to hold the line against any possible counterattack. The pressure on the flanks was exerted in the manner of a giant nutcracker.

The scheme would surely have been successful were it not for one fortunate incident—fortunate, that is, from the Southern standpoint; disastrous from the Union view. The weakest point in the Confederate line was their right flank, held by Brigadier General Robert Toombs of Longstreet's wing. Toombs, a veteran politician but an inexperienced soldier, was handicapped by being compelled to hold a large sector of the line with a single undermanned brigade. Opposite him, across the Antietam, was Ambrose Burnside and the Union IX Corps. Burnside's numerical superiority was tremendous; the only factor in Toombs' favor was the topography. The banks of the Antietam were steep and rugged at this point. One stone bridge was the only direct means of crossing the stream except for two fords which were pretty well out of the question as they were completely covered by Confederate small-arms fire. Commencing at around eight o'clock that morning, McClellan sent order after order to Burnside to cross the bridge and commence the process of rolling back the Southern right.

The battle roared on the Union right and center but Burnside on the left could not or would not move. He refused to expose troops to the direct fire which they would be under from the opposite heights if they attempted to storm the bridge.

Burnside was a handsome man of pleasing personality. He was destined soon to command the Army of the Potomac and one day to be Governor of Rhode Island. He will always be remembered for the style of wearing his side whiskers which has come down through the years under the name of "sideburns." He was not, however, on September 17, a good general or even an approximation of one. His delay at the bridge disrupted McClellan's timetable.

The plan was working successfully on the other flank and in the center. If Burnside could smash through Toombs' weak lines, it would be all over for the Army of Northern Virginia but the shouting. Morning turned into afternoon, however, before Burnside, after receiving at least four direct orders to move, finally sent Jacob Cox with the 51st New York and 51st Pennsylvania Volunteers across the bridge. The high ground held by Toombs was now stormed and the thin gray line was broken. The IX Corps crossed in force and mobilized on the far bank adjacent to the almost exposed Confederate right. The pressure against the rest of Lee's line was so intense, furthermore, that nothing could be done to divert Burnside's advance which was finally sweeping forward by 3:30 p. m. By this time the situation was such that as Alexander later wrote, "Lee's army was ruined and the end of the Confederacy was in sight."[13]

Only a miracle could save the day for Lee. That miracle had been in the making, however, since six-thirty that morning. At that time A. P. Hill received urgent orders from General Lee to move to Sharpsburg.[14] He left Thomas to complete the details attendant upon the surrender of Harpers Ferry. Then, leading his other five brigades, Powell Hill set off on the narrow hilly road to Sharpsburg.

Gregg's Brigade was in the lead. Its march, which typified that of the division, is described by one of the officers:

> Early in the morning of Wednesday, September 17, Gregg's Brigade was put in motion up the road toward Shepherdstown. The day was hot and dusty in the extreme. All along the way we heard the boom of cannon, almost in our front. Pressing forward at a rapid gait, and but two or three times halting to draw breath, we reached the Potomac about 2 p.m. at Boteler's Ford. We waded the river at once and rapidly, although the current was quite swift, and the ledges of rock, cropping out at sharp angles, rendered the passage both difficult and painful. Climbing up the slippery bank on the Maryland side, we proceeded at once to the scene of action.[15]

The seventeen-mile march, which had started at 7:30

---
[13] Alexander, p. 262.
[14] 19 O.R., Pt. 1, p. 981 contains Hill's report of the day.
[15] Caldwell, p. 44.

a. m., was completed at 3:30 p. m. Hill had ridden on ahead during the last hour to report to General Lee.

The men were dusty, tired, and footsore. But they were ready for action—and not a minute too soon. Hill had literally driven the troops at sword point. His impetuosity, that so often resulted in predicaments subjecting him to criticism, had spurred him on. It was as though he knew the fate of the Confederacy marched with the Light Division on that dust-choked road.

Powell had donned his famous bright red hunting shirt, as was often his habit on marches, so that the men could constantly have their commander in view.[16] Despite this informal uniform, Powell Hill had buckled on his dress sword. As he neared the end of the road that debouched upon an open field below Sharpsburg, he started to draw the sword but hesitated as a sight uncommon to the Light Division caught his eye. A few feet off the road, crouching behind a tree, was a young second lieutenant who had dropped out of the vanguard that was about to emerge from the thicket-bordered road upon the open field where the guns were roaring. Without hesitation Hill rode to the man and demanded his sword. The trembling lieutenant handed it to him. Hill raised the sword and brought it violently down across the lieutenant's back, shattering the weapon. Then he drew his own sword and rode on without a word.

Lee sensed that a miracle was taking place when he heard of Hill's arrival. He hastened to confer with the general who a few days before had been under arrest and relieved of his command. Lee and Hill met near the town which was now invaded by the leading Federal units. Anecdote has it that they embraced. In any event, Lee very briefly outlined the desperate situation. The Federal forces were overrunning the last of Toombs' reserve positions. Longstreet and Jackson were holding in the center and on the left but would be helpless if the Confederate right flank were turned as had seemed inevitable a moment or two before. No words were

---

[16] 19 *S.H.S.P.*, 178.

wasted as Lee told Hill to take over the right and throw as many troops as he could against the exposed and unsuspecting flank of the now boisterously overconfident Union forces.

A. P. Hill sent Pender and Brockenbrough to the extreme right, near the mouth of Antietam Creek, to anchor the line. Branch, Gregg, and Archer were deployed extending from

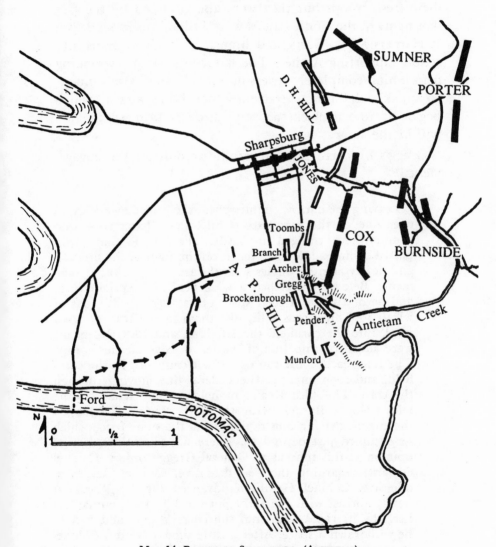

MAP 14. BATTLE OF SHARPSBURG (ANTIETAM)
The situation about 4:30 p.m. just after A. P. Hill has committed his brigades into action on the right flank.

this anchor to the left joining with D. R. Jones' Brigade which, almost overrun, was the only bulwark holding back the Union tide from enveloping the rest of Lee's army.

Archer was the first to engage. With a wild yell his men charged the totally unprotected flank of the surprised enemy. Not only were the Federals stunned by the appearance of these fresh troops but they were also confused by the fact that many of the Confederates wore Federal uniforms seized at Harpers Ferry. Gregg and Branch led their veterans into action supporting Archer. The latter now swept everything before him, completely reversing the adversaries' advantage. So quickly did events transpire that Hill's attack, which began at four o'clock, accomplished its primary mission within the hour.

Gregg's historian gives a graphic account of the engagement:[17]

> Leaving the narrow country road, the brigade was carried over one of the many steep hills that characterize that country, and arranged for battle. The 14th Regiment was posted behind a low stone fence, on the right of the brigade, and nearly at right angles with the front of the other regiments. Below us stretched a wide field of luxuriant corn, and beyond it was a clear space of varying breadth, out of which rose numerous hills, like those in the rear, clear of trees. Into the cornfield the 1st, 12th, and 13th Regiments were advanced into line of battle, to drive off the enemy. The line reached the top of a small eminence in the cornfield, and soon engaged the Federal line moving through the corn. The 13th Regiment held a stone fence on the left. Colonel Barnes, with the 12th Regiment, charged the enemy, driving him rapidly from the stone fence which he occupied just beyond us. There was some difference of opinion at this time as to General Gregg's orders, Colonel Edwards regarding them as defensive, Colonel Barnes as offensive. Colonel Hamilton advanced the 1st Regiment nearly abreast with the 12th. But the 12th soon outflanked itself by its rapid dash into the enemy's line, and had to be withdrawn a space. After a little time, however, Colonel Barnes returned to the attack, and this time drove away

[17] Caldwell, pp. 44-47.

the force which had occupied the fence on his retirement, pursuing them to the opposite hill and inflicting a heavy loss upon them.

A considerable pressure was now brought to bear upon the right of the First Regiment. Colonel Hamilton changed his front slightly to meet it, and swept the obnoxious line from the field, with great loss to it. This movement also secured Colonel Barnes' right from further molestation. Hardly, however, had it been executed, when a line of Federals came hurrying down on the right of the 1st Regiment, threatening soon to enfilade their line. General Gregg now despatched Captain Perrin with Orr's Rifles after them. The Rifles fell upon this line, almost completely flanking the flankers, and after a short, sharp fire, dispersed them in disorder.

The firing during this period, which was about an hour, was as rapid as possible, and on our side unusually accurate. So dense was the corn that the lines sometimes approached within 30 or 40 yards of each other before opening. We had somewhat the advantage, for the enemy, descending to attack us, naturally fired too high, while we had either a level or a rise to fire upon . . . it is a fact that men fire above their own levels. And when the enemy retreated they had to pass through our ground, which enabled us to kill large numbers of them.

This was an exciting field to view. Far along in front of the Confederate army, on our left, we could see the blue lines of the Federals, moving to attack over the smooth, round hills, marching in perfect order, with banners flying and guns and bayonets glistening in the sun. Never have I witnessed such accurate marching. And their appearance was greatly improved by their well-kept, loose, blue uniform, which gave them a massive look, entirely unlike the tight, light-colored, and variegated garb of the Confederates.

The Union forces began to break pellmell toward the Antietam. Now the Confederates became the attackers and pursuers. A semblance of order was soon restored to the Union left by the arrival of reinforcements. The Southern counterattack was halted.

General Branch was killed at about the time the Federal counterattack was broken.

He had just swept the enemy before him and driven them in such confusion and dismay, that all firing had ceased in his immediate front, when Generals Gregg and Archer directed his attention to a V-shaped column of the enemy that was advancing against the troops on his left. He stepped forward and formed with these generals a little group, which evidently attracted the attention of some sharpshooter on the other side. For, just as he was raising his glasses to his eyes, a single shot was fired, and a bullet was sent to do its deadly work, which, striking him in the right cheek, passed out back of his left ear, and he fell dying into the arms of Major Englehard of his staff.[18]

As the sun sank, the men of the Light Division made makeshift camp on the ground that they had taken. Powell Hill sheathed his sword and took his first breathing spell since receiving Lee's orders at six-thirty that morning. It was not an occasion for relaxation. The inevitable casualty reports were now coming in. The fight, as far as the Light Division was concerned, had been short. Only about 2,000 of Hill's men had actually been engaged,[19] but 63 had been killed and 283 wounded. Numerically the Division's losses were not heavy that day when weighed against its achievement. The names on the casualty list, however, burned more deeply into Powell Hill's thoughts than upon any other occasion in the war to date. Foremost in his mind at this time, of course, was Lawrence O'Brien Branch. As he wrote in his report of the battle, "He was my senior brigadier, and one to whom I could have intrusted the command of the division with all confidence." Then there was Maxcy Gregg, who had been knocked down by a spent ball, but who was found to be only bruised and soon was back in action. Among the killed was Colonel Dixon Barnes, greatly beloved by his regiment, and a courageous fighter. Barnes, who had commanded a regiment in Gregg's Brigade, exemplified the wealthy South Carolina planter, flowing white beard and all. The report of the Battle of Sharpsburg, written by Mc-

---

[18] *N.C. Regts.*, 2, p. 537.

[19] Alexander, p. 268, states the number as 2,700, but this might include the remnants of Toombs' Brigade.

Gowan who succeeded Gregg after the latter was killed at Fredericksburg, said of Barnes:

> Where all did so well it may not be unpardonable to declare that in this battle the palm was born off by the intrepid Colonel Barnes, who nobly fell while leading the invincible Twelfth in their last victorious charge. Colonel Barnes was as amiable and generous in peace as he was gallant and irresistible in war. Having large wealth and high position at home, he left all to fall at the head of his beloved regiment, gallantly struggling for the independence of his country.[20]

Hill's favorite artillerist, Willie Pegram, had received his first wound, which rendered him temporarily hors de combat.

The losses in the other divisions that had been fighting all day had been heavier than Hill's, aggregating a staggering 10,000. The Federals had also lost heavily—about 12,000 on the 17th.[21]

The Army of Northern Virginia was reduced to about 40,000 men as night settled over Sharpsburg. That there was an army at all, however, was sufficient to bolster the spirits of the commanders from Robert E. Lee down. And even the losses of the day could not dim the pride of every man in the Light Division. They threw themselves on the ground, too exhausted to cook their rations. Their bodies were spent but their spirits were refreshed by the exhilaration of victory. They were ready to follow A. P. Hill wherever the morrow's orders might send them.

---

[20] 19 *O.R.*, Pt. 1, p. 989.
[21] Alexander, p. 275. Total Federal losses at Sharpsburg September 16-18 were 12,410.

CHAPTER 13

Lee the Mediator

*T*HE CONFEDERATE ARMY withdrew
across the Potomac into Virginia during the
next day and night. McClellan, never very aggressive, had
now become even more cautious. He did not follow immediately. Lee, having crossed the river without mishap,
posted General William Nelson Pendleton, commander of
the Army's reserve artillery, at Boteler's Ford to ward off
pursuit. Pendleton was a minister by profession. He was
courageous enough and a fair artillery officer, but was in-
capable of exercising the relatively independent command
position now assigned him. Porter's Federal corps was sent
after the retreating Southerners on the evening of the 19th.
Their reconnaissance force crossed near Boteler's Ford and
succeeded in outflanking the inexperienced Pendleton, seizing five of his guns, and forcing him to retreat.[1] Lee decided
to wait for the following morning to take action against the
salient which the Federals were now building up on the
Virginia side of the river. Jackson, however, enraged when
he learned of the Reverend Pendleton's bungling of the
rear guard chore, ordered A. P. Hill to return to the Potomac
and drive the Union troops back into Maryland.

The Light Division went back into action at six-thirty
on the morning of the 20th. Hill formed the division into
two lines, one consisting of Pender, Gregg, and Thomas, the
other of Archer, Brockenbrough, and Colonel James H.
Lane, who had succeeded Branch.[2] These two lines then

---

[1] F. W. Palfrey, *The Antietam and Fredericksburg*, p. 128.

[2] Hill's account of this engagement, also known as Shepherdstown, appears
at 19 *O.R.*, Pt. 1, p. 982.

swept toward the Potomac with the intention of pushing the Federals into the river. Dorsey Pender's was the only brigade to become hotly engaged although Archer joined Pender in a concerted charge, breaking the Union salient, and sending the enemy troops fleeing to Boteler's Ford. The Federal forces sustained reasonably heavy losses while under fire as they crossed the ford but their casualties officially totaled only 363 men.[3] The usually factual Powell Hill, however, in a flamboyant report made what may be his most exaggerated claim of the entire war when he wrote:

> . . . A simultaneous, daring charge was made, and the enemy driven pellmell into the river. Then commenced the most terrible slaughter that the War has yet witnessed. The broad surface of the Potomac was blue with the floating bodies of our foe. But few escaped to tell the tale. By their own account they lost 3,000 men, killed and drowned, from one brigade alone. Some 200 prisoners were taken. My own loss was 30 killed and 231 wounded; total, 261.

Hill apparently returned to his customary accurate reporting in the last sentence. Why he wrote as he did with respect to the Federal losses cannot be readily explained. Perhaps he was overexuberant after his division's fine work at Sharpsburg. Perhaps the reports from his subordinates as to enemy losses became multiplied by ten in the heat of battle. One Northern regiment, the 118th Pennsylvania, known as the "Corn Exchange Regiment," lost about 300 men at the ford. Palfrey, referring to Hill's statements, quoted the following poetic lines:

> Or art thou drunk with wine, Sir Knight, or art thyself beside?[4]

Whatever may be said of Hill's official report of the affair, the fact remains that his mission was accomplished. No more Federal troops remained south of the Potomac in that area, Lee's withdrawal was able to continue undisturbed.

---

[3] Alexander, p. 272.
[4] Palfrey, p. 179.

Sharpsburg had been neither a victory nor a defeat for Lee's army. The battle had tested the mettle of both Jackson and Longstreet in heavy action against odds. They had not been found wanting. The laurels of the Maryland campaign, however, were generally recognized as belonging to A. P. Hill. In fact, one contemporary writer described A. P. Hill's arrival at Sharpsburg as "not less opportune to Lee than was that of Blucher to Wellington at Waterloo."[5] Jackson and Lee both joined in according accolades to Powell Hill and the Light Division. Longstreet, ever jealous of credit for his own troops, was inclined to belittle Hill's part on the 17th in his official reports of the campaign. Mellowing somewhat in later years, however, he wrote in his reminiscences:

> Outflanked and staggered by the gallant attack of A. P. Hill's brigades, (Burnside's) advance was arrested.[6]

New anecdotes concerning the old rivalry of Hill and McClellan for Nellie Marcy sprang up in both armies. McClellan was relieved of his command and left the U. S. Army shortly after the campaign. The wags pointed out that Hill had proved himself the better man in the final analysis by sending his successful rival in amour limping home to the little lady. For Powell Hill, however, the comparative respite in hostilities that now occurred was an occasion not to engage in thoughts of the "Sunbeam" (Nellie Marcy) but to return to Dolly and the baby.

Dolly was a true soldier's wife. No Army wife ever adapted herself to military life better than the former Kitty Morgan of Kentucky. Powell refreshed his strength in his visits with her. It was now that she began to live a transient life, following as near the army as possible. Dolly's beauty and good spirits were a tonic to the troops of the Light Division. Now, too, Powell had a chance to visit Culpeper, which was temporarily out of the hands of the invaders. In fact, the autumn of 1862 might well have been a happy interlude in his life were it not for the one thing that continuously rankled his

---

[5] 14 *S.H.S.P.*, p. 116.
[6] Longstreet, p. 261.

mind—the charges against him that had been preferred by Jackson.

The Cromwell of the South would probably have been satisfied to leave the matter in the status quo. After all, he had severely reprimanded Hill on several occasions, had embarrassed him before his officers and troops, and had punished him with a brief period of arrest. Hill had responded with outstanding achievements in battle. Jackson, therefore, had had the satisfaction of chastising Hill and had also reaped the benefits of his generalship. He must have realized, at least subconsciously, that Hill's work at Slaughter's Mountain, Manassas, and Sharpsburg had played no small part in the re-establishment of Jackson's prestige following his fiasco during the Seven Days. There is nothing in the records or manuscripts to indicate that Stonewall, under these circumstances, proposed to take any further affirmative action against the commander of the Light Division.

Powell Hill, however, had been stung to the quick by what he felt were a series of unjust and totally unwarranted accusations. His proud, fiery nature was particularly outraged by the arrest incident. During the heat of battle he was able to swallow his humiliation. During the comparative quiet after Sharpsburg he determined to seek justice in the only honorable manner available to a soldier. He demanded of Lee a court of inquiry on Jackson's charges. Actually Jackson had never preferred formal charges or specifications against him. In endorsing Hill's demands through channels to the Commanding General, Jackson still did not make formal charges, although he outlined all of his grievances against Hill covering the past several months. Lee was deeply disturbed when the matter came before him. He did not regard any of the charges as serious. His concern was for harmony in the army. He not only had little regard for the efficacy of courts-martial in cases involving personal disagreements between officers, but he feared the effect on the morale of both officers and men of what would amount to a recriminative brawl between two of the South's greatest generals. He wrote what he felt to be a tactful endorsement upon Hill's application in which he, in effect, suggested that Hill and Jackson "call it quits" in the interest of the service, adding that if Hill had done anything wrong it was unintentional and would not be repeated.[7]

Hill was not satisfied. He again applied for a court of inquiry, this time categorically denying every accusation made in Jackson's endorsement to his prior application, and going on to accuse Jackson of "black-listing" him. He then wrote a series of charges against Jackson which he sent to Stonewall in accordance with standard Army procedure, to be forwarded to Lee. These charges do not appear to have been taken seriously by anyone, and were soon lost or disregarded and destroyed. Their text never appeared in the official records.

Jackson was still reluctant to bring to a head the issue which Hill was now pressing. Nevertheless, under Hill's insistence, he had no practical alternative but to file formal charges. This he did but he attached thereto his observation to Lee that he didn't think any hearing was necessary. He did, however, set up in great detail specifications of "neglect of duty" by Hill. There were seven specifications set forth under the neglect-of-duty charge. Four of them covered the series of incidents of September 4th leading up to the final altercation between Jackson and Hill at which Hill was placed under arrest and relieved of his command. The other three specifications related to the first clash between the two generals which took place at Orange Court House back in August. These specifications, the originals of which are now on display at the Battle Abbey in Richmond, read as follows:

CHARGE—NEGLECT OF DUTY

Specification 1 In this that Major General A. P. Hill when he was directed by Major General T. J. Jackson to move early in the morning of August 8, 1862 from Orange Court House towards Culpeper Court House by way of

---

[7] The correspondence and sequence of events in this connection do not appear in the Official Records. Much of the material, however, has been found among Jackson's papers and is outlined admirably in Freeman's, *Lee's Lieutenants*, Vol. 2, p. 243 et seq.

Barnetts Ford, did fail to move in obedience to said order but did continue in the vicinity of Orange Court House until night, thus remaining a day's march in rear of the position which he should have occupied. All this near Orange Court House, Virginia on or about the 8th of August, 1862.

Specification 2   In this that Major General A. P. Hill, on the night of the 9th of August, 1862, when he had been specially directed by Major General T. J. Jackson, to move his troops as soon as the moon should rise, via Somerville Ford, did fail to obey said order, and thus rendered it necessary for Major General T. J. Jackson about two hours after the designated time, to put the said troops in motion as they had not up to that time, left camp. All this near Somerville Ford, Virginia on or about the time specified.

Specification 3   In this that Major General A. P. Hill did neglect to give all his brigade commanders the requisite orders for enabling him to move his division as soon as the moon should rise during the night of the 9th of Aug., 1862, as he had been directed by Major General T. J. Jackson. All this near Somerville Ford, Virginia on or about the time specified.

Lee "filed" this welter of charges, denials, and counter-charges and left further developments to Father Time. He had intervened once to prevent a duel between Hill and Longstreet. Now his attempts at active intervention did not appear to be successful where stubborn temperaments were concerned. He held the key to the situation, however. He took all the applications, endorsements, and other papers and let them rest quietly in a headquarters drawer. After all, he was the Commanding General and if he didn't think a court of inquiry was advisable, none could be called. Hill and Jackson had the satisfaction of openly stating their respective positions. Robert E. Lee exercised his command function in the "best interest of the service" by terminating the affair. The steam was blown off. Personal animosity might continue but the principals concerned were left with no further recourse against each other. They had nothing to do now but resume devoting their full attention to their primary duty—that of fighting a war.

Lee was fortunate at this time to have available a bit of "salve" which he could apply to the unhealed wounds in the pride of Stonewall Jackson and Powell Hill. The Confederate Congress on September 18 had formally authorized the establishment of army corps to be commanded by officers in the new rank of lieutenant general. As far as the Army of Northern Virginia was concerned, the new law would do no more than formalize the system already in effect, except that the old "wing" commanders could now be given a promotion in rank. Lee recommended Longstreet and Jackson for promotion to rank of lieutenant general. This, of course, placated Stonewall. Lee then took advantage of the situation to bestow a commendation upon A. P. Hill in such terms as to make it the next best thing to a promotion. In submitting the names of Longstreet and Jackson to Davis, the Commanding General wrote:

> Next to these two officers, I consider A. P. Hill the best commander with me. He fights his troops well and takes good care of them.[8]

Hill thus was singled out as the oustanding major general in the Army. No formal promotion was available but Lee's tactful handling of the situation caused Hill to be recognized as being on an elevation above his fellow division commanders and permitted him to retain his same relative position as far as Jackson was concerned. The Light Division in the reorganization continued to be by far the largest unit in the Army. Its commander's pride in recognition by Robert E. Lee was as much on behalf of his troops as himself.

By the middle of November the new arrangement of the army was completed. The Second Corps under Jackson now consisted of the following divisions with their respective troop strength "present for duty" on November 20:[9]

A. P. Hill 11,554
Ewell 7,716
D. H. Hill 6,944

---

[8] 19 O.R., Pt. 2, p. 643.
[9] Alexander, pp. 279-80.

211

Taliaferro	5,478
Longstreet's First Corps included the following:	
McLaws	7,898
Anderson	7,639
Pickett	7,567
Hood	7,334
Walker (2 brigades, no artillery)	3,855
Reserve artillery	623

In addition, the army included Stuart's cavalry, numbering 9,146, and Pendleton's reserve artillery of 718. The entire Army of Northern Virginia numbered 76,472. It was at a peak never before attained and never to be duplicated.

There was no substantial change made in the Light Division under the reorganization. Field's Brigade was still commanded by the durable, if unspectacular Colonel J. M. Brockenbrough. Jim Lane, who had succeeded to Branch's command, and Thomas, who had commanded the Third Brigade for some time, were now promoted to the rank of brigadier general and their commands were placed on a permanent basis.

We have already briefly examined Thomas' qualifications and found him to be highly acceptable among the leaders of the Light Division. Lane was new to the post of brigade commander. He was, however, a battle-wise regimental leader with a splendid military background. He was a North Carolinian with the traditional Southern military education. With Daniel Harvey Hill and C. C. Lee, he had been one of the ranking officers in his class at the North Carolina Military Institute at Charlotte. Lane then matriculated at Virginia Military Institute, while Hill and Lee went to West Point. The three rejoined, however, in one of the many coincidences brought about by the war, as officers of the 1st North Carolina Volunteers. D. H. Hill was colonel of this initial Tarheel regiment; C. C. Lee was lieutenant colonel; and Lane was major. They served under "Prince John" Magruder in the early Peninsular campaign. When the army was reorganized in the spring of '62, Lane was assigned to Branch's Brigade which became an early component of A. P. Hill's Light Division. Jim Lane, although a tough fighter, was always a studious fellow. Like Robert E. Lee, he was destined to carry on right through to Appomattox, and then to devote himself to higher education in the postbellum South.

The other three infantry brigades of the Light Division continued under the respective leadership of Gregg, Archer, and Pender. Hill also succeeded in retaining his artillery, although plans were afoot to create a corps artillery unit to take the place of much of the division artillery. Hill's artillery continued under Lindsay Walker's command. Powell Hill breathed a sigh of relief when he was permitted to keep Willie Pegram's battery which at one stage was slated for reassignment to a corps. The Pegram unit had been badly smashed again at Sharpsburg and its captain wounded. It was now reorganized, however, and, with Pegram on the mend, was ready to resume its place as probably the outstanding battery in the entire Confederate Army.

The bulk of Lee's army rested and recruited its strength during October and November of 1862. The only major foray on either side was a sensational cavalry raid by Jeb Stuart and 1,800 of his famed horsemen. Starting October 9th, Jeb's expedition swung up through western Maryland and into Pennsylvania where considerable damage was done to Federal installations at Chambersburg. Stuart n e x t proceeded east and then back south rejoining the army near Leesburg. The raid was of little tactical value but it did alarm Washington. Lincoln's government determined that a major victory was needed immediately to bolster morale and quiet the ever-increasing chant of the rapidly growing peace-at-any-price faction in the North.

Lee had again divided his command, Jackson's Corps now being in the Valley near Winchester while Longstreet's force was centered around Culpeper. The separation was for two reasons: one, to keep the Federals guessing; the other to be prepared for whatever approach the Union forces

213

might take, in what Lee knew must inevitably be another campaign against Richmond.

In November, Burnside accepted command of the Army of the Potomac. With little or no attempt to conceal his plans he started toward Fredericksburg with an army of some 118,000.[10] Lee thereupon brought Jackson's Corps back from the Valley. Contact was re-established between the two corps and preparations were made to "receive" the invader.

Powell Hill took Dolly for a fleeting visit to Richmond in the lull before the next approaching storm. The Southern aristocracy was striving to carry on in the old tradition at the capital. The home front situation, however, was rapidly worsening. Food was scarce. Profiteering had reared its ugly head. Political intrigue was rampant. Jefferson Davis' popularity was on the wane. Powell and Dolly attended one or two of the mockeries that passed for social functions known as "starvation balls." They did not regret soon returning nearer the front. Before they separated she told him that she was again pregnant. Dolly never suggested the question of where he might be when the baby came. No other thought could exist, however, in the mind of a line soldier about to return to duty. Dolly did her best to keep up Powell's spirits but it was with a heavier heart than usual that he left her to rejoin the Light Division on the eve of the Battle of Fredericksburg.

[10] Alexander, p. 284.

CHAPTER 14

Preparation Along the Rappahannock

IT WAS DAMP and cold along the Rappahannock those first two weeks of December, 1862. Hill returned from his leave in time to direct the movement of the Light Division from the Valley to the Fredericksburg area during late November. It had not been Lee's original plan to attempt to hold Fredericksburg against an attack in force. Following Sharpsburg, McClellan had massed the Army of the Potomac near Harpers Ferry. Lee, having withdrawn into Virginia, with Jackson in the upper Valley and Longstreet based around Culpeper, had maintained a mere token force at Fredericksburg. Suddenly, however, the picture was changed by another of the Federal government's reversals in policy. McClellan had become regarded as overcautious by the men at the capital who had sacrificed his offense on the Peninsula on the altar of the defense of Washington. Ambrose Burnside, whose dallying at the bridge at Sharpsburg had cost victory in that battle, had been picked from a group of better generals to take McClellan's place. His instructions from the War Department were to make an early move on Richmond via Fredericksburg. Still very much unsure of himself after the debacle along the Antietam, Burnside hesitantly moved his army opposite Fredericksburg where he went into bivouac despite the light opposition across the river.

The new commander of the Army of the Potomac wanted a pontoon bridge before attempting a crossing. He also wanted a little time to digest the responsibility thrust upon him. Therefore, he sat down north of the Rappahannock and thought things over. It would have been possible to cross by the fords above the town before Lee had his defenses organized, but the same feeling of insecurity, fear of the unknown, or whatever it may have been, that caused Burnside to delay at the Antietam, made him wait for the arrival of a pontoon train.

Burnside's vanguard under Sumner was opposite Fredericksburg on November 17. Lee sent into the town what few reinforcements he could muster on the 18th. At best, he hoped for a delaying action to permit him to organize his main army behind the North Anna. To his amazement, however, Burnside did not even attempt a probing movement at one of the fords. Thereupon, Lee rushed Longstreet over from Culpeper to establish positions in the town and on the heights to the west. In the meantime, Jackson approached from the Valley by one of his characteristically rapid forced marches. Lee used this unexpected breathing spell to map the defense that would prove so devastating when Burnside finally did get under way several weeks later. It also gave the commander of the Army of Northern Virginia an opportunity to evaluate his new Union counterpart. Although Lee was a generous man, who almost never disparaged another, friend or foe, his estimate of Ambrose Burnside was not high. On the other hand, he held an admiration for McClellan that was probably more than the slow-moving Little Mac deserved, at least as a field commander. Asked later which was the ablest Union general in the war, he replied without hesitation, "McClellan, by all odds".[1]

Destiny and politics had now, however, removed McClellan from the scene, and replaced him with the handsome, somewhat befuddled Burnside. The latter, over his head as an army commander, was harried at every turn by government officials who had one eye on the war and the other on the 1864 election. They wanted a victory, but they did not want casualties. They wanted a general who could win, but who would not make himself too important politically in

[1] Long, p. 233.

216

so doing. They wound up with defeat, tremendous casualties, and a general who could not win even though he commanded the greatest army the Union had yet put on the field.

Burnside's delay gave Powell Hill a chance to take stock of himself as well as of his division. The Light Division, on arriving on the Rappahannock, was posted at a place called Yerby's, near Guiney's Station, along the Richmond, Fredericksburg and Potomac Railroad, where it could be moved to support Longstreet if necessary, or could intercept Burnside if he should attempt to force a crossing below Fredericksburg. The weather was uncomfortable, but the troops were rested and generally in good spirits. Hill was proud of them. He spent hours early that December, going among his men imbuing them anew with his aggressive attitude and, in return, getting strength from their obviously sincere fondness, as well as respect, for him. Powell needed to absorb this type of strength. As usual, he was temporarily refreshed by the sojourn with his family. His spirits were high. He was optimistic about the war. Nevertheless, although he scarcely admitted it to himself, his body was weaker than ever before on the eve of a campaign. Courage and spiritual strength were necessary to make up for physical shortcomings. Hill, of course, had the requisite courage. He also had a vigor of spirit that matched Jackson's, or that of anybody in the army, despite his dislike of religious formality. Nevertheless, he welcomed the talks in his tent those cold evenings near Fredericksburg with the robust, religious Dorsey Pender and the kind, scholarly Maxcy Gregg. From them he drew an intangible sense of compensation for the inadequacy of his body to the task which it must perform. He could not resist the temptation, however, to poke a little fun at Pender's religious fervor as Dorsey and Gregg paid their respects just a couple of nights after the Light Division's headquarters had been established at Yerby's Station.

"General Pender," he smiled, "I take it your men are now becoming as full of religion as of fight."

"One and the same thing," nodded Pender. "A soldier

needs Jehovah on his side to gain victory no matter how much fight there is in him."

"A favoring Jehovah, a favoring Jehovah." Hill reached forward and prodded Pender's chest with his forefinger. "Yes, if that will win battles, teach it to your troops. As for me," he turned and smiled quizzically at Gregg, "I am not sure that the science of war is regulated by any external influence, no matter how omnipotent. Faith we must have, but on the field, I'm afraid that I lean more to the teachings of Napoleon."[2]

Pender shrugged, "I cannot quarrel with you, General Hill. Whether it comes from Jehovah, as I believe, or the science and strategy of Napoleon, as you profess, no division was ever better led than ours. My faith lies in God and A. P. Hill."

Gregg broke what almost became an embarrassed silence. "As an astronomer, I must assert," he said laughing, "that some of us put our faith in our stars."

"Whatever you say," replied Pender, "we must have faith."

Hill got up and opened the trunk at the foot of his cot. "Here's a symbol of faith that always rides with me in battle." He held up the hambone that his mother had given him so many years before. "This, gentlemen, is a talisman of faith—my mother's faith that it would keep me from harm." He laughed softly. "And I guess it has." He reached into the trunk again. "But now, if General Pender will excuse us, General Gregg and I will toast all of our faiths in this poor-grade bourbon that I brought from Richmond." He drew out a bottle.

"I'll drink with you in spirit," Pender's smile broadened as he spoke, "But I'm sure Gregg will want to know why there is poor-grade bourbon for the commander of the Light Division. Is patriotism dead among the civilians in Richmond?"

---

[2] Hill's view of Napoleon as the criterion of military leadership and his lack of faith in a "favoring Jehovah" on the battlefield are described by W. J. Robertson in a series of articles in the *Richmond Times-Dispatch,* October, 1934.

218

Hill's face became solemn as he poured the whiskey. "Everything is dead in Richmond—or at least dying. The sincere people are feeling the pangs of hunger. The selfish are flourishing with their profiteering. People in the Government are nervous. You sense you're on the edge of a volcano in Richmond these days. I think that when they started bringing the wounded into the city in great numbers last spring people received a shock from which they may never recover. It is our business to watch suffering on the field. To the women of Richmond it is something they cannot understand." His features hardened. "Yes, they are brave enough. They are patriotic. But a city overflowing with wounded soldiers for whom there can be no adequate care; a city where good food is becoming scarcer each day, and—," he smiled as he looked at his glass, "also good bourbon; well, the civilians just don't know how to cope with the situation."

Gregg shook his head. "I hadn't realized it's so bad. My friends in Columbia haven't indicated anything like that in their letters."

"It probably isn't that bad down in Carolina. As a matter of fact it really isn't that bad in Richmond. It just seems very bad because everyone is under pressure—and such a nervous feeling pervades everything."

Hill hesitated. Then banged his fist down on the table. "Damn it. What will they do if a crisis really comes? The war is not going badly." He smiled grimly, "In a few days, from what I've learned from General Lee, it's going to improve considerably. But those so-called business men, who fear their shadows, and that other group, who think they must maintain the old social front to keep up the morale of the country! They threaten our economy. The Government doesn't know what to do about it. Public officers buy in the black market and flock to balls and parties—'starvation' balls they call them. Perhaps they will be really that, some day, too."

Gregg looked up with interest, "What did Mrs. Hill think of all that?"

219

Powell laughed, "Well, she's a soldier's wife, you know. Then, too, she's a Kentuckian. It doesn't hurt her as much to watch the decline of Richmond as it does a Virginian. As a matter of fact, I think she actually admired the false front that is being kept up in the capital. I don't mean that there's defeatism in the air—except maybe for the black-market money grubbers, who know their day must surely come. Mrs. Hill thought the courage of most people was commendable. She even liked the mock frivolity that some try to maintain. To me it was macabre—grand ballrooms filled with dancing couples; everything ceremonious, but no refreshments, and feeble music played by a few septuagenarian fiddlers."

He paused to fill his pipe.

Pender shook his head glumly. "It's been a long time since my wife and I have danced, even to the music of decrepit fiddlers."

"That loss may trouble you young blades," laughed Gregg, "but dancing is one thing that I cheerfully sacrifice to the war effort."

"I don't suppose you include me in your reference to 'young blades.' General Pender is the only one here to fill that role." Hill sighed softly, "I did have my day, though."

"And you still are having your day," cut in Gregg. "Starvation ball, or what you will. I'll warrant that you and Mrs. Hill cut quite a figure on the dance floor."

Hill shook his head. "It's not just me. It's the times. Three short years ago in Washington we danced for hours on many evenings. The music at Willard's Hotel was a far cry from the squeals I heard the other night. If there had been no war, those things would have gone on." He hesitated with a chuckle. "Making allowances, of course, for the raising of a family. No, gentlemen, it's something outside of ourselves. It's—it's—" He pounded the table again. "It's just so God damned lonely sometimes."

Gregg and Pender watched their general intently. He had never before, and would never again, let himself go like that

220

in their presence. Hill immediately sensed this. He rose abruptly.

"There's work to be done tomorrow, gentlemen." His voice was soft, but it had the familar ring of its usual authority that had left it for a few moments. "Burnside is over there across the river." He pointed toward the Rappahannock. Then Powell Hill relaxed into a smile. "And, gentlemen, he was a gay blade once, who liked to dance. He's a handsome devil, and he probably still enjoys social pleasures. We shared many together in cadet days."

Gregg smiled. "Student days always seem to have a quality that later life defiles."

Hill gazed at the South Carolinian. "You're a philosopher, Gregg. You philosophers often ascribe complex meanings to simple events. You might be right about this one, though. Burnside was a tortured man at Antietam. I'll wager he's pacing the ground over there tonight." He nodded toward the river. "But there was never a cadet so hell-bent for fun and with such little concern for the consequences as Ambrose Burnside at the Academy. And do you know," Powell paused to light his pipe, "Burnside was the only one of our bunch of good-time boys to become a captain of cadets?"

"The devil takes care of his own," grunted Gregg.

"Yes," went on Hill, "Harry Heth and Burnside got away with murder. Julian McAllister and I roomed over the commandant's office. We were so close to headquarters as to be presumed out of the way of temptation. That was perfect for Heth and Burnside. They cached in our room wine, cigars, turkeys, hams, and anything else they could steal from the commissary."

Hill smiled faintly at Pender. "But perhaps I shouldn't use the word 'steal' in reference to one of our own officers, General Heth. I don't know though," his smile broadened, "It was a long while ago and they did steal those things. I guess I was an accessory after the fact."

"Were they ever caught?" asked Pender.

"Burnside was court-martialed on one occasion, but it didn't upset him. It apparently didn't upset the authorities

221

either, because they just looked at his smiling confident face and made him a cadet captain. I was lucky to be a lieutenant."

"Heth seems to have made the grade," said Gregg.

"Yes," answered Hill, "but he was anchor man in the class—number 38 out of 38 cadets who graduated in the class of '47. Well, we're all here now—except McAllister. He never stayed in the army. Burnside is over there commanding the Army of the Potomac. We've just completed our business with McClellan, my earlier roommate. General Heth is with our forces. There are others, many others."

"General Jackson?" prompted Gregg.

Hill looked at him quizzically. "Yes, General Jackson." He paused to puff on his pipe. "The class of '47 has produced many of us who never dreamed we'd be enemies on the field of battle." He smiled slightly. "I remember Heth and I carrying Burnside to his quarters one night. Poor fellow had too much to drink. He managed to come to, though, just as we dumped him on his bunk. He pushed up on his elbow and gave us that famous smile. He could hardly talk but he managed to apologize for his condition and to thank us for helping him. He was quite a fellow."[3]

There was a long pause in the conversation.

The lines of Powell Hill's face hardened again. "Ambrose Burnside is now my enemy. I think, gentlemen, that in a few days we shall destroy his great army. General Lee is sure we shall if Burnside attacks Fredericksburg. I know Burnside. He is not the type of general whom Napoleon would select for the science of war. But," he opened the tent flap for Gregg, "he is a brave man. He will attack."

After the others had left, Hill stood outside the tent in the cold, damp air. Many thoughts flashed through his mind. He reproached himself for his display of emotion to Pender and Gregg. He would have to exhibit better self-control in the future. Then he smiled. After all, it was lonely in his position, but it would be much more lonely if he didn't

---

[3] Incidents of West Point days based on Harry Heth's unpublished manuscript.

have friends such as Gregg and Pender. Perhaps it was just as well that he had given them a quick glance into his heart. They would be even closer now. He shook his head. No, that wouldn't do. You might love your subordinates, but they must not become too close personally. There were so many with whom he'd like to be friends. For example, there was young Willie Pegram, a soldier if there ever was one. Best artilleryman in the world, mused Powell. After his wounding at Sharpsburg, the boy had bounced back, ready for action. Hill had praised Pegram in his official reports and had commended him before the troops, but somehow it would have been more satisfactory to sit down and talk with him over a pipe or a glass of bourbon. William Johnson Pegram, he thought—can't be much over twenty years old, shy, studious. But what a gunner! Hill looked up toward the stars. War is my business, but why should it be the business of a lad like Willie Pegram? Still, he shrugged his shoulders, Pegram seems to love battle more than any man I ever saw.

Hill's reverie was broken by the sentry passing on his rounds. The sentry halted and saluted.

"Good evening, son," Powell Hill said softly as he returned the salute, and entered his tent.

He sat down on his cot, but he had no desire to sleep. There were too many things on his mind concerning the Light Division. The one thought that had disturbed him most ever since Manassas, returned. What about Charlie Field's Brigade? Field had been badly hurt; he had lost a leg. From the medical reports there was every indication that Field might never be back with his brigade. He certainly would not be available for a long time. The command of the brigade had fallen on the shoulders of Field's senior colonel, John M. Brockenbrough, commander of the 40th Virginia regiment.

Brockenbrough was a good regimental leader, but he seemed slow to grasp the rudiments of a brigade command. He was courageous enough and seemed sufficiently intelligent, but there was something lacking. Hill hoped that Brockenbrough appeared to be short of the mark only be-

223

cause he was trying to fill the place of a really first-class officer. Brockenbrough had assumed command on the field of Second Manassas at the height of battle and in a driving rainstorm. His new command was advancing on Branch's left at the time, but was soon stopped and pushed back, leaving Branch isolated and open to a flanking counter-attack by the Federals. It was a bad start, probably not al-together Brockenbrough's fault, but it certainly did not help him secure the self-confidence necessary for successful command.

At Sharpsburg, Powell Hill committed his other available brigades ahead of Brockenbrough's. The latter, nevertheless, got into action in that battle as did every fighting unit that Lee commanded north of the Potomac. The brigade, a good veteran outfit, well trained by Field, conducted itself at least adequately, so that there was no occasion to consider any steps as drastic as seeking a replacement for Brockenbrough elsewhere in the army. Brockenbrough was to continue for a long period as a brigade commander with the rank of colonel. He was never to be a conspicuous failure on any field, but neither was he ever to attain a mark of distinction. Hill had him well sized up as he ran over his commanders in his mind that night near Fredericksburg.

Just as Hill was skeptical of Brockenbrough's ability in higher command, he had no misgiving whatever about his other new brigade commander, Jim Lane. Lane took over Branch's command without a trace of disturbance in the operation of the brigade. Branch had been a good soldier, respected by his men and superiors alike. His replacement would have been difficult except for the fortuitous circum-stance that Lane was a natural soldier. He was a rough and ready, down to earth individual, who had a way of instilling spirit and confidence in the troops. O'Brien Branch, the man, would be missed. His brigade, however, under Colonel James Lane was as strong as ever.

After pondering these matters for a while, Powell Hill got up and again left the tent. The stars were now obscured by the fog that so often drifted in over the Valley of the

Rappahannock at that season of the year. He took a long breath. His features relaxed. He'd keep an eye on Brockenbrough. The rest of the Light Division was really in fine fettle. No division in the army was as strong numerically. None had better brigade commanders. Lee was right when he forecast the destruction of that army commanded by his old friend, Ambrose Burnside.

General Edward J. Stackpole in his excellent treatise entitled *The Fredericksburg Campaign*[4] enumerates the events which transpired between November 6 when Halleck issued orders designed to move the pontoons required by Burnside from Harpers Ferry to Fredericksburg, and December 1, when all elements of Lee's army had arrived around Fredericksburg, with the pontoons still not in place. Everything went wrong. Orders were mailed rather than telegraphed. Mud and rain slowed progress. Orders were misinterpreted. The overall plan was apparently never understood by the engineer officer directing operations. These things were not Burnside's fault. Much of the blame can be assessed to Halleck, who, General Stackpole relates, was roundly berated in articles published in the *Providence* (Rhode Island) *Journal*. It must be remembered, nevertheless, that Burnside could have moved much earlier across the fords against a practically undefended Fredericksburg. With respect to criticism of Halleck, in palliation of Burnside's indecisiveness, it should be noted that Burnside was already building local political prestige in Rhode Island where he would eventually be elected governor. Whether or not the *Journal* articles were early political propaganda or proper criticisms of Halleck is immaterial. The fact remains that the Union chance for easy victory at Fredericksburg vanished in early December. By the time the preliminary bombardment of the town was ordered by Burnside on the 11th, the Confederates were so strongly entrenched, and so well organized, that they eagerly awaited the long-delayed river crossing by the Army of the Potomac.

---

[4] Military Service Publishing Co., Harrisburg, Pa., 1957; pp. 97-98.

CHAPTER 15

Victory and Tragedy

*F*OG, which shrouded Fredericksburg on Saturday morning, December 13th, concealed from Lee the Union movements on the opposite shore. The Confederates, however, already had been given ample opportunity to watch Burnside mass his troops across the Rappahannock. The points of concentration and the preliminary artillery barrages of the 11th and 12th indicated the probable avenues of attack. Such a bombardment was laid upon Fredericksburg by Burnside's guns that Lee evacuated the town and drew up his army in a crescent on the surrounding high ground, Jackson's Corps on the right, Longstreet's on the left. Fredericksburg was a shambles by the afternoon of the 12th. Every building had been damaged, many completely demolished, in what had been a prosperous, bustling little city. The residents had, of course, long since fled. It was a smoldering ghost town into which Burnside's vanguard cautiously moved on the 12th.

Lee had placed Longstreet's Corps on the heights to the west which commanded the town and the river. Longstreet's strong point was Marye's Heights, a steep eminence from the base of which open fields sloped down to Fredericksburg. At the foot of Marye's Hill (one of the two hills comprising the Heights) was a sunken road running north and south. The east boundary of the road was a sturdy stone wall four feet high; the west was a retaining wall along the base of the hill. In this road Longstreet placed his front line of infantry. The riflemen there had superb protection as well as an unobstructed field of fire toward Fredericksburg. Back on the hill, the Confederate artillery was massed, and reserve infantry was held in readiness. It was the grim hope of the Confederate defenders, all the way from Robert E. Lee down to the last rifleman, that Burnside would move against Marye's Heights. No dismay was expressed in the Southern camp, therefore, when it became apparent late on the 12th and early on the 13th that the Federals were forcing their way across the Rappahannock via pontoon bridges despite the devastating fire that was poured upon them.

There was considerable uneasiness in the Federal ranks as the shape of the coming battle developed. They had a numerically superior force, but this advantage was far less than on other occasions. It was also apparent, even to the line private, that the Confederate positions were strong. Among Burnside's staff and corps and division commanders there was much opposition to the plan of attack. As a matter of fact, it was felt by some that Burnside had no definite plan at all, that he had merely determined to cross the river, strike at the enemy, and see what developed.[1] In any event, as the fog began to lift during the morning of the fateful 13th of December, 1862, part of the Army of the Potomac was in and around the ruins of Fredericksburg arrayed for battle. The rest was in readiness on the plains south of the town. Burnside had divided the army into three "grand divisions" under the respective commands of Franklin, Hooker, and Sumner. Hooker's command was broken into two approximately equal parts, one being assigned to Sumner, the other to Franklin. As the sun broke through around ten o'clock that morning, it was apparent that Franklin was preparing to attack the Confederate right below Fredericksburg in force while Sumner was about to move against Longstreet on the Southern left. Longstreet was pleased. He could not anticipate, nevertheless, the full extent of the slaughter of Federal troops that would take place before Marye's Hill that day.

On the Confederate right, however, the picture was somewhat different. Jackson's Corps did not have as a base

---

[1] See Palfrey, pp. 143 et. seq., for Northern contemporary criticism.

any natural strong point such as Marye's Hill, though it was in position on a low, wooded ridge. On the right was an excellent position for Lindsay Walker's artillery, under whose fire the Federal attack would be compelled to proceed across open fields toward the woods in which the Confederates were concealed. Jackson's lines were so arranged, furthermore, that there were sufficient reserve elements to afford the depth that had been so badly lacking in previous campaigns. A. P. Hill's Light Division covered the one-and-a-half-mile front opposite the main point of Franklin's concentration. Powell Hill established a front line of Archer, Lane, Pender, and two regiments from Brockenbrough's Brigade. Walker's artillery was protected by earthworks, and was high enough to fire over the defending infantry. The reserves were the balance of Brockenbrough's Brigade, in support of the artillery, and Gregg and Thomas forming, in effect, a second line of defense.[2] Behind the lines manned by the Light Division were Taliaferro's and Ewell's Divisions, the latter temporarily commanded by Jube Early. Then came D. H. Hill's Division, forming a fourth and final line.

Jackson experienced some of Longstreet's anticipation at the prospects of the battle when he noted that Franklin was massing for a frontal assault rather than attempting a flanking maneuver in which his numerical superiority would stand him in good stead. The Confederate four-line depth behind a narrow front would obviously be most effective against a direct attack. Jackson took one more precaution relative to his troops that morning. He ordered his Provost Marshal, Major D. B. Bridgeford, "To shoot all stragglers who refused to go forward, or, if caught a second time, upon the evidence of two witnesses to shoot them."[3]

In the meantime, Powell Hill moved among his troops exhorting them to the heights of effort which they never failed to attain. No dire threats to cowards or stragglers

[2] 21 O.R., p. 645. A. P. Hill's report on Fredericksburg appears here.
[3] 21 O.R., p. 641.

were necessary in the Light Division. Hill then made a final inspection of his position while his men intently watched the awe-inspiring spectacle of the great Union force maneuvering in battle formation on the fields before them. He noted a gap between Archer's and Lane's Brigades and placed Gregg in rear of it to cover the interval, so that any breakthrough could be promptly smashed. Unfortunately, however, Maxcy Gregg did not seem to grasp the precise nature of the situation. A tragedy thereby resulted later that day which should have been averted. Tragedy, however, is one of the fortunes of war.

Hill held his artillery fire in abeyance until the enemy advanced within point-blank range. The Federal attack was in such force, nevertheless, that, despite heavy casualties, one of George Meade's brigades was able to penetrate the Confederate lines through the gap between Archer and Lane. The artillery on the right, with the doughty Pegram's battery pre-dominating, was able to punish the Northern units in the open field, but could not be brought into play against the advance through the marshy, wooded gap in the Southern line. Thomas came promptly to the support of Lane's sector of the line and the advance was halted there. Archer held despite heavy pressure against his flank. Meade's foremost brigade, however, was now well within the Confederate lines. The situation was developed to the point at which Hill had anticipated that Gregg would move up and plug the gap. It is not clear just why the usually astute South Carolinian did not comprehend what was happening. He may have misunderstood Hill's orders, or perhaps those orders were not clearly passed on to him with a sufficiently detailed description of the gap between Archer and Lane. In any event, for the first time in the War, Maxcy Gregg was not ready to meet a crisis.

His men were resting along the newly-cut military road, thinking they were well behind the combat lines. Meade's foremost brigade, after getting in between Archer and Lane, moved swiftly several hundred yards up the slope and came upon Gregg's men without warning. Many had stacked their arms and could not reach them before they were overrun by the Federals. Gregg himself mistook the enemy for retreating elements of Archer's Brigade. Orr's regiment was the first Southern unit to move against the advance. Maxcy Gregg, however, rode in front of Orr's riflemen as they started to fire, knocking their muskets up toward the sky and shouting that they were firing on friends.[4] In the

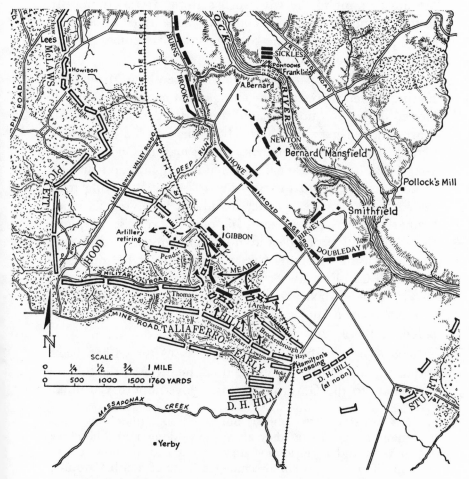

MAP 15. BATTLE OF FREDERICKSBURG—ACTION ON SOUTH FLANK

[4] Alexander, p. 299.

231

confusion that now became rampant, Gregg was hit and fell in front of his troops, mortally wounded. The brigadier who had been at the very heart of most of the Light Division's battles thus became the victim of a tragic mistake, one of the few battlefield errors which he ever committed.

Gregg's unfailing courtesy and thoughtfulness of others prevailed until the very end. Even when he knew he was dying he became disturbed at the thought that Jackson might consider some of his actions to have been impolite. He didn't want to die with such a thing, trivial though it seemed to others, upon his conscience. He asked an aide to see if Jackson would come by to receive his apology. Stonewall hurried back with the aide.

Gregg, in severe pain, his spine shattered by a Minie ball, haltingly tried to explain the cause of his mental discomfort. Stonewall Jackson now became transformed from the stern, sharp-tongued martinet of the battlefield to his other, and perhaps truer self—the patient, gentle man of God. He told Gregg that he had never been offended by him and that he could not even recall the occasion to which the dying man referred. As a matter of fact, incidents involving flares of temper between Jackson and his officers, were so frequent that Stonewall probably did not even remember any particular occasion involving Gregg. In any event, he counseled the South Carolina lawyer to "turn [his] thoughts to God." Gently he held Maxcy Gregg's hand until the pain-contorted features relaxed into a smile. "I thank you", Gregg whispered, "I thank you very much."[5]

Maxcy Gregg wrote his own obituary. After he had been wounded, and shortly before he died, he dictated the following report to the Governor of his beloved South Carolina:

> I am severely wounded, but the troops under my command have acted as they always have done, and I hope we have gained a glorious victory. If I am to die now, I give my life cheerfully for the independence of South Carolina,

---

[5] 43 *S.H.S.P.*, 34 gives account of Gregg's death which affords basis for foregoing description.

232

and I trust you will live to see our cause triumph completely.

Gregg's death followed one of the few mistakes that A. P.
Hill ever committed as a division commander. The gap
between Archer and Lane should not have existed. Hill
knew about it, and it would seem that Gregg should have
understood the situation. Nevertheless, it was Hill's command responsibility that nothing should have been taken
for granted. If he had wanted to leave a cavity in which the
enemy might become ensnared as they had in the railroad
cut interval between Gregg and Thomas at Manassas, he
could have done so while supplying complete information
and instructions to his brigadiers. At Manassas, Sam Mc-
Gowan's regiment, which had been in reserve, came up to
smash the Federal advance through the break in the lines.
At Fredericksburg, Gregg's entire brigade was the reserve
element, but it had not been sufficiently alerted for the
breakthrough.

The damage to the line caused by Meade's assault was
quickly repaired as Hill called for support from Early.
"That gallant old warrior," wrote Hill later, "came crashing
through the woods at the double-quick." Sam McGowan,
having succeeded automatically to Gregg's command, was
able to reorganize the brigade. Then, supported by Early's
men, McGowan's troops struck out for vengeance and hurled
the Federals back. As Meade's regiments fled back through
the breach in the Southern line, the whole Federal advance
on the south flank wavered and then broke into a general
withdrawal. Archer, Lane, and Thomas joined in a counter-
attack along Jackson's entire front. Pender on the extreme
left was exposed to artillery fire and was unable to move
out with the others. The fire, pinning down the Confederate
left, became so severe that the casualties which Pender now
suffered exceeded those of the other brigades that were
openly counterattacking. Another tragic blow to the Confederacy nearly occurred in this sector, too, when Dorsey
Pender was hit in the left arm by a bullet. He went to the

rear for treatment but was soon back with his troops. The wound was not unlike that which Stonewall Jackson was destined to receive in the next major battle. Fortunately for the South, however, infection did not get into Pender's injured member, as it did in Jackson's case. The death of one brigadier was enough for the Light Division that day.

Jackson made no serious attempt to press the counter-attack. The Federals were driven back to their reserve lines. The men of A. P. Hill's and Early's Divisions, having done their jobs well, were permitted to stabilize their lines and observe the progress of the battle on Longstreet's flank of the army.

For Powell Hill, however, it was again time to take stock of his losses. The casualty lists showed 1,976 enlisted men and 146 officers. One of those officers, moreover, represented a loss that far transcended a mere number on a casualty sheet. Hill mourned the death of every good soldier to fall for the Cause, but when Maxcy Gregg passed on there was something deeper that affected him as never before. The ring of sincerity resounds in his tribute to his friend's memory:

> A more chivalrous gentleman and gallant soldier never adorned the service which he so loved.[6]

Gregg's was the hardest hit brigade, too, with Orr's Rifles having lost 170 men.

As Hill surveyed the field, still smoldering after the battle, he found some things to cheer him up. Willie Pegram had come through unscathed. Powell had to smile as he looked upon the buoyant young artilleryman. He wrote in his report: "Pegram, as usual, managed to find the hottest place." Then there were the cheers of the troops to lift his spirits. They had held their side of the line and looked with anticipation to the hills behind Fredericksburg where Longstreet waited.

It was the fight at Marye's Hill—if it can be called a

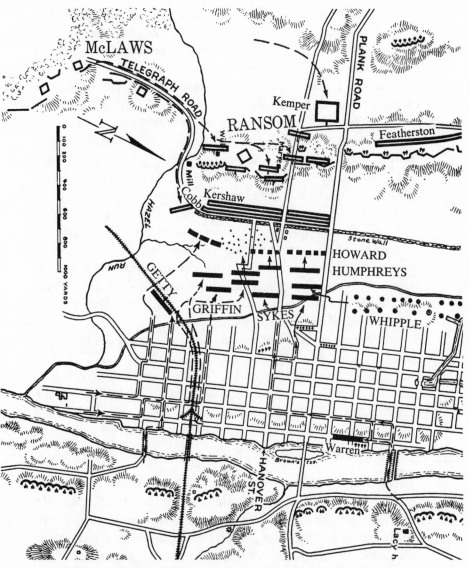

MAP 16. REPULSE OF FEDERAL ATTACK AGAINST MARYE'S HEIGHTS

fight—that monopolizes most of the literature and history concerning the Battle of Fredericksburg. Suffice to say here, that Burnside sent six separate waves of troops up the slope toward the sunken road and six times the remnants fell back, leaving the field covered with Union dead and dying.

235

This was the most senseless slaughter of the war, exceeding Gettysburg and Cold Harbor in this respect, because at Marye's Heights the attackers had no conceivable chance of success. Burnside had been criticized because of his inactivity at the bridge along the Antietam. His innate humanity had kept him from exposing his men to fire there and this had put him in trouble. He was determined to avoid a repetition at Fredericksburg. Psychology, or perhaps psychiatry, may be able to explain the reversal in Burnside's battlefield attitude. The dead on the slopes behind Fredericksburg, however, were not interested.

Half of the Army of the Potomac had been repulsed by Jackson's Corps. The rest was now pulverized by Longstreet. In the rain, during the night of the 15th, Burnside withdrew across the river. He had lost 12,647 men, over 12 percent of his army.[7] Lee's total losses were 5,309,[8] nearly half of which, it will be noted, were in the Light Division. It was another Confederate victory.

Lee's army now established winter quarters, keeping a wary eye on the camp across the Rappahannock. The frustrated Burnside made a couple of feeble passes at opening a new campaign but soon found himself immersed in the criticism of Washington politicians, much of it justified this time. He was succeeded in his command by "Fighting Joe" Hooker.

After the Battle of Fredericksburg, Powell Hill spent much time, as was his custom, visiting his field hospitals, looking after the comfort of his wounded, and with his own hands lifting some of the poor fellows into more comfortable positions. As Dr. Jones recalls, "No general during the war was more careful to make proper provision for his sick and wounded, gave more personal attention to them, or was more tender and sympathetic."

---

[7] Alexander, p. 313.

[8] Lee's final official figure, reported at 21 O.R., p. 652, was over 1,000 fewer, stating the discrepancy to be in "slightly" wounded men who returned to the ranks within a few weeks. Alexander's figure appears to be correct in the strict sense of the word "casualty." Lee was inclined to minimize his losses.

236

Lee has been criticized for not taking the offensive after Fredericksburg. His troops needed rest after their long series of intensive campaigns, however. Their commander felt that a refreshed Army of Northern Virginia would be much more effective after a respite. He was satisfied that the possible advantages to be gained by hitting the Federals while in their disorganized state immediately after Fredericksburg would be outweighed if he failed to recognize this human equation.

The winter of 1862 was far from a pleasant sojourn for the Confederates, officers and enlisted men alike. Food was scarce and clothing insufficient. This was occasioned by congestion on the limited railroad facilities available, coupled with the South's lack of resources to replace rail equipment as it wore out. The situation became so acute that the Richmond Government detached Longstreet with two of his divisions, Pickett's and Hood's, to go on a foraging campaign south of the James near Suffolk, taking them several days' march from Lee's army around Fredericksburg.

Since Lee did not know what plans were brewing in Hooker's headquarters, he again had to spread out his army along the Rappahannock to watch all possible crossing sites. There was still some indication that the Federals might attempt a crossing near Port Royal, where they would have the powerful support of their gunboats. Lee moved Jackson's Corps back to that area. This corps now consisted of four divisions: A. P. Hill's, D. H. Hill's, Early's and Trimble's, the latter commanded by Colston.

In describing Lee's strenuous efforts to secure more food for his army, Jed Hotchkiss, Jackson's cartographer, writes,

Agents were sent out through the country drained by his army, and in conjunction with the authorities at Richmond, gathered supplies in every quarter. These were collected at various depots convenient to the troops. And when the usual method of procuring supplies by purchase and tithe failed, General Lee issued an appeal to the people which soon filled his commissariat. The reserve artillery and all the surplus transportation of the army was sent to the rear, where it was more easy to forage them. The

237

arsenals at Richmond were kept constantly at work to re-equip his army, and arm the men coming in. Much of his field artillery was replaced by new and improved guns. Careful attention was bestowed upon discipline. Many regulations were introduced to promote that system and order which is the life of armies. When the weather permitted, the troops were constantly engaged in field exercises. Prompt measures were taken to prevent desertion, and those who had deserted were brought back in large numbers. The number of absentees was very large in the beginning of the year. By spring it was cut in half. The Conscription Act, now fairly in operation, increased the strength of the army daily. Jackson's corps grew in three months from twenty-five to thirty-three thousand muskets.

Many changes were made in organization, especially in the staff. The staff was made a complete organization in itself, extending from regimental to army headquarters, and ceased to be a mere appendage of brigade, division, and corps commanders. Several of its departments were extended in their operations and more fully developed. The artillery, which heretofore had been attached to the different divisions, was now consolidated into one corps under General Pendleton. A similar organization was adopted for the engineers and cavalry.

Morale was splendid, unimpaired by privation.

Powell Hill devoted the winter to reorganizing the Light Division and preparing for the next campaign. He was heartsick at the insufficient rations available for the men. He maintained his own headquarters on a Spartan basis, sharing with his troops all food and supplies that might have been within his prerogative as a division commander.

The Federals, in their withdrawal after the Battle of Fredericksburg, had abandoned large numbers of tent flies, which were eagerly appropriated by the Confederates. Powell Hill issued these flies to his men on the basis of one per twenty men. The soldiers used this canvas to roof the miserable log huts which they erected as winter quarters.

Some clothing was issued at this time, but it was exceedingly flimsy, and wore out within a few weeks. Despite the lack of adequate food and shelter, as well as warm clothing, the health of the command was surprisingly good.

A little scurvy appeared, and there was no diminution in the number of vermin, but Confederate surgeons noted that there was not as much sickness during the winter as when the weather was better. This probably was largely due to the disappearance of flies and mosquitoes.

Hill did what he could for his men and officers and, where he couldn't provide enough food or clothing, he bolstered morale with promotion. Willie Pegram was made a major, becoming second in command of the division artillery. David McIntosh, whose battery had vied for honors with Pegram's at Fredericksburg, also was promoted from captain to major. It was apparent by now that General Field would not be able to resume command of his brigade in the foreseeable future. Hill would have liked to obtain promotion for one of the colonels. Lee, however, sent him Harry Heth, a most capable soldier, who had been campaigning in the west. Heth (pronounced Heath) was well received by the Light Division, although he was senior to Pender, Archer, and the others, and so immediately became the ranking brigadier in the division. McGowan, in the meantime, had formally succeeded to the command of Gregg's Brigade.

Samuel McGowan was born in Laurens district, South Carolina, in 1821. After graduating from South Carolina College twenty years later, he entered a law office at Abbeville Court House. Within six years he had acquired a substantial law practice. When the war with Mexico was on the horizon, he entered the Palmetto Regiment, in which he served in Mexico as a captain in the Quartermaster Department. After the Mexican War he resumed his law practice, which continued to grow. He became a major general in the state militia and served a term in the state legislature. In 1860 he raised a brigade, but his commission as a major general lapsed when his unit was inducted into the Confederate Army. Shortly afterwards he was elected to the command of a regiment of volunteers. He served with distinction in the early battles, being wounded at the Second Manassas. After Gregg was killed, he received the brigade, being promoted over Colonels Hamilton and Edwards.

239

McGowan was a smooth politician, a good speaker, and popular. Though not as rigid a disciplinarian as others, he was a competent drillmaster, and succeeded in inspiring confidence in his command. He survived the war.

Thomas and Lane continued as the other two brigadiers under Hill. The troop strength received only partial replenishment during this period. Thus, because of the losses on December 15, the official "for duty" strength of the Light Division stood at 10,400 men on March 21. [9]

The period of comparative idleness also served to revive the quarrel between Hill and Jackson. During January, Hill renewed his demand for a trial on the charges pending against him which Lee still fervently hoped would be forgotten. Lee again endorsed Hill's demand for a trial with an observation to the effect that the matter should be dropped in the "interests of the service."[10] Powell Hill, however, was adamant. He wrote to Lee's Adjutant General:

> The General must acknowledge that if the charges preferred against me by General Jackson were true, that I do not deserve to command a division in this army; if they were untrue, then General Jackson deserves a rebuke as notorious as the arrest.[11]

As if the situation were not bad enough, another incident occurred during April that brought the trouble between Hill and Jackson to an absolute and unavoidable climax. An intercepted enemy communication was referred up through General Lane's brigade headquarters instead of being sent directly to army headquarters as ordered by Lee. This transpired because Powell Hill had ordered that all communications be handled through channels in the Light Division and only passed on to higher headquarters by himself. The officer who had obeyed Hill's instructions in contravention of Lee's standing order was a Captain Adams. When word of the incident reached Jackson, he relieved Adams from duty and sent him to Lee. Hill, violently inter-

---

[9] Alexander, p. 321. Hotchkiss gives the strength as 11,100.
[10] 19 O.R., Pt. 2, p. 732.
[11] Ibid.

vening, rushed to Adams' defense. It then developed that Hill had, on a previous occasion, specifically told Adams to disregard an order from Jackson and to obey future orders from the corps commander only if they came through Hill himself.

Jackson had no alternative. He reiterated his charges against Hill, adding the details of Hill's defiant instructions to Adams. He then asked Lee to relieve A. P. Hill from duty as commander of the Light Division. Lee had worked miracles before in averting a climax to the quarrel, but there was nothing he could do now. The issues were drawn so that either Jackson or Hill had to be upheld, with the result that the services of one or the other would be lost to the army. This ultimate choice was averted by the opening of the Battle of Chancellorsville, during which Jackson was mortally wounded. Powell Hill, the senior division commander, succeeded him on the field and was later made a corps commander. Thus it required the death of one of the principals to end forever one of the most unfortunate quarrels in the annals of warfare between great leaders of a common cause.

CHAPTER 16

"Let Us Cross Over the River-"

POWELL HILL became a changed man on the field of Chancellorsville. The sequence of events during those first days of May, 1863, would have had a sobering effect on any man under similar circumstances. Hill's state of mind immediately before the battle, combined with the almost simultaneous mental and physical shocks of Jackson's mortal wounding and his own injury, effected a transformation that marked his outlook and actions until his death two years later.

It was not that his basic character or even his temperament was changed. Powell Hill was of an innately genial and friendly nature. A certain degree of aloofness was required of his role as a division commander by his concept of the duties and responsibilities of military leadership. He had true affection for his men and deep friendship for many of his officers. He was never, however, on a first-name basis with the brigadiers, not even those whom he loved, including Dorsey Pender and the late Maxcy Gregg. Elevation to higher command, he felt, required a degree of aloofness from personal ties with his subordinates. He didn't like this way of life. He hated loneliness, but to him duty dictated the course and he would not deviate therefrom. The self-imposed exile from the close personal society of his officers was the chief factor in his intense desire to have his wife with him as much as possible, even on occasions when prudence indicated the inadvisability of this.

There were, however, deeper changes in A. P. Hill, the explanation for which must be found in the circumstances surrounding his next promotion. He had been convinced that Jackson was badgering him with false accusations. His nature as a gentleman and a soldier, whose performance of duty was paramount to all else, made him resent Jackson's actions with a bitter intensity that was beginning to color his life during the early spring of 1863. He wanted to go to the mat on the issues burning between him and his corps commander. On the other hand, Powell Hill was a soldier "by the book," and he subscribed to the principle that duty requires a soldier's unqualified allegiance to his commanding officer. An emotional tug of war was, therefore, being fought within him when Hooker opened the campaign in late April. There was no question but that in battle Hill's sense of duty would have prevailed over personal hatred, regardless of the outcome. On the other hand, his inner conflict prevented him from being psychologically prepared for the promotion and increased responsibility which were about to be his. The speed with which things happened, furthermore, did not smooth the transition from one of many major generals in the Army of Northern Virginia to one of three lieutenant generals, second only to Lee himself.

During the early spring of 1863, Hill and Jackson had been preparing for a campaign of testimony against each other before a court-martial, instead of getting ready to fight their common foe. The enemy, in the person of General Hooker, intervened by opening the campaign of Chancellorsville. Hooker's rejuvenated Army of the Potomac had a strength of 134,668 officers and men.[1] General Hooker planned to envelop Lee from the west with the bulk of this force, while holding the Confederates in place with two corps, under Sedgwick, which were to "demonstrate" in the Fredericksburg area. Accordingly, Hooker on April 27 sent three corps, numbering 42,000 men, on an encircling march via Kelly's Ford, thence southeast across the Rapidan at Ely's and Germanna Fords, to the vicinity of Chancellorsville. This force arrived there about noon on April 30.

---

[1] These figures are from the tables given in the Appendix of E. J. Stackpole's new book, *Chancellorsville, Lee's Greatest Battle*. The Stackpole Co., Harrisburg, 1958.

Meantime his cavalry corps, under Stoneman, was on a foray which went as far south as the area between Gordonsville and Richmond. Within the next two days Hooker's right wing in the Chancellorsville area was reinforced by two more corps, and eventually by a third. Thus he had 42,000 men in Lee's rear, which force was built up rapidly to almost 90,000. In addition, he had Sedgwick's two corps, initially over 40,000 strong, opposite Fredericksburg.

Lee's total strength was only about 60,000, perhaps 61,000,[2] as two divisions were with Longstreet near Suffolk, and half the cavalry were absent on recruiting duty or in the Shenandoah. Lee not only was badly outnumbered, but he did not have accurate information of Hooker's movements. Furthermore, with Hooker's right wing, numerically as strong as Lee's whole force, to the west, and Sedgwick with another powerful force to the east, Lee was faced with fighting in two directions.

By April 29, however, the picture had begun to clarify for Lee. On that day he started to move some of his divisions nearer Fredericksburg. Since the Federal left wing under Sedgwick was obviously about to cross the Rappahannock below Fredericksburg, Lee moved A. P. Hill's and Early's divisions some ten and fifteen miles, respectively, northwest to the old positions near Hamilton's Crossing. This was the area which they had occupied during and after the Battle of Fredericksburg, and which by now had been strengthened with earthworks.

As the situation continued to develop, and it became increasingly evident that Hooker had concentrated a considerable force near Chancellorsville, Lee made another bold decision. Leaving only Early's Division opposite Fredericksburg, he ordered Jackson's Corps to march west to join Anderson and McLaws, who were facing the Federals from an intrenched position astride the Plank Road near Tabernacle Church. Lee now had the two fronts which he had hoped to avoid—one facing west, the other east. But

---

[2] *Ibid.*

245

he was not dismayed. Instead of "fleeing ingloriously" as Hooker had boasted that he would do, he was already planning to sally forth and attack his opponent.

Jackson's Corps marched northwest from the Hamilton's Crossing position early on Friday, May 1. A. P. Hill rode at the head of his division, which was second in the column, Rodes being in the lead and Colston bringing up the rear. As they approached Tabernacle Church cannon could be heard firing to the front, for contact had been made between Anderson's and McLaws' leading brigades and elements of the Federal Twelfth and Fifth Corps. Jackson had been Hill's antagonist in the war of words which they had been conducting, but now he was Powell's commander. The situation was changed radically. Personal differences were set aside in the common effort against the enemy.

The fighting on that day was a "feeling-out" operation, in which the Light Division did not participate. A. P. Hill's brigades were held in reserve on the left rear of the concentrated Confederate force.

That night Lee and Jackson met in their famous conference near the intersection of the Orange Plank Road and the road leading southwest to Catharine Furnace. They crouched beside a small fire and discussed the information which had been gathered during the day by the cavalry and by Jackson himself in a personal reconnaissance. Stuart rode up with the vital news that the Federal right flank, consisting of Howard's XI Corps, was "in the air" near Wilderness Church. A plan of operation for the next day was evolved, a scheme which has been hailed by historians and tacticians as a model of boldness and brilliance.

The encircling maneuver which resulted from this plan is regarded as Stonewall Jackson's greatest accomplishment. Full credit for the success of the day, and ultimately of the whole battle, has been accorded Jackson by some. There is no intention here of entering into a debate as to where the chief accolades belong for the Southern victory at Chancellorsville. Colonel Marshall, who was present at the Friday night meeting between the commanders, gives full credit

246

for the plan to Lee. He even says that Jackson at first opposed it as too hazardous.[3] Be that as it may, the execution of the plan was Jackson's. The flanking movement around the Federal right on Saturday, May 2, was personally han-

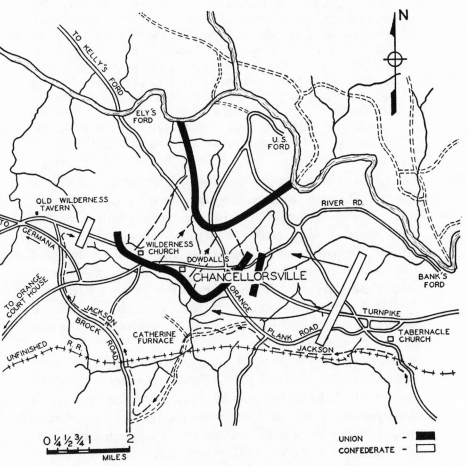

MAP 17. BATTLE OF CHANCELLORSVILLE—JACKSON'S FLANK ATTACK

dled by Stonewall Jackson in every detail. Its success won the battle.

The advance was to start before daylight, but it was eight o'clock before it got under way. One of A. P. Hill's soldiers has left an account of this momentous occasion:

[3] Marshall, p. 170.

247

At daylight (May 2) everything was astir. Blankets were rolled up; the coffee we half made over a handful of sticks was drunk scalding hot; cold rations were swallowed hurriedly, and everything was made ready for the battle just before us. The brigade was moved a little forward, knapsacks piled up and committed to a guard of the sick, and other preparations were made. After we had started, Jackson moved along the column. He rode in his usual unstudied manner, wearing a common oilcloth over his shoulders, and with his cap drawn low over his eyes. He looked forward more eagerly than I had ever seen him do, and there appeared to be a more than wonted contraction of the thin, firm lips. We were on the point of breaking out in the old cheer, but reading battle in his haste and stern look, we contented ourselves with gazing at him and speculating.

Hill's Division was at the rear of the column, still in reserve. The two rearmost brigades, Archer's and Thomas's, had a skirmish near Catharine Furnace, where they had been detailed to protect the artillery and wagons at the rear of the column, but otherwise the march, a hot and tiresome affair, was made without incident or interference from the enemy. The route followed the Furnace Road past Wellford's, then into the Brock Road, running north across the Plank Road, and into the main Turnpike running east toward Chancellorsville.

When Jackson reached a point on the Turnpike west of Wilderness Church he deployed Rodes' Division astride the road, with Colston in support. Hill's Division was partly deployed and partly in column on the road. The two rearmost brigades were still coming up. The deployment was completed at 5 p. m., and a few minutes later Jackson ordered the assault.

The impetuous advance of the Confederates took Howard's regiments completely by surprise. In a few moments the broken XI Corps was streaming east in great disorder and even panic. Jackson pressed the pursuit relentlessly, knowing well that the lateness of the hour was working against him in achieving a complete victory before dark. But by 7:30 p. m. Rodes' attack had spent its force. The

248

companies were intermingled and had lost their sense of direction in the dense woods and tangle of underbrush. Only the Light Division was still concentrated, well in hand, and in shape to continue the assault. Jackson, who was at the very front, was attempting to straighten out the lines and prepare for a resumption of the advance. He soon saw that fresh units would have to be brought up for a passage of the lines. He sent for A. P. Hill.

Hill came up quickly with his staff. Personal differences were now entirely cast aside. He was eager to get into the fray. He reported to Jackson in the gathering darkness, and received orders to take over the front of the attack. At once Hill moved quickly among his units, arranging Lane's Brigade, in the lead, in line of battle along the west edge of a small clearing. While he was so engaged, Jackson again rode up, shouting, "Press them, Hill! Cut them off from United States Ford. Press them!"

Hill shook his head. "My staff is not familiar with the ground."

Jackson shouted to Captain Boswell, his Engineer Officer, "Report to General Hill. Show him how the ground lies."

With that, the two generals separated, each desperately hurrying on his respective mission of reorganization and reconnaissance. In the darkness, among the thickets and trees of the Wilderness, visibility was negligible. One's sense of direction was easily lost. Jackson, moving north from the main road, came upon an apparently deserted woodland road as an uncertain moonlight broke through the trees. He turned back toward his own troops. A short distance west on this road an advance detachment of Lane's Eighteenth North Carolinians lay in the underbrush awaiting a possible enemy counterattack.

The story of the wounding and later death of Stonewall Jackson has been told many times, but the name of A. P. Hill, and the fortunes of his men, were so closely associated with the event, that the account is worth repeating here.

Stonewall had ridden outside the Confederate lines without notifying his own skirmishers. He now bore down upon

249

Lane's men, who could see nothing but forms on horseback in the dim moonlight. Their orders were to fire at anyone approaching from the east.

As Jackson, followed by a portion of his staff, clattered up the road a long, blinding flash erupted almost in their faces. Powell Hill, in the meantime, had ridden up behind the men who had fired. He sensed what was happening, although he could not make out Jackson's party for certain.

"Cease firing, cease firing!" his voice rang out.

"Who gave that order? Pour it on, boys," came back a shout from the bushes.

Another volley roared. Jackson was hit in the left arm and right hand. An aide grabbed his horse and led him within the Confederate lines. Hill helped place Jackson on the ground under a tree, and with a handkerchief stanched the flow of blood from his injured hand.

"Is the wound painful?" he inquired, his voice expressing a tenderness entirely foreign to his former bitterness toward his commander.

"Very painful," answered Jackson. "My arm is broken."

Hill held Stonewall in his arms while he directed two of his young staff officers in arresting the hemorrhage and adjusting a sling to support the shattered arm.[4]

Someone brought a bottle of whiskey. Jackson at first shook his head. Then, his head propped on Powell Hill's breast he permitted the bottle to be brought to his lips. He took a long swallow. This was the first liquor he had tasted in years. Some of the staff officers who knelt about their leader thought of the comment he had made some months earlier when he heard Kyd Douglas observe he didn't like the taste of liquor. Jackson had smiled at his young aide on that occasion and said: "In that I differ with you and most men. I like the taste of all spirituous liquors. I am the fondest man of liquor in this army and if I had indulged my appetite I would have been a drunkard. But liquors are not good for me. I question whether they are much good to any-

---

[4] The description of Hill's ministration to Jackson's wounds is detailed by Dabney, pp. 687-688.

one."[5] Aside from the temperance advice, Jackson's views on drinking, in the light of his own taste for liquor, are indicative of that trait of his character evidenced by his comment to an officer who asked for leave to visit his dying wife. Jackson refused the leave and said coldly: "Man, do you love your wife more than your country?"[6] The officer's wife died and Jackson, a tender, loving husband and father himself, earned the officer's undying hatred. Stonewall would not digress from his code no matter what the cost to those around him, or to himself.

These incidents give insight to the cold, iron self-discipline of the man which marked him apart from his fellows. It was part of a character so entirely foreign as to be almost incomprehensible to the warm, understanding nature of the officer in whose arms Thomas J. Jackson now lay. On the arrival of a regimental surgeon, Powell Hill relaxed his grip on his suffering leader and turned his attention toward the skirmish line just a few feet away.

Jackson was then moved by litter toward the rear. Hill had given instructions that Stonewall's identity should not be revealed to the men. The word, however, was brought to Dorsey Pender, through whose lines Jackson was now being passed. Pender, himself wounded, expressed a word of consolation to Jackson, then hesitated as if wondering whether or not to discuss a field problem with his leader. The problem was major, however, and A. P. Hill was not nearby. Finally, he spoke, just as the litter bearers started to move on.

"I fear I shall not be able to hold my ground."

Jackson turned his head toward Pender and issued his last military order: "General Pender, you *must* keep your men together. You *must* hold your ground, sir."[7]

In the meantime, Powell Hill returned from where he had been ministering to Jackson, to continue directing the deployment of Lane's Brigade for a resumption of the advance. Suddenly a volley of enemy artillery fire, accompanied by

[5] Douglas, p. 186.
[6] *Ibid.*, p. 236.
[7] Dabney, p. 690.

musketry, swept down the road and through the trees. Hill experienced a sharp, numbing sensation across the calves of his legs. He fell to the ground, fingering the place where he had been struck to determine whether he was bleeding seriously. But there was no blood. Probably he had been struck by the flat side of a shell fragment, or a limb of a tree, or a spent ball which failed to cut through his boots. His legs, however, were severely bruised and for the moment partially paralyzed.

The precise nature of Hill's injury was never diagnosed. Henry Kyd Douglas, of Jackson's staff, who was with him at the time, thought that a bursting shell had been the cause, for his own boot top and stirrup strap were cut at the same instant.[8] A few moments after he was struck, Hill found that he could stand erect and even hobble about, so he decided that he was able to function. Realizing that he was the senior officer on the field—Rodes and Colston being brigadiers—he turned over the command of his division to his senior brigade commander, Henry Heth. Then he assumed command of the corps.

Soon Hill noticed that the pain in his legs was growing more intense. He found it difficult to ride, and almost impossible to walk. In justice to the troops he felt that only a man in full possession of his faculties should exercise so important a post at this time. So he conferred with Rodes, nearby, who agreed that command of the corps should devolve upon Stuart, the only other major general in the area. It was a disappointment to Rodes to be passed over for another, especially one who was inexperienced in commanding infantry, but he acquiesced gracefully, as his official report indicates:

> General Stuart's name was well and very favorably known to the army, and would tend, I hope, to re-establish confidence. I yielded because I was satisfied the good of the service demanded it.[9]

Major General J. E. B. Stuart, who had used his cavalry

[8] Douglas, p. 223.
[9] 25 *O.R.*, Pt. 1, p. 942.

for screening Jackson's flanking march, was then some five miles distant, on the road to Ely's Ford. On being sent for, he rode rapidly to report to Hill, who formally turned over to him the command of the corps.

The troops were sufficiently well trained and ably commanded by the brigade and regimental commanders that no panic or confusion resulted from the almost simultaneous disablement of Jackson and Hill. Hill remained on the field throughout that night and during the next day despite his inability to take active part in the campaign. That Stuart appreciated this and did not regard it as interference with his new authority clearly appears from his report:

> Maj. Gen A. P. Hill, who had the misfortune to be wounded soon after the command devolved upon him, remained near the field next day, notwithstanding his wound, for which I was very grateful, for circumstances might have arisen making his presence necessary.[10]

The following day Stuart ordered the renewal of the attack. Now it was the turn of the Light Division to relieve Rodes' Division and to spearhead the advance. Harry Heth led Powell Hill's old troops brilliantly, inflicting a devastating defeat upon Hooker's men, who had been badly demoralized by the surprise maneuver and attack of the preceding day. The fighting that day was savage but the Confederate onslaught was irresistible. The Light Division, under General Heth, was not able to carry out Jackson's injunction to cut off the enemy from United States Ford. It did, however, engage in some violent infighting during the next two days, which resulted in seizing the key terrain features of Hazel Grove and Fairview. The attacks of Heth's brigades then forced the Federals back through Chancellorsville, clearing that area for a junction of Jackson's Corps with the other divisions which, under Lee, were advancing from the east.

Hooker was evidently tremendously impressed with the power and tenacity of the Confederate attacks, for he soon

---

withdrew his force to the vicinity of United States Ford, and then back across the Rappahannock.

Heth wrote in his report:

> The Light Division (A. P. Hill's), although unfortunately deprived of the presence of their gallant commander, showed on this day that the spirit with which he had inspired them by success on so many battlefields was still present, and each and all did their duty.[11]

Heth was wounded, though not incapacitated for long. He was compelled to temporarily yield command of the division to Dorsey Pender before the Chancellorsville campaign ended.

During the battle of May 3 there occurred an extraordinary example of symbolism. Hooker's house literally came down around him. At the time of the incident he still had 37,000 troops uncommitted to battle. While he was weighing his decision as to what course to take in the face of the attack by Jackson's Corps, a pillar of the Chancellorsville House, against which he was leaning, was struck by a cannon ball and toppled over.[12] "Fighting Joe" was injured and what little he had of decisiveness left him. He ordered general retreat. Even the relatively successful Union troops at Fredericksburg who had finally carried Marye's Heights, lightly held in this campaign as compared with the battle of the preceding December, were withdrawn. After taking Marye's Heights, General Sedgwick, if properly directed and reinforced, might have been able to overrun Lee's rear. The generalship to coordinate the necessary maneuver, however, was lacking. Hooker quit the field with 37,000 men still not engaged in the campaign.

It was on May 3 that Brigadier General James Archer achieved his most important single success during the war. There was irony in the situation because Archer, astute veteran though he was, failed to realize the significance of what he had done. On the morning of May 3, 1863, his bri-

---

[11] *Ibid.*, p. 892.
[12] Abner Doubleday, *Chancellorsville and Gettysburg,* p. 53.

gade was advancing through the woods near Chancellorsville. Coming upon a Union battery on a hill "near a spring house," Archer promptly ordered an attack at the double-quick.[13] His men took the hill, four guns, and 100 prisoners. They then pressed on, but were forced back when they hit superior enemy forces. Lee, in the meantime, rode up and appraised the situation. He noted that the hill near the spring house commanded that entire sector of the field and constituted the strategic strong point of the phase of the great battle that was fought that day. Jeb Stuart, who was still in command of Jackson's Corps, then rushed batteries to that little hill, which appears in the maps and reports of Chancellorsville as Hazel Grove. The Confederate victory which followed was due, in no small measure, to Acher's rather lucky seizure of Hazel Grove, a name which Archer apparently never did learn, because he never used it in his report.

The next day Pender was wounded as Heth had been. The command of the Light Division then devolved upon Archer. The hard-working, somewhat stolid Archer, having directed a spectacular attack that, by little more than chance, eventually led to one of the great Confederate victories of the war, was thus rewarded by Fate's giving him, albeit temporarily, the highest command he was ever to hold.

Archer's worth was reflected in many other campaigns. His ability to lead his brigade in a smashing attack had been demonstrated at Slaughter's Mountain.[14] His courage and determination to stay on the battle line, come what might, was also demonstrated at Sharpsburg, where he had himself brought on the field in an ambulance, and then mounted his horse, although he was so terribly ill he could scarcely stay in the saddle. Nevertheless, the greatest day which lay before him, as he reported to A. P. Hill at the end of May 1862, was to come a year later when, almost by accident, he took that hill "near a spring house."

By the fifth of the month, as the battle came to an end,

---

[13] 25 *O.R.*, Pt. 1, p. 924, et seq. Archer's report of his part in the entire Chanvellorsville campaign appears here.
[14] 12 *O.R.*, Pt. 11, p. 218.

Powell Hill had sufficiently recovered to confer with Lee. Hill was now the second ranking officer on the field. He made no attempt that day, however, to resume command of Jackson's old corps. Jeb Stuart had done the fighting on the third and fourth, and Hill was glad to have him remain in command for the accolades as the campaign came to its victorious close—victorious, that is, from the South's strategic viewpoint in that Hooker's vastly superior army had been beaten. From the standpoint of casualties it was a close contest. Confederate losses totalled 13,156 (the hardest hit division again being the Light Division). The Northern casualties were 16,804.[15] On May 6, the fight over, Lee restored A. P. Hill to temporary command of the Second Corps and returned Stuart to the cavalry.

In the meantime, Jackson's life ebbed away. His arm had been amputated shortly after he was wounded. Under the care of his surgeon, Dr. Hunter McGuire, an attempt was made to take Old Jack to Richmond. Pneumonia set in, however, so that the trip had to be halted at a little place on the railroad between Fredericksburg and Richmond called Guiney's (now spelled Guinea) Station. The end came on Sunday, the tenth. During his last hours, Jackson was in a delirium. Early that morning he had been told plainly that he would die that day. He expressed satisfaction that he would die on Sunday. At three-fifteen that afternoon his voice suddenly rang out: "Order A. P. Hill to prepare for action! Pass the infantry to the front—."

Then there was a pause. It seemed to those around him that a storm within the dying man had reached its pitch and was subsiding. "No, no," now came his barely audible words, "let us cross over the river and rest under the shade of the trees."[16]

Thomas J. Jackson was dead.

There is a large stone along the road near Chancellorsville which marks the place where Jackson fell. The battle itself, however, is its own monument to the all-time master

---

[15] Alexander, pp. 361, 362.
[16] Douglas, p. 228.

of the flanking maneuver. Chancellorsville was his master-piece of execution.

For those who lived on to fight another day for their doomed Cause, however, there were other rivers to cross. Ambition and jealousy reared their heads as the question of who would permanently succeed to Jackson's rank and command became the topic of the day. The most prominent names mentioned were obviously those of A. P. Hill, who held the temporary corps command, and Jeb Stuart, who had handled the situation so well after both Jackson and Hill fell the night of the second. Then there was Ewell, Jackson's best lieutenant in the early days of the war, who had been denied further prominence only because of the loss of a leg at the Second Manassas. Harvey Hill also had some support, notably from Longstreet, who wrote:

> General D. H. Hill was next in rank to General Ewell. He was the hero of Bethel, Seven Pines, South Mountain and the hardest fighter at Sharpsburg. His record was as good as that of "Stonewall" Jackson, but not being a Virginian, he was not so well advertised.[17]

Longstreet did not have much support in his campaign for Harvey, however, and Stuart as a cavalry officer never seemed to be seriously considered by the high command. The choice lay between Powell Hill and Ewell. The princi-pals conducted themselves decorously during this period but their respective adherents often carried arguments to the point of intense bitterness. Dorsey Pender, who worshipped Powell Hill, thought that jealousy existed toward Hill and the Light Division chiefly because they had been so success-ful. This probably accounted for many of the recrimina-tions against Hill, he claimed. The tactful Robert E. Lee, however, was not swayed by any consideration except the good of the service. He finally settled the problem with something of a stroke of genius. He reorganized the Army of Northern Virginia into three corps, retaining Longstreet, of course, in command of the First, and then appointing

---

[17] Longstreet, p. 332, note.

Ewell and A. P. Hill to the respective commands of the Second and Third Corps.

A. P. Hill was called to Lee's tent on the morning of May 24. There, the Commanding General told him that he was being promoted to the rank of lieutenant general and given command of the new Third Corps, to consist of the Light Division, R. H. Anderson's Division, now transferred from Longstreet's Corps, and a new division about to be formed.

This promotion immediately caused a new problem in which Lieutenant General Hill was vitally interested. The Light Division now needed a commander. Harry Heth was temporarily in charge. Hill told Lee that he liked and admired Heth but pointed out Dorsey Pender's great record. He expressed the view that under Pender, with whom the troops had fought and bled—Pender had been wounded four times—the division would be much more effective than under the comparative stranger, Heth, capable though he was. Then Powell Hill made a most tactful suggestion on his own hook. He said that both men should be promoted and each should have a division.

Lee and Jefferson Davis went along with this plan. As a result, Pender was given McGowan's, Lane's, and Thomas Brigades along with his own. Heth received Archer's Brigade, together with that formerly commanded by himself, now under Brockenbrough, plus two brigades reassigned under the reorganization of the army. The new brigades were Johnston Pettigrew's North Carolinians and Joseph R. Davis' Mississippi Brigade. Neither brigade had seen much action, and some of the officers assigned to them were, as Lee tactfully put it, "uninstructed."

Hill, always loyal to his own, then obtained the command of the Third Corps Artillery for Lindsay Walker. The old Light Division was, therefore, no longer a single fighting unit. Its component parts were still under the command of the Cavalier from Culpeper, and the remaining months of the war would hear much from Lieutenant General A. P. Hill and the Third Corps. The old color and flamboyance of the division as well as its commander, nevertheless, were never to be quite restored. Stonewall Jackson's soul was not the only thing to cross over the river into eternity during the spring of 1863.

The events that had transpired late on May 2 seemed to have taken some of the fire out of Powell Hill. His reaction to the sudden developments was heightened by the fact that within a few moments he had been wounded himself and, in turn, was forced to relinquish command. He was, therefore, not quite himself when he wrote his report of the battle, which was both his first as a corps commander, and his last as commander of the Light Division. Jackson was still alive on the date of the report, although the seriousness of his condition was fully recognized. Nevertheless, it is unlikely, even if Hill had written the report later, and with better retrospect, that he would have paid Jackson a tribute such as had flowed from his pen when Maxcy Gregg was killed. In common with every officer and man in the army, Powell Hill knew that the South suffered an irreplaceable loss when Jackson fell. Hill, however, had too much integrity to express a sentimental personal feeling which he did not experience. Lee, who loved Jackson as a man as well as a soldier, wept openly. But A. P. Hill, though he regretted the loss to his Cause of a great soldier, could shed no tears for the individual who had fallen.

The irony that so frequently marks the battlefield had put the Southern Cromwell literally in the arms of the Cavalier from Culpeper that fateful night of May 2. Jackson's final battle orders, furthermore, were to Pender, lieutenant to the man whom, a few days earlier, Stonewall had sought to have relieved of his command. The last name which he mentioned in his final delirium a week later was that of A. P. Hill. These things must have blended in Hill's subconscious mind with the other circumstances of that day. At any rate, with one or two possible exceptions, at Bristoe Station and perhaps for an hour or two the first day at Gettysburg, Hill was never again the flamboyant, impetuous leader of troops that he had been during the past year. He was a good corps commander and was often a masterful tactician even in the desperate hours of the late winter and early spring of 1865. As a corps commander, nevertheless, he failed to achieve the status of greatness which was his as commander of the Light Division. Serving with Jackson he had played no small part in Stonewall's success. In fact, one wonders what Jackson's place in history would be today without A. P. Hill's presence at such places as Slaughter's Mountain, Manassas, and Sharpsburg. Some will argue, and with excellent authority, that Hill "made" Jackson.

No one will contend, however, that Hill as a corps commander was able to fill Stonewall's place.

CHAPTER 17

Two Successors to the Light Division

*P*OWELL HILL, during the days following Chancellorsville, was not spending his time philosophizing about what might happen because Jackson would not be present at a little Pennsylvania town, the name of which then meant nothing to him. He was busy looking into the organization of his new command. The arrangement of his divisions was of more immediate concern than the fact that he and the Light Division had played such a prominent part in bringing the scent of success to the Confederacy and an air of defeatism to the North. He was more concerned with the problem of whether Brockenbrough would make the grade, than he was with the deteriorating political situation in the North. He had a corps to plan for, but he could not bring himself to look into details of the rest of his command until he was satisfied with the disposition of the Light Division. Pender's new division, of course, appeared solid. Pender, Thomas, Lane, and McGowan were members of the original cast, so to speak. Only Pender had commanded a brigade at the start, but the others had been with the Light Division all the way, in one capacity or another.

Lane had proven his worth at Fredericksburg, when his brigade was outflanked by Meade's breakthrough between Archer and himself. He had been hard pressed, but had recovered and was instrumental in closing the gap with the aid of reinforcements from Thomas. Much has been made of the near-disaster caused by the gap in Hill's line at Fredericksburg. No blame attaches to Lane, who informed Gregg

261

of the situation at least a day before the Union attack. Lane also advised Hill of the situation, but thought nothing further of it, because Gregg was designated as his support, and he assumed that Maxcy's South Carolinians would move up to plug the hole if necessary.[1] The breakthrough would never have occurred had Maxcy Gregg been fully alert to the situation.

The Confederate right wing at Fredericksburg was fortunate that Jim Lane was on the scene to seal off further damage. Lane was a tough and capable fighter, who had a deep-seated dislike of the enemy as men, aside from the question of opposing ideologies. In his report of the Battle of Fredericksburg, he wrote as follows of an incident in which he felt that one of his captured officers had been unnecessarily manhandled:

> The Yankee wretches dragged Lieut. J. W. Pettus, Company C, Thirty-seventh Regiment, some distance by the legs after he had been wounded in the head and leg.[2]

Lane's losses were by all odds the heaviest in the Light Division at Fredericksburg. He officially reported 535 casualties, including prisoners and missing. Subsequent figures submitted for the entire army indicated Lane's losses were even higher.[3] It was a rough baptism of fire for a new brigadier, but he was a good soldier and would be an even better one in the future.

Lane was a graduate of the Virginia Military Institute, class of 1854. Jackson took an interest in all VMI men, including Lane. Stonewall stopped to talk with him before riding out from the lines on the fatal night of his accidental wounding at Chancellorsville. Lane was looking for Hill at the time to ascertain whether or not he should move ahead. The tangled wilderness had made communications difficult, and he could not locate Hill. He asked Jackson if he wanted to order an advance.

Jackson nodded, "Push right ahead, Lane," he said,

---

[1] 21 *O.R.,* pp. 653-4.
[2] *Ibid,* p. 655.
[3] *Ibid.* p. 560.

262

shoving his hand forward as if pushing the enemy back bodily. Jackson then rode into the night.[4] Lane thus became another member of the Light Division to figure in a final episode of Jackson's life. Stonewall's last words were of Hill. His last command while being carried away, wounded, was to Pender. His last order before the fatal accident was to Lane. Finally, the accidental volley that brought down Jackson was from the Eighteenth North Carolina Regiment of Lane's Brigade.

McGowan, who had succeeded Gregg, had also fitted into the picture well. Sam McGowan first came into relative prominence during the Seven Days, commanding the Fourteenth Regiment under Maxcy Gregg. He was commended by Hill for conspicuous gallantry on the Peninsula.[5] He soon assumed the position as Gregg's number one regimental commander and was recognized as one of the outstanding officers of the Light Division, despite his lack of formal military training. Like Gregg, he was a "civilian soldier." He did not possess all of Gregg's cultural background, but he was a gentleman in every sense of the word, and he had the burning ardor of all South Carolinians for the Confederate cause. McGowan had been wounded during the heavy fighting at Second Manassas, where his brigade did such heroic work in holding the left of Jackson's line, but he was back in harness at Sharpsburg.

After the Battle of Fredericksburg, Lee had offered command of Gregg's Brigade to Wade Hampton, a cavalry officer.[6] Hampton had been successful with cavalry in action, but there was some criticism of his handling of the horses of his brigade. In addition, Hampton had indicated earlier that he did not want his cavalry assignment to be permanent. Nevertheless, he declined Lee's offer. Gregg's Brigade, therefore, had been assigned to the man best suited to handle it, Sam McGowan. McGowan's South Carolinians were prominent in the fighting at Chancellorsville. They had the mis-

---

[4] Lane's account is recorded in 8 *S.H.S.P.*, p. 494.
[5] 11 *O.R.*, Pt. 2, pp. 838-9.
[6] 21 *O.R.*, p, 1067.

fortune, however, to run into a strong counterattack in their sector of the line on the last day of the battle. They were forced into what they regarded as an ignominious retreat. Actually, it was an orderly withdrawal before a superior force. McGowan himself was wounded, but his men did not panic, and eventually held fast on a new line. They were humiliated, however, when the Stonewall Brigade from Virginia, coming up in support, passed over them and drove back the Union advance.[7] For Virginians of the Valley to succeed where South Carolinians had failed hurt their pride to the quick. It had been a tough, confusing campaign, however, and their command was in a chaotic state when first McGowan, and then the next two colonels to succeed as commander, were shot down in relatively quick succession. Colonels Edwards and Perrin followed McGowan as casualties. The tired and smashed, but not dispirited, brigade wound up the battle under its fourth ranking officer, Colonel D. H. Hamilton.

Powell Hill was thus more than satisfied with the manner in which Pender's new division shaped up. The old order of the Light Division would be well carried on by Dorsey with the veteran Thomas, and the newly appointed, but well-seasoned, Lane and McGowan, as brigadiers. The only question here was the extent of the seriousness of McGowan's wound.

The other new division, Heth's, was more of a problem. This division included Heth's own brigade, now under Brockenbrough, still something of a question mark, along with the redoubtable Archer's troops, plus two newly assigned brigades. Heth, therefore, had a command the ranks of which were filled only to about fifty percent by soldiers of the old Light Division. He also had Brockenbrough to watch, and he had to orient two new brigade commanders, together with troops that lacked the campaign background of the Light Division. On the positive side, however, Heth had Archer. More important, Harry Heth himself was an

---

[7] 25 O.R., Pt. 1, pp. 942-4.

able soldier and an old-line Virginian, who fitted well into the hierarchy of Robert E. Lee and A. P. Hill.

Harry Heth and Powell Hill had been acquaintances since boyhood. Harry's uncle, Richard Cunningham, owned a fine home in Culpeper County, near Brandy Station. The boys thus had a chance to strike up a friendship that endured through West Point and into their Regular Army careers. Heth had experienced a rather tempestuous career at the Military Academy. He roomed with Burnside, who was the demerit champion of his day. Thus Heth, who was not averse to rule-breaking where fun was involved, was subject to constant temptation. He yielded to that temptation almost as often as did Burnside. Nevertheless, Harry Heth graduated with the class of 1847 and entered the Army, a handsome, dashing lieutenant. He served in the same outfit with Lewis Armistead and Winfield Hancock in Mexico. The three struck up a friendship that would have endured through the Civil War, except for one of those quirks of fate which war so often brings about. Armistead was killed by Hancock's men at Gettysburg, while, on the same field, Hancock was badly wounded by Armistead's troops. Heth survived all hostilities, but had had a previous opportunity to read his own obituary after an incident at Blue Water during the Indian fighting of 1855. He was reported to have been killed on September 3. Newspapers carried the report. Several of his classmates, including Powell Hill, joined in a resolution of sympathy to his family. Heth showed up, however, very much alive. On April 7, 1857, he was married in an elaborate ceremony at which the groomsmen included A. P. Hill and John Pegram, Willie's older brother.

As was the case with Lee, Hill, and most old-line Virginians, Harry Heth left the Union with his state. He experienced bitter pangs, however, when the choice had to be made. He was serving in the West at the time and enjoyed his command and his associations. He had no complaints concerning the Army or life in general. Jefferson Davis had known Heth before the war and had an eye upon him from the start. Early in the hostilities he discussed with Heth the proposition of putting him in command of the Trans-Mississippi army, with the rank of major general. Heth had plenty of self-confidence and was certainly not a shy, retiring individual. Nevertheless, realizing his limitations, he told the President that he would prefer to prove himself first as a brigadier general. He felt, and Davis agreed, that he would be better able to accept higher responsibility after obtaining more experience. Heth thereupon was commissioned a brigadier general and received an assignment in West Virginia, where he served until Lee brought him into the Army of Northern Virginia after Fredericksburg.[8]

In October of 1862, Davis apparently thought Heth was ready for promotion, and so nominated him a major general. He was not confirmed by the Senate, however, for reasons which are not at all clear. Heth's memoirs do not go into the point. It is likely that his name came up when the issue of "too many Virginians" was raised by representatives of other states. In any event, when again nominated by Davis, in 1863, upon Hill's recommendation, approved by Lee, he was quickly confirmed a major general. After Fredericksburg, Lee had given him Charlie Field's Brigade in the Light Division. The question of Brockenbrough's ability was temporarily solved by this move. At Chancellorsville, however, circumstances of battlefield casualties gave Heth, having senior date of rank, temporary command of the division. He handled the job well, despite the fact that he was a newcomer to the other brigadiers, as well as to the troops. When Heth took over the division command, of course, Brockenbrough again assumed temporary command of Field's old brigade. As a result, Heth obtained valuable experience as a division commander at Chancellorsville, and Brockenbrough had another battle under his belt as a brigade leader. The command echelon of the new division, carved in part out of the old Light Division, was thus considerably better seasoned than before the great battle along the Rappahannock.

---

[8] These incidents, and other material on Heth herein, are taken from his unpublished autobiographical manuscript.

Heth has been characterized as an unlucky soldier. He was unquestionably a brilliant officer. Lee expressed his confidence in him by giving him a brigade just before the battle of Chancellorsville, though he lacked combat experience at that level of command. He did well at Chancellorsville and was to prove a good division commander after that. Nevertheless, he never quite seemed to attain the high degree of success for which he appeared qualified. Something always seemed to go just a little awry when he appeared to be on the threshold of greatness.

A. P. Hill, however, was satisfied that Heth would be a good major general at the head of a good division, if his two new brigades measured up to the standards of the Light Division. These troops were Johnston Pettigrew's North Carolina Brigade and Joseph R. Davis' Mississippi Brigade. The men were without extensive combat experience. Davis, nephew of the President, had had no experience at all in battle. Pettigrew, however, was a campaign veteran, who had fought on the Peninsula with many of his new colleagues in the Army of Northern Virginia. Hill realized that time alone would tell how the new division would stand up in battle.

The other division assigned to A. P. Hill's new Third Corps was that of the highly capable Major General Richard Heron Anderson, affectionately known throughout the Army as "Dick." Anderson's greatest success was yet to be achieved, but he brought a good record into the Third Corps. His career during the early stages of the war generally paralleled that of Hill. He fought as a brigade leader on the Peninsula. Subsequently, after successful performances during the Seven Days, he was given Huger's old division and was assigned to Longstreet's command at about the same time as Hill and the Light Division went under Jackson in the midsummer of 1862. Anderson served with Longstreet until the reorganization after Jackson's death. He was a West Pointer, class of 1842, saw action in the Mexican War, and served in the peacetime Army as a captain of dragoons in the west. He was later to succeed to Longstreet's command when the latter was wounded in the Wilderness campaign. Anderson

267

eventually was promoted to the rank of lieutenant general and was a colorful combat figure during the last days of hostilities. His brigadiers, when he joined A. P. Hill, were Cadmus Wilcox, William Mahone, Ambrose R. Wright, E. A. Perry, and Carnot Posey. They were all capable men who were to distinguish themselves in action at Gettysburg. Wilcox was destined to succeed Dorsey Pender. He and Harry Heth would be the last division commanders to lead the battered remnants of the old Light Division as the war ended in the spring of 1865. Anderson's Division, all things considered, was a solid, experienced unit that would be a good complement to Heth's veterans in the Third Corps.

It was a new Army of Northern Virginia, but it was a confident army, fresh from victory and determined. Early in June, the three corps commanders, Longstreet, Ewell, and Powell Hill, learned of Lee's planned invasion of the North. Plans were secret, but somehow, as it does in all armies, rumor seeped down through the command echelons to the troops. The men were ready to join their great leader, Robert E. Lee, in taking the initiative. They would have been even more confident if they had fully appreciated the strength of the "peace at any price" movement in the North, the fears of Washington politicians, and the power wielded by men like Vallandigham. On the other hand, they were a bit inclined to underrate the enemy's fighting forces. They had met and beaten the Army of the Potomac, but they had never seen it at its best under proper leadership. In any event, the Confederates, from Lee, through A. P. Hill, Ewell, Longstreet, Heth, Pender, the wholly inexperienced Joe Davis, and the other generals, down through the ranks of the Light Division veterans, to the recruits from Mississippi, expected to strike at the North and were ready to do so.

Dorsey Pender wrote to his wife: "All feel that something is brewing and that Gen. Lee is not going to wait all the time for them to come to him." Then he expressed the sentiment of the whole Army as he wrote, "Have no fear we shall not beat them."[9]

---

[9] Pender Papers.

268

CHAPTER 18

Debut as Corps Commander

IMMEDIATELY after the promotion of Ewell and Hill, a final tribute to Jackson was staged by Robert E. Lee in the form of a grand review of Stonewall's old corps. The three divisions were drawn up one behind the other with seventy-five-yard intervals separating them. Then, Lee riding Traveller and attended by his full staff and numerous generals including A. P. Hill and the three division commanders of the Second Corps, Edward Johnson, Rodes, and Jube Early, swept around the entire corps at full gallop. Thereafter, without breaking pace, Lee led the entourage around each division separately. The course of the review covered over nine miles and the pace was such that generals and staff officers began falling out one by one. When the breathless Traveller was finally reined in by Lee, there were only two of the entire reviewing group still with him. One was a young cavalry staff officer; the other was Lieutenant General A. P. Hill.[1]

The review was followed by an interlude in hostilities which afforded Powell Hill a modicum of home life with Dolly and the children, for there were now two. The baby born during the spring of 1863 was named Lucy Lee for the commander of the Army of Northern Virginia. These intervals with Dolly always were a tonic to the general. Her cheerful manner afforded an antidote to the lonely, reticent life that he felt compelled to live during field campaigns and in camp. The troops also responded to Dolly's infectious charm. News of Lucy Lee's birth spread rapidly through

---

[1] Edward A. Moore, *Story of a Cannoneer under Stonewall Jackson*, p. 184.

the new Third Corps. Some of the men of the old Light Division constructed a rough-hewn cradle which they presented to the Hill family.

A mist settled over Powell Hill's eyes as he accepted this token from men he had led into battles from which their comrades had not emerged, and whom he would send under enemy fire many more times. He treasured that cradle and, until she outgrew it, it would be the only bed which baby Lucy Lee would know. Dolly's pleasure at the gift was less sentimentally expressed although it was equally heartfelt. She laughed and joked with the soldiers who made the presentation and sent them back to their camp quarters with a sense of the radiance that had long been denied them during the bitter months of battle, marches, and countermarches far from their own loved ones.

True to the Cavalier tradition, Powell would not permit his wife to share the austere manner of living that he had adopted. She had two trusted family servants constantly with her until the very last days at Petersburg. She took her jewelry and other valuables with her as she traveled about Virginia, always staying near her husband's post of command. When the journey became dangerous she rolled her hair into a chignon and kept her most valuable possessions hidden there. These occasions of danger were many, too. Powell Hill, of course, would not submit his family to unnecessary hazard. Dolly, however, possessed the adventurous spirit of the Morgans of Kentucky. She not only would refuse to avoid danger but she would actually expose herself to risk if she thought she could be helpful either to Powell or to their Cause. According to one story, during the latter part of the war, she learned that Phil Sheridan was expected one evening at a hotel not far from the Confederate lines. Dolly, probably with the aid of her womanly wiles, crossed over into enemy territory and went to the hotel. She didn't know precisely what her mission would be but she felt that she might pick up some useful military information by getting close to the Federal general's temporary headquarters. Despite her charms, or perhaps because of them, she became

270

an object of suspicion. Sensing that she would be taken into custody before Sheridan's arrival she hurriedly left the hotel and fled into the night toward the Confederate lines. Several shots rang out behind her. One wonders, however, if the Union soldiers who fired those shots took very careful aim or made a serious attempt to overtake their beautiful quarry.[2]

Plans for a rather elaborate christening ceremony for Lucy Lee, with Robert E. Lee as godfather, were interrupted by the exigencies of the war. By the end of May, Lee felt that the army was sufficiently refreshed, and the reorganization well enough completed, so that the campaign could be renewed. After defeating Hooker's great army, the Army of Northern Virginia from Lee, through Lieutenant Generals Longstreet, Ewell, and Hill, down to the last private in the ranks, was ready to press the attack against the North.

As preparations got under way for the new campaign, A. P. Hill put aside the colorful dress uniform and French kepi which he wore while promenading with Dolly on the home front. Now he donned his gray field uniform and substituted a black soft hat for the kepi. He made one concession to his new rank as far as uniform was concerned. He allowed considerable heavy gold braid and other similar ornamentation to be placed on his hat. He also secured a new horse. His old iron grey, "Champ," was worn out by the rigors of the campaign. Powell's new mount was a jet black stallion named Prince. He continued to wear his hip-length boots with a polished brass spur on the right heel. His elevation in rank, furthermore, did not affect his superstition. He always carried the hambone his mother had given him when he left for the Mexican War. In addition, he was never without another talisman, a pipe, handmade by a soldier of the Light Division. He didn't smoke it often but, like the hambone, it was a symbol of devotion from which he would not be separated when he went into battle.

The fateful field of Gettysburg was to be the next princi-

[2] Robertson, *op. cit.*

271

pal scene of action. Before that, however, an incident took place that was to foreshadow the Confederate disaster in Pennsylvania. Jeb Stuart, flushed with the victory of Chancellorsville, permitted his love of show and pomp to overrule his judgment. The result was that the fate of the Confederate Army at Gettysburg was probably sealed by a pageant put on by Jeb at Brandy Station, near Culpeper, on June 5. A great review of all the cavalry was staged. People came from miles around to watch and wonder at Stuart's hard-riding men guiding their beautifully groomed mounts through intricate formations, simulating wild charges, and the like. The pageantry continued with brilliant dances and dinner parties in the evenings. The show lasted through June 8. Then orders came to pack up and prepare to move north. The rumor of an advance into Pennsylvania spread through the army like wildfire. Longstreet's and Ewell's corps were now around Culpeper and Brandy Station with the cavalry, poised for the move north. A. P. Hill's Third Corps alone confronted Hooker's entire army. Lee was deftly manipulating his troop movements so that the enemy would not observe the changes of position which were being effected. Stuart's "circus," however, created such a furor that word reached Hooker that something was in the air.

On the night of June 8, while Stuart's men were dividing their attentions between a final fling of celebration and preparations for the following day's departure, Buford's Union cavalry struck. The redoubtable Grumble Jones, in charge of the Confederate picket lines, first observed Federal cavalry infiltration about 2 a. m. He rushed word to Stuart that enemy in force were crossing the Rappahannock. Jeb, apparently dazzled by the brilliance of his own show, ignored the warning. Buford broke through to Brandy Station and a serious cavalry engagement was on. The Union attack was never intended to be more than a raid. Buford, accordingly, soon withdrew. He had obtained information, however, that gave the Union high command at least a general idea of what Lee's plans were. More important than this, however, as far as the Gettysburg campaign was concerned, was the fact that

Stuart's pride was injured by the humiliating surprise attack which made a mockery of his great parade ground spectacle. Nothing would suit Jeb now but revenge in the form of a large-scale spectacular raid against the enemy.

As a result, Stuart chose to interpret subsequent orders to fit his own fancy. Instead of using his cavalry to screen the army's advance toward the north, Jeb went off on a circuitous raid which, though spectacular, took him completely out of touch with the rest of the army. Ultimately it caused him to be so late in arriving at the scene of the Battle of Gettysburg that Lee lacked the vital enemy information with which Stuart usually kept him supplied. No attempt will be made here to engage in the controversy concerning Stuart's orders or his obedience thereto. Suffice to say that he interpreted the orders as sanctioning the raid. Stuart's "paths of glory" led to the grave for thousands of brave men who did not feel the right to exercise "discretion" with respect to their orders. The insult to Stuart's pride at Brandy Station destined to failure the Confederates' battle at Gettysburg. The three days of savage fighting there forever sealed the doom of the Confederacy.

In the meantime, during the last sweltering days of June, 1863, Lee led his three infantry corps into Pennsylvania, Longstreet following well to the rear. The march, as usual, had left many of the troops with little more than rags to be used for shoes. Many were barefoot. Harry Heth's division reached Cashtown on the 30th of June. Heth heard there were shoes to be had at Gettysburg not far to the southeast. Heth himself, needing a hat, had his quartermaster locate several for him at Cashtown. He found them all too large, however, and so had to be content with an oversize headgear, into the sweatband of which he stuffed some paper.[3] Thereupon he rode over to A. P. Hill's headquarters and told his superior about the shoes in Gettysburg. Hill had been advised that there was Union cavalry near the town but not in force. He nodded when Heth spoke of the shoes. As usual, Hill was thinking of the footsore troops. He was

[3] Heth Mss,

273

well aware that Lee's strategy was to avoid a major battle at this time, but from all reports there were not enough enemy in the vicinity to cause serious trouble. So, when Heth now asked permission to go down for the shoes, Hill concurred with an emphatic, "Do so!"[4]

At five o'clock the next morning, July 1, Heth started for Gettysburg. The die was irrevocably cast. The Battle of Gettysburg was about to begin. Hill had indicated that he did not think there were many Federal troops in the vicinity. In the absence of Stuart's cavalry, however, neither Hill nor Lee nor anybody else in the Army actually knew the exact whereabouts of the Army of the Potomac. Although Lee had some cavalry with the army, most of it had been ranging farther north with Ewell and Early. It occurred to the new corps commander that perhaps Heth might run into something unforeseen. As a result, he ordered Pender to immediately follow Heth. Hill has been criticized for sending a division to support what was in effect a reconnaissance force. He had, however, developed the sort of seventh sense of impending conflict that often comes with long campaign experience. It is difficult to tell whether or not his decision to dispatch Pender after Heth was fortuitous to the Confederate arms. Had Heth been without support his division might have had even more serious trouble from the Federals. On the other hand, if only one division had gone down to Gettysburg that day the fateful battle might have been averted. This would have been a good thing for the Confederacy because it is doubtful if there was any place in the State of Pennsylvania better suited to the Union strategy about to be employed than Gettysburg.

In any event, Heth ran into some of Buford's cavalry. This was not unexpected, so Harry pushed on in to attack. What was not anticipated by the Confederate command, however, was the fact that behind the cavalry at Gettysburg was coming up the vanguard of the entire Army of the Potomac, now commanded by George Meade. The major engagement which Lee did not want, and which Hill had been

---

[4] *Ibid.*

274

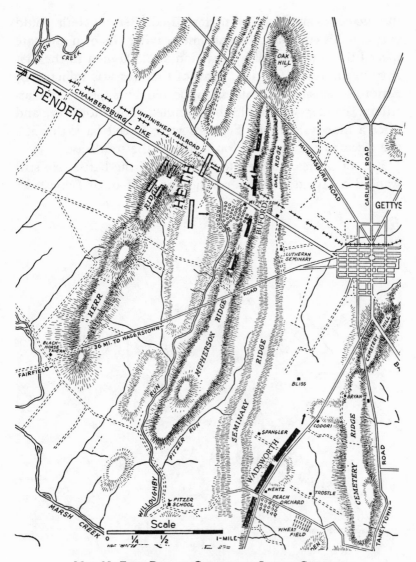

MAP 18. First Day at Gettysburg—Initial Contact

Heth's Division of A. P. Hill's Corps, moving on Gettysburg from the direction of Cashtown, encountered Buford's Federal Cavalry division along Willoughby Run at about 8 a.m. At once a fierce fight ensued for the possession of McPherson's woods and ridge. Buford resisted the Confederate attack until about 10 a.m. when the leading elements of Wadsworth's division arrived. Pender's Division of A. P. Hill's Corps is still moving eastward along the Chambersburg Pike, having bivouacked near Cashtown. The third division of this corps, Anderson's, is just starting out from Fayetteville, on the west side of the Cashtown gap.

275

instructed to avoid, now materialized. Before Heth could extricate his command he had lost heavily. His own estimate placed the casualties of his division at 2,300 men in the first thirty minutes of fighting. Most of this loss was inflicted by Buford's repeating carbines, supported by superb light artillery. Pender was up in line immediately, however, and after a bloody fight the Federals were forced back through the town to the cemetery on a hill to the southeast.

Lee, of course, hurried to the scene of the battle. He still wanted to avoid a major conflict, at least until Longstreet

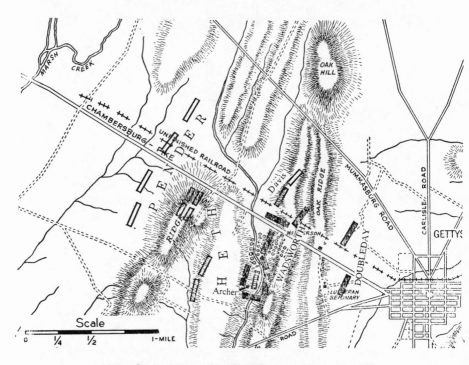

MAP 19. SITUATION ABOUT 10:30 A.M., JULY 1, 1863
Buford's defense of McPherson's and Seminary Ridges has been taken over by the infantry of Wadsworth's and Doubleday's divisions. Archer's Brigade, which has charged into the woods, has been boxed in by the Iron Brigade of Wadsworth's division; Archer and most of his men are captured. Two other brigades of Heth's Division are moving around to the south to outflank the Federals; but Lee, who has arrived on the high ground to the west, is restraining Pender and Heth from pushing home their attacks because Longstreet, is not up, and Ewell, coming in from the north, has not yet arrived. Davis' Brigade and Heth's Division has had a costly see-saw fight for the railroad cut north of McPherson's. Heth has been taking heavy losses.

276

arrived. At two o'clock, he conferred with Powell Hill at temporary headquarters which were hastily set up along the ridge to the west of Gettysburg, which was named for the seminary on the high ground near the northern end thereof. Stuart's absence and the lack of enemy information which he customarily supplied continued to handicap both generals in making their estimate of the enemy's strength. The fighting had become somewhat stabilized by now on Heth's and Pender's fronts. Both had driven forward as far as they could, their divisions resting generally along Seminary Ridge. The men of the old Light Division were divided between these two commands. Now, with A. P. Hill riding along the lines urging them on, it was like an echo of the earlier campaigns. They were finally held at bay, however. Harry Heth was among the casualties. He was hit in the head by a Minie ball but the wadding in the band of the ill-fitting hat which he got at Cashtown saved his life.[5] Ewell now came up with two divisions of the Second Corps to form on the left. Lee immediately ordered Ewell to carry Cemetery Hill.[6] A flank attack upon the hill from the north through the town into which Rodes' men were already infiltrating would probably have been successful. The bulk of the enemy were still heavily engaged on their front by Hill's Corps. Ewell, however, for one reason or another, procrastinated. Night fell with the issue still undecided.

Longstreet did not arrive to join in a council of war until nearly dawn the following day. His corps was not in line and ready to attack until the next afternoon. Only Hill and Ewell met with Lee that night to plan the next day's strategy. Volumes have been written on what the South *should* have done at Gettysburg. Other volumes have been directed toward placing the blame for the debacle that was to follow. Thousands of words have been devoted to the various plans proposed and arguments entered upon during conferences between Lee and his three lieutenant generals. Sorrel, who served under both Longstreet and Hill, and who saw very

---

[5] *Ibid.*
[6] Maurice, p. 228.

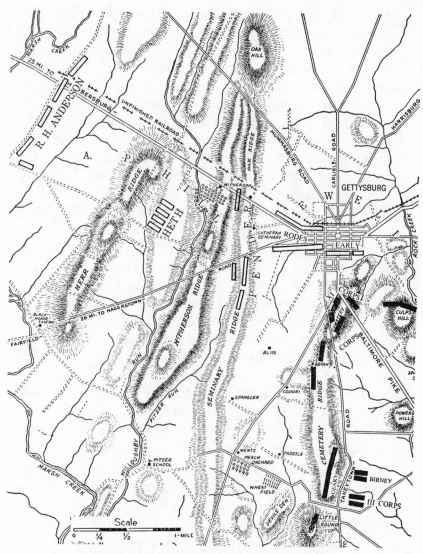

MAP 20. SITUATION ABOUT 7:30 P.M., JULY 1, 1863

During the day Ewell's Corps, arriving from the north, attacked Howard's Eleventh Corps which had taken up positions from Oak Hill eastward to where the Harrisburg Road crossed Rock Creek. Ewell drove the Federals south and, in conjunction with Hill's Corps, took Gettysburg and several thousand prisoners. The Federals retreated to Cemetery Hill and Culp's Hill. Other Federal units are arriving and taking up positions along Cemetery Ridge or are in reserve after a hard day's march. Similarly Anderson of Hill's Corps has arrived within sight of the battlefield, but is in reserve. Heth's Division, badly damaged during the fighting of the day, is bivouacked west of McPherson Ridge, and will remain there during the rest of the battle.

278

active service at Gettysburg, pointed out that these generals and Ewell never seemed to work well together. Inexperience of Hill and Ewell as corps commanders, however, probably, accounts for the lack of coordination during these three July days more than their divergent views as to what course should be followed. All suggested plans, as well as that which Lee finally adopted, moreover, had to proceed on the theory that the cavalry was not available. Sorrel asserts that this was the prime cause of the defeat.[7]

Of the alternatives rejected by Lee, historians have perhaps been most kind with respect to Longstreet's plan. He wanted to pass around the Union left and cut off Meade from his communications with Washington. This might well have been a happy proposal. Ewell's position was not altogether clear, but at least he did not seem to oppose proceeding the next morning with the attack on the Union right which he should have made that afternoon. Lee would not go along with Longstreet's proposal, a fact which later caused Longstreet to lay the cause of the disaster of the third day at Gettysburg squarely at the commander's doorstep. Longstreet attributed Lee's indecision and "uneven temper" during the campaign to vexation at Stuart's "wandering" cavalry.[8] Others thought Lee was ill. There is good authority for reports that he was suffering from diarrhea during the three days of Gettysburg.[9]

In any event, Lee would have none of Longstreet's advice. Ewell offered none. Hill expressed the view that an attack through the town from the positions now held by Rodes would still be the best avenue of approach the next day. Lee appeared to toy with the plan but then seemed to summarily reject it by announcing his decision that Longstreet would attack on the right the following afternoon.

Powell Hill ordinarily was not one to argue with battlefield orders, but he continued to urge his views until the first evening's council of war was dissolved by Lee. He returned

[7] Sorrel, p. 167.
[8] Longstreet, p. 359.
[9] W. W. Blackford, "*War Years with Jeb Stuart,*" p. 230.

to the lines manned by the men of Heth and Pender and related the general orders for the morrow. The Third Corps had borne the brunt of the first day's fighting. They were seasoned veterans. Hill nevertheless wanted to assure himself that his men would be ready to support Longstreet's attack on the 2nd. He slept but little and, early in the morning, returned to his commander's headquarters to make a final protest. Ill health or not, the commander of the Army of Northern Virginia was in the saddle the morning of July 2 awaiting Longstreet's attack on the right. Some of the tenseness of the previous evening seemed to have left Lee as he greeted Hill. Powell's gray eyes lit up as he perceived one last chance to dissuade his leader from the day's program.

"If this attack could not have been made sooner," he said, "it should not be made now, for if Longstreet gains a victory he will not be able to reap the legitimate fruits; night will put an end to the fighting and we shall find the Federals entrenched tomorrow morning in probably as strong or stronger position, and we will be compelled to go over the same thing again."[10]

Lee's jaws hardened. He merely shook his head. Longstreet had already argued the point with him that morning. He was not to be dissuaded. Hill rode away to command his corps, although his was a rather negative part in the battle which raged throughout the next two days. He and two of his divisions had precipitated the fight and pressed the enemy to the full extent of their resources on July 1. It was a flash of the old days, but fate did not decree a recurrence of brilliant exploit for A. P. Hill during the rest of the battle.

History relates how Longstreet's attack that afternoon was repulsed on the rocky slopes of Little Round Top, and how Ewell still was inactive on the left. Hill's plan might not have been any more successful. His warning with respect to Longstreet's attack, however, was literally fulfilled. Night fell on the 2d of July with the Federals in "as strong or

[10] Heth Mss. pp. 148-9.

280

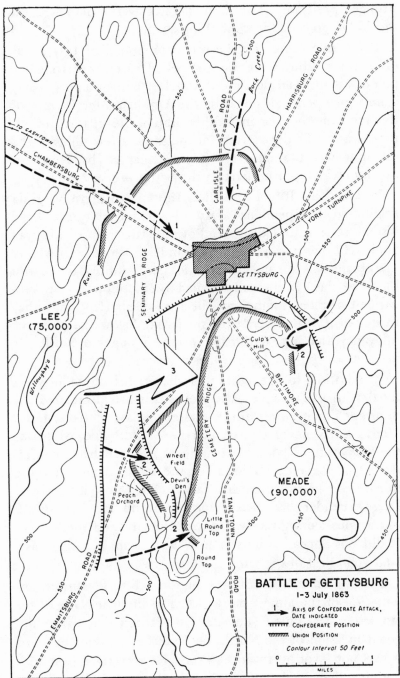

LEE
(75,000)

MEADE
(90,000)

BATTLE OF GETTYSBURG
1-3 July 1863

1 ──► AXIS OF CONFEDERATE ATTACK,
DATE INDICATED

CONFEDERATE POSITION

UNION POSITION

Contour Interval 50 Feet

0
MILES

MAP 21. ACTIONS ON THE THREE DAYS AT GETTYSBURG

281

stronger position." The Confederates were compelled on the 3d "to go over the same thing again."

The "same thing" on the torrid afternoon of July 3 was even worse. Longstreet was compelled to make his famous nod of assent, sending Pickett and 15,000 men across nearly a mile of open fields against the Union center in one of the most heroic yet incredibly impossible charges of all times. Stuart finally arrived on the scene a few miles to the east but was too late. He was intercepted by Northern cavalry and played no part in the battle proper.

It rained on July 4 and the Army of Northern Virginia celebrated Independence Day by commencing the long, dismal retreat to Culpeper. Powell Hill was on his way home. His debut as a corps commander had not been wholly inauspicious. He came pretty close to winning the battle that first day. If his counsel had been followed, the subsequent disasters might have been avoided. Hill made that long journey, however, with spirits far below the point of buoyancy that marked many of the much more difficult marches of the old Light Division days.

In addition to the odium of defeat, his thoughts were filled with the terrible casualties which had decimated his divisions during those three sweltering days at Gettysburg. Heth's Division, of course, had been badly chewed up at the very outset. Thousands more of his men had been attached to Pickett's Division for the fateful charge on the third. Over half of them had fallen. Then, too, his beloved Dorsey Pender had been mortally wounded. The loyal, courageous Dorsey received a leg injury from a shell burst. It did not appear serious at first, but, as in Jackson's case, fatal complications set in.

Dorsey Pender's death was signified by the abrupt termination of the almost daily letters to his wife. One of his last letters was dated June 22. He realized that Fanny opposed invasion of the North, because she felt that the Lord would not favor an invading army. He secretly agreed with her view that the defense of their land was as far as the Con-

282

federacy should go. He wrote that he knew the crossing of the Potomac would cause her grief. Then he added:

The advance of our column is at Chambersburg, Penna., tonight. May the Lord prosper this expedition and bring an early peace out of it. I feel that we are taking a very important step but see no reason why it should not be successful. We have a large army that is in splendid condition and spirit and the best Generals of the South.

Then he seemed to realize that this campaign might be his last, in spite of the optimism he was expressing. He added:

I have written very regularly up to this time but, of course, after this my letters will be exceedingly irregular. My love to all and now, my own darling, may God in his infinite mercy watch over you.

Your Loving Husband.

Pender had been the most deeply religious man in the Army, not excepting Jackson. He had also been the most inspirational and fiercest of all Confederate generals in leading a charge. He was not a man who could be replaced. Powell Hill had lost not only his best fighting soldier, but his staunchest supporter and friend. The commander's life that had been lonely before would be even lonelier hereafter. Hill also lost another capable and faithful general at Gettysburg when Archer was taken prisoner. There wasn't much left now of the group of brigadiers that embarked on that first campaign with A. P. Hill at Mechanicsville so many months before.

CHAPTER 19

Keeping the Enemy Moving

B Y THE SPRING of 1863, the war was two years old. The original Light Division had completed its meteoric existence of barely one year. A. P. Hill had established himself as the foremost division commander in the Army of Northern Virginia. The Seven Days, Slaughter's Mountain, Second Manassas, Sharpsburg, Fredericksburg, and Chancellorsville were the highpoints of that year of the Light Division. Four of the six campaigns, Slaughter's Mountain, Second Manassas, Fredericksburg, and Chancellorsville represented Confederate victories. The other two might be termed draws. There was certainly nothing resembling a decisive Federal victory in the entire series of battles. Never again, however, would the Confederacy have such success. After Jackson fell, the pattern was changed. The Gettysburg campaign marked the beginning of the end.

The high-water mark of the Confederacy at Gettysburg in 1863 represented the closest approach in our history to the permanent dissolution of the Union. The South, of course, had no strong economic backbone. It lacked resources of all sorts. Manpower was limited. The Federal naval blockade was reasonably successful in keeping out munitions from abroad. Weapons were wearing out. Broken-down railroad equipment could not be replaced. Food was becoming scarce. King Cotton was, in effect, a deposed monarch because of the blockade. Efforts that might better have gone into food production were wasted on cotton, now a drug on the market, while hunger pangs began to be experienced by soldiers and civilians alike. Nevertheless, the series of successes during the first two years kept Southern spirits

285

flaming. A sense of confidence was being engendered by the successes of Robert E. Lee. This made people forget the many material shortcomings of the Confederacy.

On the other hand, repeated defeats, climaxing at Chancellorsville, sank many Northerners into a feeling of despair. Casualties were heavy. The draft was being constantly increased. Fighting was taking place north of the Potomac. Many Northerners, led by a few political rabble-rousers, looked at the current frontline situation and forgot that they possessed in abundance everything that the Confederates lacked. Manpower was plentiful, even though the draft was, as it has always been, very unpopular. Materials of war were being produced in many mills and factories. There was no shortage of food or civilian goods. Even the physical aspect of the war was propitious when one looked at the campaign in the West, where only Vicksburg prevented complete Union control of the Mississippi Valley. As long as Lee was winning, however, everything else took on a gloomy look to a considerable number of Washington politicians, and to many otherwise solid Yankee citizens, who had never thought much of the war in any event.

Lincoln wanted, and needed, a victory now more than ever. McClellan had been removed from the strategic scene, but it was too late to prevent him from becoming a formidable political foe. England, piously neutral on the surface, fervently hoped for a Southern victory and the opening of a cotton trade that would have her mills humming in competition with those of New England and the other Union manufacturing states, which presumably would get less favorable trade consideration from the South after a bitter war. Clement C. Vallandigham, a former Congressman from Ohio, and currently leader of the peace movement in the North, had denounced Lincoln's administration for some time with apparent impunity. His utterances against the war effort were patently treasonable. Nevertheless, he developed a substantial following and was regarded generally as an "opposition political leader" rather than a traitor. In fact, he was the spokesman of some important factions of

286

the rather disorganized Democratic party. He was eventually arrested for inciting resistance to the government in the prosecution of the war. Thereupon there arose a storm of protests that offered almost as much threat to the stability of the government at Washington as did Robert E. Lee's army.

A series of resolutions were adopted at a public meeting of New York Democrats held in Albany on May 16, 1863, which severely criticized the Administration for its handling of Vallandigham. These resolutions represented such a potent point of view that they received a long public reply from Lincoln. The resolutions were forwarded to the President over the signature of a distinguished and patriotic citizen, Erastus Corning,[1] a leader of the Democratic party in the state and former mayor of Albany, who was president of the New York Central Railroad. Some of the pertinent resolutions follow. It may be noted that while they state adherence to "the cause of the Union," they recognize the current "adverse and disheartening circumstances," and then flatly denounce the action taken in the seizure and confinement of Vallandigham.

> Resolved, That the Democrats of New York point to their uniform course of action during the two years of civil war through which we have passed, to the alacrity which they have evinced in filling the ranks of the army, to their contributions and sacrifices, as the evidence of their patriotism and devotion to the cause of our imperilled country. Never in the history of civil wars has a government been sustained with such ample resources of means and men as the people have voluntarily placed in the hands of the Administration.
>
> Resolved, That as Democrats we are determined to maintain this patriotic attitude, and, despite of adverse and disheartening circumstances, to devote all our energies to sustain the cause of the Union, to secure peace through victory, and to bring back the restoration of all the States under the safeguards of the Constitution.
>
> Resolved, That while we will not consent to be mis-

---

[1] The great grandson of Mr. Corning, Erastus Corning II, is Mayor of Albany today.

287

apprehended upon these points, we are determined not to be misunderstood in regard to others not less essential. We demand that the Administration shall be true to the Constitution; shall recognize and maintain the rights of the States and the liberties of the citizen; shall everywhere, outside of the lines of necessary military occupation and the scenes of insurrection, exert all its powers to maintain the supremacy of the civil over military law.

Resolved, That in view of these principles we denounce the recent assumption of a military commander to seize and try a citizen of Ohio, Clement L. Vallandigham, for no other reason than words addressed to a public meeting, in criticism of the course of the Administration, and in condemnation of the military orders of that General.

Resolved, That this assumption of power by a military tribunal, if successfully asserted, not only abrogates the right of the people to assemble and discuss the affairs of government, the liberty of speech and of the press, the right of trial by jury, the law of evidence, and the privilege of habeas corpus, but it strikes a fatal blow at the supremacy of law, and the authority of the State and federal constitutions.

Regardless of the views one might have of Vallandigham, these resolutions represented strong sentiment by sound, loyal Union citizens who, in the vernacular, were becoming "fed up" with things.

Lincoln sent back a long reply under date of June 12, 1863. The essence of the President's reply was that Vallandigham was a traitor who was counseling desertion from the Army and otherwise directly hindering the war effort. Lincoln asked, "Must I shoot a simple-minded soldier boy who deserts, while I must not touch a hair of a wily agitator who induces him to desert?"[2] All prominent publications in the North joined in the controversy. The conservative pro-Lincoln *Harper's Weekly* said in its May 30, 1863, issue;

> The President enjoys the power of commuting or remitting [Vallandigham's] sentence altogether; and it is the unanimous hope of the loyal North that he will remit it. For, whether the arrest of Vallandigham was or was not a wise

[2] Vallandigham incident discussed in detail from extreme Southern viewpoint by Pollard in *The Lost Cause,* at p. 464 et seq.

step, there can be very little question but his imprisonment for months, and perhaps years, in a military fortress would make a martyr of him, and would rally to his side, for the sake of liberty and free speech, an immense number of sympathizers. It would probably make him governor of Ohio, and would impart great strength to the Copperhead sentiment of the Northwest.

There was, therefore, a critical political situation in the North brought about entirely by the fact that the war was not going well. A successful invasion of the South or some other portent of an early victory would have given such men as Vallandigham no basis upon which to mount their anti-war, peace-at-any price campaign. It is only in the light of this generally turbulent internal situation in the North that the full effect of the year's successes by the Army of Northern Virginia can be appreciated.

An analysis of the six major engagements fought by Lee's army from June 1862, to June 1863, indicates the reason for the successes, and gives the clue to Lee's subsequent defeats which eventually brought the remnants of the Army of Northern Virginia to Appomattox. There was one common denominator to the victories of those twelve months. That this denominator was not present at Gettysburg, where the tide turned, or during the dreary months around Petersburg, where the Confederacy died, seems to prove the case. That fact also establishes the importance of the part played by the Light Division in the victorious era, and points up the failure of the Army without a Jackson, and without an A. P. Hill leading a Light Division to execute the stratagems of Jackson's style of warfare.

The common denominator of the victories at Slaughter's Mountain, Second Manassas, Fredericksburg, and Chancellorsville was that they were all battles in which the Union forces were compelled to "move." This also applied to the Seven Days and the Antietam where, although the South failed to gain clear-cut decisions, nevertheless, vastly superior Union forces were deprived of anything resembling victories. In all of these campaigns, the Federal generals were obliged

289

to keep moving in order to prevent being outflanked, or were forced to move head-on into battle for which they were not prepared, or were enticed into moving, at the expense of terrible casualties, against strongly prepared positions which they could not overcome. During this period, the Union troops, as a general rule, Malvern Hill being an exception, were never permitted to dig in and use their superior man and gun power against massed attacks that would become suicidal, such as Burnside's repeated charges against Marye's Heights at Fredericksburg.

A brief review of the six campaigns in question illustrates the different methods by which the Union troops were forced to "move." It is to be noted that the controlling factor is not necessarily Confederate movement, although this was several times the device employed to set off the enemy movement, which resulted each time in Union failure.

At the start of the Seven Days, Hill was forced to open the campaign by attacking a defensive line set up by Porter along Beaver Dam. Lee's plan to force Union movement, however, had been based upon Jackson's hitting Porter's flank from the north, thus causing him to withdraw in front of Hill. Jackson's delay prevented this from being done on Lee's schedule. Nevertheless, when Porter was finally forced to pull out, Longstreet and Hill followed in pursuit along the Union flank, literally herding McClellan's army toward the James. Thereafter, the Battles of Gaines' Mill and Frayser's Farm were waged against Union troops that were kept off balance because they were forced to protect the constant retrogressive movement of their supply trains. At Malvern Hill, McClellan made a temporary stand and had his only successful day of the seven. Nevertheless, he was now in retreat and was committed to a withdrawal to the James, where his supplies were accumulating.

The Battle of Slaughter's Mountain, known in the North as Cedar Mountain, was actually the start of the Second Manassas campaign. It was, nevertheless, a complete battle in itself and it occurred some time before the fighting around

290

Manassas, many miles to the north. Here again, the Federals were on the move when they were encountered. Jackson ran into Banks somewhat by chance. Banks was outnumbered badly and should have withdrawn. Nevertheless, he elected to engage in a head-on fight. This was a battle of movement on both sides, with the issue being decided when Powell Hill raced up in time to put the Union troops to rout.

The actual Second Battle of Manassas was a masterpiece of maneuver planned by Lee, with its opening phases performed by Jackson, and with Longstreet arriving on the scene in time to seal the victory. Jackson marched around Pope's flank and got behind him. Pope was then forced to turn around and move against the concealed and entrenched Confederates. The Light Division magnificently held the left, where the main Union effort was made. Then Longstreet came up through Throughfare Gap and smashed the flank of Pope's massed line which was concentrating in movement against Jackson.

Along the Antietam, Lee established a defensive line and and let McClellan attack. This strategy nearly proved a fatal mistake for Lee, because McClellan moved in with an overwhelming force, which would have destroyed the Army of Northern Virginia had not A. P. Hill arrived at the last possible moment and charged into Burnside's moving and exposed flank. Hill's attack broke up the left phase of the Union attack and permitted Lee to extricate the rest of the army.

At Fredericksburg, Lee's tactics were somewhat different, but they resulted in forcing the Union troops to move where he wanted them. Longstreet was firmly entrenched on Marye's Heights. Jackson was deployed in a semicircle on the right. Burnside moved into the same type of viselike formation as Pope had at Manassas. The result was a resounding defeat for the Army of the Potomac. The Light Division bore the brunt of the attack on the Confederate right.

Finally, at Chancellorsville, Lee and Jackson conjured

another great flanking movement that surprised Hooker and knocked him so far off balance that he had to move out of previously planned positions to attempt to counteract Jackson's attack. Again he was outmaneuvered so badly that he never was able to put a great part of his army into action. Hooker lost a battle that he should have won against less talented opposition. As usual, A. P. Hill's Division was in the thick of the battle, sustaining the heaviest losses on the Confederate side.[3]

The strategic pattern by which Lee forced the enemy to move to its own destruction in these six campaigns was discontinued after Chancellorsville. The tide turned a few weeks later at Gettysburg. There, Lee met his first great defeat. There, the Southern victories that had spawned the likes of Vallandigham, and had caused such great consternation, even among the most loyal elements in the North, came to an abrupt end. The end occurred at Gettysburg because Lee adopted new tactics. He attacked superior strength in strong defensive positions. Meade was permitted to dig in and make preparations that were sufficient to smash a suicidal attack, just as Lee had done at Fredericksburg. The Union won, and assumed the initiative as Grant arrived on the scene to conduct the last stages of the war against Lee. After Gettysburg, with one notable exception, the Confederates were kept on the move and were unable to employ the "enemy movement" pattern that had been so successful from the Seven Days through Chancellorsville. The one exception was at Cold Harbor, where Lee maneuvered Grant into attacking extremely well-fortified positions. The result was a terrible defeat for the North with the most concentrated casualty rate of the war. By then, however, it was too late. Lee had to retreat to Petersburg to stand a long siege that ultimately led to the surrender at Appomattox.

The immediate question, as one reviews these six battles, is why did Lee change his successful campaign pattern? No

---

[3] Alexander, p. 361 (although Rode's division suffered slightly more proportionately).

one can safely attribute the great Confederate leader's reversal of policy to any single factor. There are a number of obvious ones, however. For one thing, in Meade, Lee met a far sounder general than he had faced, at least in Pope, Burnside, or Hooker. Another factor was the absence of Stuart's cavalry at Gettysburg. This practically eliminated his intelligence-gathering agency and kept him from being able to anticipate Meade's movements and thus entrap him as he had ensnared the other Union commanders. The inception of the Battle of Gettysburg was an accident, which good information would have prevented. This was not true of the six preceding battles, except possibly Slaughter's Mountain. Many other sound reasons have been advanced for Lee's failure at Gettysburg in the countless words that have been written about that battle.

The fact that stands out, however, is that Lee at Gettysburg, and in subsequent campaigns, did not have at his command the same army that had been so victorious during the previous twelve months. Jackson was no longer with him. The men of the Light Division were divided into two parts, each competently commanded, but the whole lacking the cohesiveness and fierce pride of the original unit when it was under the direct command of A. P. Hill. Then, too, the new three-corps army was different and more unwieldy than the old two wings, especially from the command viewpoint, as there were now three instead of two elements to be coordinated and given orders. Besides, neither A. P. Hill nor Ewell had a chance to gain experience in higher command before going into action at Gettysburg.

Lee, therefore, was not only deprived of Jackson's counsel and unique flanking ability, but he also had two newly organized corps, led by inexperienced men, to take the place of the single streamlined command that Jackson had handled so well, at least after he got over the "spell" of the Seven Days. The old Light Division was not there. "Tell A. P. Hill to come up," would now be a meaningless order. Had Jackson been at Gettysburg, it is impossible to believe that Meade would have been able to set up his defenses on Culp's Hill and along Cemetery Ridge. The Jackson of Manassas and Chancellorsville would have had the Light Division in the town and smashing at Meade's troops while they were recoiling from the first encounter. This would have prevented Meade from organizing his defenses as Ewell permitted him to do. Ewell lost the advantage by waiting for orders which Lee never issued. Jackson would have held the initiative. Robert E. Lee, accustomed to Jackson, might well have thought further orders to Ewell unnecessary under the circumstances.

In any event, after the first day at Gettysburg, Lee found himself in an unaccustomed position and without some of tools he had previously employed. He then made the same paramount mistake that his opponents had made on the other occasions. *He* did the moving against the superior force in a superior position. Pickett's charge is history.

CHAPTER 20

Bristoe Station and
The Wilderness

*B*Y *AUGUST 1, 1863*, the Confederate withdrawal from Pennsylvania to south of the
Rapidan had been completed. The next two months were
devoted to resting and reorganizing the veterans as well as
training and integrating the recruits. Powell Hill had always
been effective along these lines. He soon had the Third
Corps restored to a position of fighting competence, although
its numerical strength remained well below par. The Army
of Northern Virginia, however, was not given time for full
recuperation. Meade had cautiously followed the retreat and
the Army of the Potomac now ranged only a short distance
to the north of Culpeper. Hill was not far from home, but
the enemy was too near at hand for comfortable visits and
reminiscences of happier days. The Federals had to be attacked and moved before relaxation at the old homestead
would be in order. By this time Longstreet had been detailed for service in the west. Lee turned to A. P. Hill and
Ewell for the mission of driving Meade back. The plan, as
usual, called for a flank attack, this time by Hill's Corps.
Now Jeb Stuart's cavalry was on hand for screening and
scouting. Gettysburg and the retreat had taken a lot out of
the army but it was with amazing resilience that the troops
commenced the Bristoe Station campaign on August 9, 1863.

Before the Bristoe Station campaign, however, Powell
had another brief peaceful interlude with Dolly and the
children. The cumulative effects of nearly three years of
active service, together with the added responsibility of

commanding a corps, now weighed heavily upon Hill's comparatively frail constitution. More and more lines creased his brow. Hollows began to develop in his cheeks. The long beard hid some of the traces of strain but the tired gray eyes told their own story. The body that had first evidenced a weakness, not shared by his spirit, many years before at West Point, exhibited warning signs. The breakdown that would follow in a few months, nevertheless, was temporarily arrested by Dolly's ebullient presence. The respite with his family, following the weary retreat from Gettysburg, actually made Hill feel like his old self.[1] His impetuous, driving aggressiveness seemed to return. Perhaps this, as much as anything, was the cause of the debacle that was to follow. Bristoe Station was the scene of A. P. Hill's first defeat by a comparable Federal force.

The general plan of the campaign was for Ewell to approach the enemy on a direct northerly line, with Hill swinging to the west and then coming in against the Federal right flank. Meade, however, took advantage of the good parallel roads running toward Washington and pulled back as far as Bristoe Station without permitting himself to become engaged by either Ewell or Hill. The Confederate attacking formation became confused by the swiftness of the Federal withdrawal. Ewell, who was to make the frontal assault, was unable to keep up with the retreat. Hill and the Third Corps found the pursuit easier coming in from the west and made the initial contact with the enemy. It seemed like old times to Hill's men especially the veterans of the Light Division. The infectious zeal to overrun the enemy spread rapidly through the Third Corps. Hill, impatiently riding with the vanguard, did nothing to dispel the troops' eagerness when the Federals were finally sighted on the 14th. They were literally racing pell-mell to the attack, the rebel yell ringing through the clear fall air.

A. P. Hill moved out with the skirmishers, well ahead of the main body of his troops. He observed the scene at

___

[1] No doubt Hill's liver was also helped by a respite from the fried bacon and dough "babies" on which he subsisted in the field.

Bristoe Station from an overlooking hill long before Harry Heth was able to get up with the leading infantry division. Powell saw for himself that the Federal III Corps, which he had been pursuing, was engaged in fording Broad Run. The enemy appeared to be in full retreat. Engaged as they were in the cumbersome fording operation, they appeared to offer a most inviting mark. In fact, the only possible obstacle to the annihilation of the enemy which Hill could see was the chance that they might escape before Heth got up.

With the impetuosity he had not exhibited since his days with the Light Division, he sent courier after courier to Heth telling him to hurry and to immediately deploy for the attack. Heth's Division had been reorganized during the summer as the result of casualties at Gettysburg and in subsequent minor actions. Pettigrew, who had shown considerable ability in taking over the division at Gettysburg while Heth was incapacitated, was fatally wounded a few days later. Davis contracted fever shortly after Gettysburg and was rendered hors de combat. The ranks of both brigades were badly depleted. The remnants of Davis's command were reassigned to other units. John R. Cooke's Brigade joined Heth as replacement for Davis.

Cooke's Brigade had been formally assigned to Heth on May 30, 1863. It had, however, been on detached service in the Department of North Carolina and around Richmond until mid-September. Now it was ordered to fill the vacancy in Heth's Division. Cooke was one of the unfortunates whose family was divided by the war and who had to fight against his own flesh and blood. His father, an old Army Regular, Philip St. George Cooke, served as a Union general. John Cooke was Jeb Stuart's brother-in-law. He was not a West Pointer, having attended Harvard. Nevertheless, the family military tradition soon made him dissatisfied with his civilian occupation as an engineer. He entered the regular army and was serving as a lieutenant when the war broke out. He fought with distinction in early engagements and was a seasoned campaigner when he led his North Carolina brigade at Bristoe Station.

Pettigrew's Brigade received what reinforcements were available and continued in action under one of its regimental commanders. Colonel W. W. Kirkland of the 21st North Carolina succeeded Pettigrew and was promoted to the rank of brigadier general. Kirkland, who had served under Ewell in the Valley, was a battle experienced officer even before joining Heth as a field officer in Pettigrew's Brigade.

Cooke's and Kirkland's brigades were Heth's foremost units at this time. Henry Walker was in close support. Hill,

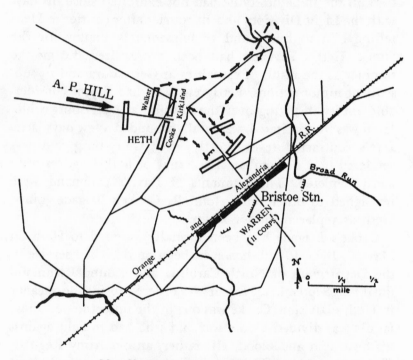

MAP 22. ENGAGEMENT AT BRISTOE STATION

A. P. Hill was a victim of incomplete information on the enemy. As his corps approached Bristoe Station from the west he saw what appeared to be enemy detachments trying to evade him by withdrawing east of Broad Run. He had Heth, in the lead, quickly deploy two brigades to pursue, then followed with a third brigade. As the first two brigades, those of Cooke and Kirkland, passed across the front of two of Warren's divisions concealed behind the railroad they received heavy fire in the flanks. Instead of withdrawing, as they should have done, they wheeled and attacked. Meantime the third brigade, Walker's, continued on across Broad Run until Walker, learning that Cooke and Kirkland were in trouble, turned back to help them. But it was too late; in the half hour that had elapsed, Cooke and Kirkland were repulsed with very heavy losses, losing a battery, too.

298

now desperately urging these brigades forward, shouted at Heth to press the attack across Broad Run, beyond which almost all of the visible Federals had by this time retreated. The men rushed ahead gleefully. Walker crossed the stream as planned. But, suddenly, the men of Cooke's Brigade experienced a terrible, chilling sensation as they reached the crest of the last rise of land in front of Broad Run. The Orange and Alexandria Railroad ran along their right flank in the direction in which the Union III Corps was retreating. To the Confederates' horror they observed thousands of Union troops now emerging from behind the railroad embankment where they had been hidden while A. P. Hill had made his personal observations of the field. The agonizing truth now also dawned upon Powell Hill as he rode along the crest of the hill with his advancing men. The Federal III Corps' retreat had been little more than a ruse. The entire Union II Corps was along that railroad embankment, extending the length of the Confederate right flank and well to its rear.

Cooke, of course, was now exposed to overwhelming firepower. Kirkland attempted to come to the other's aid but was similarly smashed by enfilade fire. Desperately Hill sent back for reinforcements. Cadmus Wilcox, commanding Pender's old division, had been intended to serve as Heth's support, but had been left behind by the urgent speed with which the latter had been rushed to the attack[2]. Dick Anderson's Division appeared over the horizon and hurried to the aid of what was left of Cooke's and Kirkland's Brigades. It was too late to save them, however. Both brigadiers were casualties and the losses in their respective brigades numbered about 700 and 600.

In his official report Hill stated simply that he was unaware of the presence of the Federal II Corps behind the railroad embankment. He went on to say:

> I am convinced that I made the attack too hastily, and at the same time that a delay of half an hour, and there

---

[2] For details of Wilcox's succession to this command, see chapter 21.

would have been no enemy to attack. In that event I believe I should equally have blamed myself for not attacking at once.[3]

It was Heth's Division that was crushed that October day but it was Lieutenant General A. P. Hill, commander of the Third Corps, on whom the blame fell. Reconnaissance is ordinarily the responsibility of the forward troop element. At Bristoe Station, however, Hill took it upon himself to ride ahead of the troops and personally reconnoiter. In fairness to Heth it must be pointed out that he never had a good chance to observe the field or to have the railroad embankment investigated. He was ordered to hasten to the attack, disregarding all precautions. The question might be raised as to why Stuart's cavalry had not located the II Corps and advised Hill. The fact remains, however, that Hill had received no report from Stuart in this connection one way or the other and, therefore, had no right to rely on lack of intelligence as indicating freedom from danger.

Hill's statement that the attack was justified in order to prevent the enemy's escape was as unsatisfactory to the Confederate high command as it has been to the historians of that terrible day. It was simply a question of impetuosity and uncontrollable eagerness to hit the enemy while they were off guard. Perhaps Hill was the victim of the Union command's good fortune. Heth refers to the strong position of the II Corps behind the embankment as "accidentally occupied."[4] The report of the Union General, Gouverneur K. Warren, however, clearly indicates that the battle was carefully planned.[5] Use of the cover afforded by the embankment was deliberate. The fact that Hill completely overlooked one army corps while planning the destruction of another cannot detract from Warren's generalship that day. A. P. Hill was not outgeneralled on many occasions, but this was one of them. One moment he had been the aggressive, inspirational leader of old, driving his men forward. The

[3] Hill's report in full appears at 29 *O.R.* Pt. 1, pp. 426-7.
[4] 29 *O.R.*, Pt. 1, p. 432.
[5] *Ibid*, pp. 235-247.

next instant he was transformed to the status of a despairing officer desperately attempting to extricate his troops from a position which threatened to result in their annihilation. The fortunes of war turned against Hill at Bristoe Station as suddenly and dramatically as he himself had reversed them against the Union over a year earlier by his arrival on the field at Sharpsburg.

Lee made the following endorsement to Hill's report of the campaign:

> General Hill explains how, in his haste to attack the Third Army Corps of the enemy, he overlooked the presence of the Second, which was the cause of the disaster that ensued.[6]

Secretary of War Seddon seized upon Lee's use of the word "disaster" in appending his endorsement to the Bristoe Station campaign report in the official records. Seddon wrote:

> Respectfully submitted to the President. The disaster at Bristoe Station seems due to a gallant but overhasty pressing on of the enemy.[7]

Jefferson Davis climaxed the document as follows:

> Returned to the Secretary of War. There was a want of vigilance, by reason of which it appears the Third Army Corps of the enemy got a position, giving great advantage to them.[8]

Hill and Lee rode over the field the next day. The Union forces had continued their withdrawal north along the railroad. The Confederates were in no shape to press after them following the devastating engagement. Hill aimlessly conducted his commander around the scene of the slaughter, halfheartedly explaining what had happened. Lee had nothing to say for some time, although his face showed his bitter disappointment at the ending of what he had hoped would

---

[6] 29 *O.R.* Pt. 1, p. 428.
[7] *Ibid.*
[8] *Ibid.*

develop into a major offensive. Finally, he looked at the crestfallen Powell Hill.

"Well, General," came his soft words, "bury your dead and let us say no more about it."[9]

The Conferedate lines now became increasingly tightly drawn toward Richmond. There were no major battles during the next few weeks but the results of two comparatively minor engagements were gloomy portents of what was in store for the Confederate cause. First, Jube Early met defeat at the hands of General John Sedgwick, commanding the right wing of the Army of the Potomac, at Rappahannock Bridge. Then there occurred a rather desultory standoff at Mine Run. Powell Hill's Corps saw some action at Mine Run, but neither the fighting nor the result was sufficiently noteworthy to warrant chronicling with the detail given the campaigns of the Light Division or the earlier engagements of the Third Corps. Suffice to say, late autumn found Lee's army being mildly pressed along the Rapidan and in the vicinity of Orange Court House while the Northern high command laid long-range plans for a series of climactic campaigns in both the Virginia and western sectors of the war.

At this point, Longstreet publicly expressed the view that the Union successes in Tennessee were such as to threaten the lifeline of the Confederacy regardless of what happened in Virginia.[10] As a result, Longstreet, with a portion of his corps, was sent to the west. The rest of the Army of Northern Virginia settled down for the winter.

Powell Hill's Third Corps was, perhaps, in the best shape of any component of the army. The strain, however, began to tell heavily on the troops after three years of war. The eager, aggressive spirit of the men of the old Light Division was gone. It was supplanted by a sort of dogged determination to hold on. The courage of the men had not weakened, but resignation had taken the place of the optimism that had flared so brightly after Chancellorsville. The rest of Lee's army was handicapped, not only by lowered morale

[9] Heth Mss.
[10] Longstreet, p. 433 ff.

among the troops, but by problems in the command echelon. Ewell was not well. His wooden leg, which was of poor construction, caused him such physical distress that his mental condition deteriorated. Early, his senior division commander, was lacking in both natural capacity and command experience to satisfactorily substitute as corps commander. Then, of course, Longstreet was absent in the west. As against this deteriorating Confederate force, the North began to amass a mighty army for a spring and summer campaign. At the head of the troops now being moved into position for a new blow against Richmond was the man who had been so successful in the West, U. S. Grant.

As usual, Powell Hill took advantage of the war's interlude in late 1863 and early 1864 to be with Dolly and the children. His never rugged constitution showed increasing signs of being sapped of its strength. The circumstances of his temporary disablement at Chancellorsville was the first outward indication that something serious was wrong. After Bristoe Station, Hill knew that he was extremely tired[11] but he felt that a sojourn with his family was sufficient to refresh him for the next campaign. He began to worry about his health, however, only because he feared being forced out of active duty. From time to time he brooded about the strange illness that had struck him down at West Point. It occurred to him that the pressure of cadet days, which had resulted in the illness that prevented him from graduating with his class, was nothing as compared to the stress and strain which now was part of his everyday life. His mirror showed that the hollows were deepening in his cheeks and under his eyes and that the lines on his forehead were more pronounced. These, however, were marks that were becoming increasingly common in the Army of Northern Virginia. He determined that he would be ready for full duty as usual as the reports came in that spring of the big Union offensive that was about to get under way.

The sudden departure of the army for the Gettysburg campaign the previous summer had prevented the formal

---

[11] A typical symptom with liver or kidney infection.

christening services for baby Lucy Lee. Now, in late April, 1864, the ceremony was arranged. General Lee was the godfather. Lee was apprehensive at Union activity along the Rappahannock but did not hesitate to set aside a couple of hours for the ceremony. For a brief interlude the war left the thoughts of Lee, the commander, and Hill, the lieutenant, as Lucy Lee was christened. The festivities that followed, however, were interrupted by distant gunfire. The two generals looked at each other knowingly. Another campaign had begun.

On May 4, 1864 Grant crossed the Rapidan at Ely's and Germanna Fords. From this date forward, until Appomattox, almost a year later, the rival armies were to be constantly engaged on fronts that shifted but always remained within rifle fire of each other. Grant's campaign was to be one of attrition. No quarter was to be asked or given. No prisoners were to be exchanged. That last year of the war saw the Army of the Potomac and the Army of Northern Virginia meet head-on at various points—The Wilderness, Spotsylvania, Cold Harbor, Petersburg, Five Forks. These, nevertheless, were just names of places at which the continuous fighting flared especially high during the next eleven months. After May 4, 1864 the war in Virginia was actually a single titanic battle.

The strength of the Confederacy waned, temporarily was recouped, then diminished again during those months. So it was with the officers and men of the C.S.A. Powell Hill was no exception. He felt mentally and spiritually refreshed as he left the christening ceremony with Lee. His body, however, would never recoup the vigor that years of campaigning had drained from it. He became conscious that he was not a well man as he commanded the Third Corps in the dense, tangled thickets west of Fredericksburg appropriately known as The Wilderness.

In that maze of woods and brush, the two armies literally groped toward each other. Heth's Division, as at Gettysburg, was Hill's foremost unit. Heth collided with Hancock's Union corps along the Plank Road, one of the thoroughfares that cut through the junglelike wilderness.[12] Lee had instructed Hill to avoid a major clash until Longstreet arrived from Orange Court House about twenty miles to the west. Longstreet had been rushed back from Tennessee as Grant's intentions became clear. He had been temporarily held at Orange Court House, however, to reorganize his corps and to determine where the battle would develop. Now Lee ordered him up. Hancock spoiled the Confederate timetable by pressing Heth so hard that Powell Hill had to send Wilcox to his support. The two divisions were able to stand off Hancock throughout May 5th, but that night found them precariously extended along the Plank Road, confronted by a superior force and with their flanks exposed. Hill came up personally to direct the action. A feeling of weakness and nausea came over him as he reached the front. Heth and Wilcox met him and explained that their divisions were halted side by side and that, although the enemy was in force before them, they believed they could hold out until Longstreet arrived. Hill felt so ill that it was impossible for him to do anything but return to his temporary headquarters.

It was probably fortunate for the morale of the ailing Hill, as well as his men, that they didn't know the full strength of the enemy nor of the danger threatening their exposed flanks. The fighting became more intense as the day came to a close. Casualties were mounting rapidly on the Heth-Wilcox front and ammunition began to run low. Darkness about 8 p.m. ended the day's battle. Both Heth and Wilcox then attempted to reorganize their formations but found that their divisions had become badly disorganized and intermingled in the brush and thickets. Hill had left orders to keep the men in their present position until dawn when Longstreet was expected. Heth and Wilcox became afraid that the confused, disorderly position of their men would make them highly vulnerable to any kind of attack. They also knew that the enemy's lines were only about fifty

---

[12] Alexander, p. 500 et. seq. Hill made no official report of this or any later campaign.

305

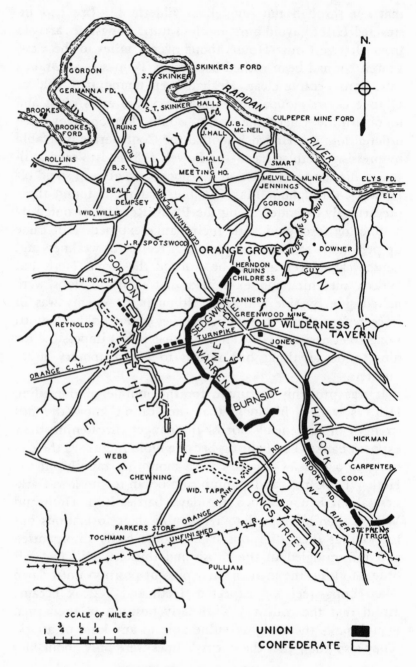

N.

GORDON

S.T. SKINKER

SKINKERS FORD

GERMANNA FD.

RAPIDAN

S.T. SKINKER HALLS
FD.

BROOKES

RUINS

J.B.
MC.NEIL

CULPEPER MINE FORD

BROOKES
FORD

J.HALL

RIVER

ROLLINS

B.S.

B.HALL

MEETING HO.

SMART

MELVILLE MLNE

JENNINGS

ELYS FD.

BEALE

DEMPSEY

GORDON

ELY

WID. WILLIS

GERMANNA PLANK RD.

J. R. SPOTSWOOD

GRANT

ORANGE GROVE

WILDERNESS RUIN

DOWNER

H. ROACH

GORDON

HERNDON
RUINS
CHILDRESS

GUY

TANNERY

REYNOLDS

SEDGWICK

GREENWOOD MINE

OLD WILDERNESS
TAVERN

EWELL HILL

TURNPIKE

PLANK

JONES

ORANGE C. H.

WARREN

LACY

LEE

BURNSIDE

HICKMAN

WEBB

BROOKS RD.

HANCOCK

CARPENTER
COOK

CHEWNING

WID. TAPP.

ORANGE PLANK

NY RIVER

RD.

LONGSTREET

PARKERS STORE

R.R.

STEPHENS
TRIGG

TOCHMAN

UNFINISHED

PULLIAM

SCALE OF MILES

¾ ½ ¼ 0   1

UNION
CONFEDERATE

MAP 23. BATTLE OF THE WILDERNESS

306

yards in front of them. Heth determined to go to Hill for authority to reorganize the troops and to separate his own men from Wilcox's by forming the two divisions on opposite sides of the road under cover of the pitch darkness.

Heth shook his head as he walked about the men on the firing line, sprawled out sleeping where they had fought all day. He feared what the dawn would bring to those men if by any chance Longstreet did not arrive that night. Leaving the entangled front line in charge of Wilcox, Heth hurried back to Hill. The commander of the Third Corps was seated on a camp stool before a small fire. A smile lighted his pain-lined features when he saw Heth.

"Your division has done splendidly today. Its magnificent fighting is the theme of the entire army."[13] He shook Heth's hand as he spoke.

Heth acknowledged the compliment to his troops but did not hesitate before describing the present situation on the front. He told Hill of the manner in which his men and Wilcox's were mixed, lying at such angles that they could not fire a shot without risking injury to their own comrades.

"We shall certainly be attacked early in the morning," he said. "Let me take one side of the road and form a line of battle and Wilcox the other side and do the same." He pointed out that this was the only way to establish an organized line that could withstand an attack.

Hill looked into the fire before replying. He was weary and sick himself. He knew how the men who had been on the road or in combat all day must feel. One of A. P. Hill's greatest virtues had always been his consideration for the comfort of his soldiers. That consideration guided him now against Heth's arguments.

"Longstreet will be up in a few hours," he said slowly. "He will form in your front. I don't propose that your division shall do any fighting tomorrow. The men have been marching and fighting all day and are tired. I do not wish them disturbed."[14]

---

[13] Heth Mss.
[14] *Ibid.*

Heth returned to discuss the situation with Wilcox. They agreed that something had to be done or their troops would be exposed to carnage at dawn. Wilcox went to Hill to back Heth's request. Hill was adamant. He complimented Wilcox on the showing of his men that day but told him they should be permitted to rest where they were.

Heth conferred with Hill twice more that night. The last time that they discussed the situation, Heth's voice rose with urgency. It was late and becoming apparent that Longstreet might not arrive before dawn. Hill, thoroughly exhausted and wracked by the attack of illness, exploded.

"Damn it, Heth," he shouted, "I don't want to hear any more about it. The men shall not be disturbed."[15]

Harry Heth turned on his heel and went in search of Lee. He could not find the commander in the confusion of The Wilderness, however, and finally returned despondently to await the dawn.

At five o'clock that morning the worst fears of Heth and Wilcox were realized. Portions of Hancock's II and Sedgwick's VI Corps began a careful, methodical assault on the scrambled Confederate lines as the hour struck. The Confederates broke. There was no organization to keep them together. Longstreet was not yet on the scene. Wilcox, at Lee's direction, madly rode down the Plank Road looking for Longstreet. Powell Hill, after a sleepless night, was too ill and weak to do anything. He insisted on remaining at the front but had to be transported along the lines in an ambulance. There was no red-shirted, sword-waving horseman on the field to rally the troops as in the old Light Division days. A rallying point was precisely what they needed. As the disorganized retreat began to gain impetus, Lee saw McGowan trying to stem the flight of some of the veterans of the Light Division.

"My God, General McGowan," said the commanding general, "is this splendid brigade of yours running like a flock of geese?"

McGowan answered, "General Lee, the men are not

---

[15] *Ibid.*

308

whipped. They only want a place to form, and they will fight as well as ever they did."[16]

Powell Hill had made a mistake the night before. In his helpless illness he fully realized that Heth had been right. He had been told, however, that Longstreet would be up in time and he wanted to spare his spent men. He had not been far wrong with respect to Longstreet's arrival. At five o'clock the First Corps, with Longstreet riding ahead, was only three miles down the road. The news of approaching help restored a semblance of order to the Confederate retreat. The line was finally stabilized as Longstreet's men joined in the pitched battle. The close-range fighting was as wild and bloody as any during the entire war. Hill was heartsick at his men's plight and enraged at his own helplessness. The training and seasoning which he had given his troops, nevertheless, stood them in good stead. Given Longstreet's Corps as a rallying point, they struck back at the enemy and gave an account of themselves that would have done credit to the old Light Division.

As the battle now developed, a repetition of the Bristoe Station disaster was averted. Hancock's advancing troops themselves became disorganized and entangled in The Wilderness. Longstreet's fresh soldiers proceeded to punish them. The close-range fighting continued throughout the day and ended in a stalemate as night fell. There were 17,000 Federal and 12,000 Confederate casualties during the two days. Longstreet was seriously wounded near the end of the engagement when he was accidentally shot by his own men under circumstances similar to Jackson's fatal wounding a year earlier near the same place.

Bristoe Station and The Wilderness saw the only two major tactical errors ever committed by A. P. Hill. There have been excuses offered for both occasions. His subordinate commander or Stuart's Cavalry should have provided better reconnaissance at Bristoe. Longstreet should have arrived earlier at the Wilderness, or Hill should have been advised that he would be late, so that his two divisions could

---

[16] Alexander, p. 503.

309

have been prepared. The ultimate responsibility of a commander, however, transcends errors by others. He alone must bear the blame when plans misfire. Powell Hill did not shirk his responsibility. He had been at fault twice according to the book. As a book soldier, therefore, the two incidents weighed heavily upon him as he proceeded by ambulance with his troops toward Spotsylvania and the continuation of the battle that would never cease until April, 1865. Hill's spirit was as willing as ever but the strength of body which had begun to wane alarmingly was further weakened by these two successive debacles.

CHAPTER 21

The End Approaches

THE HISTORY of the war has designated Spotsylvania Court House, a few miles southeast of The Wilderness, as the site of the next battle. The fighting there, however, was no more than a continuation of the action of May 5-6. Lee was attempting to outmaneuver Grant. The Northern general was endeavoring to cut Lee off from Richmond and precipitate a fight to the finish. On the evening of the 10th of May the commander of the Army of Northern Virginia met with Heth and the still ailing A. P. Hill in the church near the court house at Spotsylvania. Powell Hill had to be transported in an ambulance but he had himself carried near enough to the front to observe the fighting. He had watched Heth's men hold the line that day. His pride in the men of his command glowed in his eyes.

"General Lee," he said, "just let them continue to attack our breastworks; we can stand that very well."[1]

Heth smiled in agreement. "You witnessed Burnside's attack on me this morning. Our losses were light compared to theirs."

Lee shook his head. He liked the confidence that Hill and Heth exuded but he appreciated the enemy's strength better than the others.

"No," he said, "this army cannot stand a siege; we must end this business on a battlefield, not in a fortified place."

This was the keynote of the days that followed. From Spotsylvania the army moved southeast toward Richmond. Movements were quick and well concealed. Grant was out-

---

[1] Heth Mss.

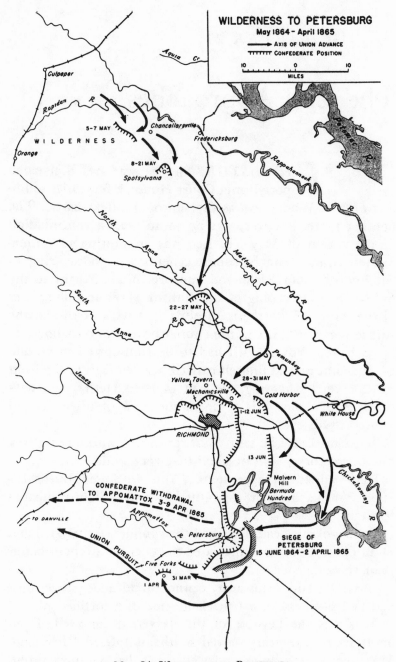

WILDERNESS TO PETERSBURG
May 1864 – April 1865

AXIS OF UNION ADVANCE
CONFEDERATE POSITION

10   0   10
MILES

Aquia Cr.

Culpeper

Rapidan R.

5-7 MAY

Chancellorsville

WILDERNESS

Fredericksburg

Orange

Rappahannock R.

Potomac R.

8-21 MAY

Spotsylvania

North Anna R.

Mattaponi R.

South Anna R.

22-27 MAY

James R.

Pamunkey R.

Yellow Tavern

Mechanicsville

28-31 MAY

Cold Harbor

White House

1-12 JUN

RICHMOND

13 JUN

Malvern Hill

Bermuda Hundred

Chickahominy R.

CONFEDERATE WITHDRAWAL
TO APPOMATTOX 3-9 APR 1865

TO DANVILLE

Appomattox R.

UNION PURSUIT

Petersburg

SIEGE OF
PETERSBURG
15 JUNE 1864-2 APRIL 1865

Five Forks

31 MAR

I APR

MAP 24. WILDERNESS TO PETERSBURG

312

generalled to the extent that he could not cut Lee's avenue of withdrawal toward the Confederate capital. On the other hand, Lee could never completely escape to the point of breaking off contact with the Federals. Time, furthermore, favored the North. The Union army was far fresher and better equipped, besides being vastly superior in numbers. The Confederate troops were not only battered and tired but their morale was now shaken by news of the suffering being undergone by the civilian population. The once gay capital toward which they fell back had become a bitter, hungry community. Profiteering and crime were rampant. Food riots were common.

Powell Hill's failing health seemed almost a symbol of the impending collapse of the Confederacy. Yet, like Hill, the South maintained a dogged determination and hung on. Again, as in the case of the Third Corps commander, spirit occasionally flared high enough to overcome material handicaps. A. P. Hill "came back" to see plenty of action during the final year of the war. The Confederate Army rallied for more than one victory before the inevitable end came at Appomattox.

The first and undoubtedly heaviest blow which the dying Confederacy struck against Grant came at Cold Harbor, almost on the outskirts of Richmond, on June 3. Grant probably made the greatest mistake of his military career at Cold Harbor. Lee performed one of his masterpieces of maneuver there, both in getting his army into position to crush the Union attack and in later extricating his troops and spiriting them south of the James to Grant's amazement and consternation.

Lee did a miraculous job during May in keeping his army intact while fighting a running battle from the Wilderness, through Spotsylvania and on down to Cold Harbor. The Confederate losses were not as heavy as the enemy's, but they were more than the diminishing army could stand. Casualties among the high officers were especially severe. Jeb Stuart had run into his cavalry nemesis, Phil Sheridan, at Yellow Tavern on May 11. Here Sheridan achieved the first

313

of a series of accomplishments that, more than anything else, ended the war. He trapped Stuart, annihilated a good portion of his command, and killed the colorful Southern cavalry chief. Also during that bloody month of May, no less than nine Confederate brigadiers were lost, along with Major General Ed (Allegheny) Johnson, who was captured. Ewell joined Hill on the sick list. Longstreet had been knocked out of action during the first day that he arrived on the battle scene at The Wilderness after returning from the west.

Nevertheless, Lee devised such magnificent defenses on the wooded hills near Cold Harbor that Grant's bull-headed onslaught resulted in the most terrible carnage of the war. As the stage became set for the battle during the latter days of May, Powell Hill literally forced himself from his sick bed and took the field. This was not only a tonic to the troops but it gave Lee at least one senior officer on whom he could rely.

A. P. Hill was back personally to lead the Third Corps in standing off the Federals along the North Anna River from May 23 to May 27. Then, during the three days culminating with the great assault of June 3, Hill stood with Lee directing the defense that became more devastating than any offense of the war. The Federal Army literally impaled itself upon the sharply angled woodland redoubts set up by the Confederates. The Union losses were nearly 10,000 for the three days, seventy percent occurring during a comparatively few minutes on the 3rd.[2]

Despite the success of the battle, Lee was under no illusion that the Army of Northern Virginia could continue to slug it out on that field with Grant's constantly reinforced army. He adhered to the theory that he had expounded to Hill and Heth several weeks before. The enemy could be met, if necessary, on an open battlefield, but there was simply not enough strength left in the Southern forces to attempt to hold a fortified position, even after a success like Cold Harbor. Lee therefore called Hill to his side and gave him orders for a well-camouflaged withdrawal south of the

---

[2] Alexander, p. 542.

James toward Petersburg while Grant was still recovering from the losses he had suffered at Cold Harbor.

Lee still clung tenaciously to the hope of precipitating a panic in the North through the medium of surprise offensive operations. He sent Early to the Valley to strike at Hunter, who had taken up the scorched-earth policy begun by Sheridan. The last Confederate force in the Shenandoah Valley had consisted of about 5,000 men under the veteran Grumble Jones. These troops were crushed by Hunter and Jones was killed. The Valley now was completely in the hands of the North. Early's raid was somewhat effective and, at its climax, actually threatened Washington. It had, however, no effect on the overall course of the war. Grant was not compelled to weaken the Army of the Potomac in any respect as he pressed toward Petersburg after Lee.

Despite the acute pressure against Richmond there were certain factors that kept the spark of hope alive in the Confederacy during the last months of 1864 and early 1865. The North was getting sick of the war. Union enlistments had ceased except at bounties of $1,000 or more per man. The civilian population was outraged at Grant's heavy casualty lists, especially at Cold Harbor. Then, too, the Confederate positions around Petersburg were the strongest and best prepared of any occupied during the war. In fact, were it not for a brilliant river crossing by Grant, Lee might have met the attack on most favorable grounds and caused a repetition of Cold Harbor. Grant surprised the Confederates by crossing the James well downstream and then swinging up to attack Petersburg from the south. As it turned out, the latter part of June found the armies drawn up facing each other around the perimeter of the Petersburg fortifications. The stabilization of the front without another major disaster or heavy casualties terminated the peace-at-any-price movement in the North and set the stage for the final death struggle.

A. P. Hill's health failed again as the Petersburg campaign developed in late June. Nevertheless, Hill stayed at the helm of the Third Corps and personally led his worn, ragged troops into Petersburg on June 18. Hill was rushed to the rescue when it was finally determined that Grant had crossed the James in force and was attacking Beauregard, now in charge of little more than a skeleton force at Petersburg. As Hill's men, and then the rest of the Army of Northern Virginia, arrived to man the Petersburg fortifications, Beauegard asked Lee to mount a full-scale counter-attack against the Federals. A year or two earlier this might have been possible, but the exhausted troops could not do it now. Hill felt that the men would do well if they could only get up to take over the manning of the fortifications. Lee agreed. The days of major offensive operations by the Army of Northern Virginia were over forever.

Powell Hill now established Dolly and the children in the cottage of Colonel Charles Venable in Petersburg. Venable was an aide of General Lee's who reflected his commander's views by doing everything possible to keep the sick Powell happy through enabling him to keep his family with him virtually on the front lines. There wasn't much of Virginia, though, that was not pretty much a part of the front in those days. Despite the nearby roar of the guns, Dolly and the children carried on their daily life as if they were in peacetime Washington or placid antebellum Culpeper.

An occasional few hours, however, were all that Powell Hill could spare from his line duty. The threat of attack was constant. The first major Union operation was based upon a 500-foot mine, dug under the Confederate positions and exploded with tremendous force on July 30 in Hill's sector of the front. This episode ended with little more loss to the Confederates than the 278 men, including 22 from Pegram's batteries, who were killed or wounded by the actual explosion.[3] The Federals bungled the followup by not forcing a major break through the "crater" which resulted from the explosion. By the time the Union troops were organized, the Confederates had sufficiently recovered to hold the line. And so it went, generally speaking, during the following months. Grant probed the defenses of Petersburg from time to time.

[3] Alexander, p. 572.

Lee feinted or raided the Union lines occasionally but never in such force as to constitute a serious counteroffensive. The stalemate obviously favored the North. But for the urgings of one of his generals, Grant probably would have "sat it out" indefinitely in a campaign of attrition. Phil Sheridan was a man of action, however. Having eliminated Stuart from the war he wanted to bring things to a head. He finally talked Grant into planning a definite offensive for the spring of 1865.

The noose around the neck of the Confederacy was tightened during the winter by Joe Johnston's return to the command of the remnants of what had once been the Army of the West. Hood had succeeded Johnston the previous summer but had been unavailing against Sherman's superior forces. Now Johnston again took over the reins at a time when the South needed a vitalizing tonic if it were to continue. Johnston was not aggressive. He had been a defensive fighter on the Peninsula years before and he had not changed. His return to command in Georgia forecast the rapidly approaching finale.

Lee still had hopes of uniting the Army of Northern Virginia with Johnston. With this in mind he attempted to balk Grant at every possible turn around Petersburg. Although Longstreet returned to active duty, Lee continued to rely heavily on A. P. Hill in the campaign which now had become a struggle for mere existence. With Mahone, Heth, and three of Pegram's batteries, Hill won a notable, although somewhat local victory at Globe Tavern on August 14. Later that month, Hill cooperated with Hampton's cavalry to achieve another victory at Reams' Station. Then, on October 27 at Burgess' Mill, along Hatcher's Run, Powell Hill personally directed the divisions of Heth and Mahone in the repulse of an attack which otherwise might have developed into a major Union offensive. These battles, however, were little more than incidents in the main campaign around Petersburg. Neither Hill nor any Southern general could mount any attack sufficient to follow up successfully an initial advantage. The men were too tired and the lines too attenuated. Like Powell Hill himself, the spirit was there but the flesh was simply not up to it.

A. P. Hill, despite his poor health and the requirements of his official duties, continued to look after the welfare of such of the officers of the old Light Division days as still survived. Lindsay Walker was chief of artillery for the Third Corps, with the redoubtable Willie Pegram, now a colonel, next in rank under him. Hill, having been successful in securing Walker's promotion as a brigadier, now sought the same elevation for young Pegram. He also convincingly demonstrated that he bore Moxley Sorrel no grudge because of his part in the old quarrel with Longstreet, by successfully recommending Moxley's promotion to brigadier general in November of 1864. Even while Powell Hill fostered the advancement of old comrades, word came of the death of another of the original old guard of brigadiers of the Light Division. Archer had died in late October. He had been a prisoner of war and was exchanged. His health had been so impaired, however, that he survived only a short time after his return to the Confederate ranks.

Heth joined Hill in the quest for promotion of Pegram. They succeeded only to the extent of having him promoted from lieutenant colonel to full colonel. The reason for Lee's failure to make him a general is one of the ironies that are part and parcel of any system of military promotion. Pegram was too good as a subordinate artillery commander to be promoted to brigadier general and placed at the head of a brigade of infantry. Pegram's qualifications as a fighting man are well summed up by Heth:

> William Pegram was one of the few men who, I believe, was supremely happy when in battle. He was then in his element.[4]

Hill endorsed Heth's recommendation as follows:

> No officer of the Army of Northern Virginia has done more to deserve his promotion than Colonel Pegram.[5]

---

[4] Heth Mss.
[5] 14 *S.H.S.P.* 17.

Lee returned the application with the notation that "the artillery could not lose the services of so valuable an officer."[6]

In the meantime, civilian life went on in battered Petersburg and destitute, if physically unscathed, Richmond. There was not enough food for either soldiers or civilians, let alone both. Confederate currency was practically worthless. Riots continued to be common in the capital as attempts were made by mobs to storm the government warehouses. A black market based on hoarded gold sprang up. Prices of services as well as commodities skyrocketed. Kyd Douglas reported paying a Petersburg dentist $260 to look after a couple of teeth.[7]

Dolly Hill uncomplainingly made the best of it. She gave Powell a home where he could rest in the brief interludes allotted him. His mysterious illness became worse during the privations of wintertime Petersburg. Lee urged him to take a leave of absence but Hill declined. The fact that he could spend an occasional few hours with his family was all that prevented a complete collapse. Finally, under persuasion by Dolly and officers of his staff, Hill determined to visit the members of his family who had temporarily made their home in Chesterfield County with his cousin and brother-in-law, Tom Hill, who had married Powell's oldest sister, Margaret. These relatives were refugees during the Federal occupation of Culpeper. Powell not only wanted to visit his kin but he desired to have another look at Richmond. Travel facilities being what they were, it was decided that Dolly and the children would remain at Petersburg. Hill could take as much leave as he felt necessary for his health, but he intended to be away only a few days. He didn't foresee any large-scale fighting until later in the spring and figured that the family would be as safe at the Venable cottage as anywhere. Thus, on the bleak winter day March 20, 1865, he kissed Dolly and the children goodbye and took off for his last sojourn with the Hills of Culpeper, and his final salute to the dying capital of the Confederacy.

---

[6] *Ibid.*
[7] Douglas, p. 322.

Powell spent a few days at Chesterfield reliving the childhood days at Culpeper. He then went into Richmond. The city was in worse turmoil than ever. Rumors were rife that the capital was about to be evacuated. Food rioting was at its peak. Powell Hill was disgusted. He hated quitters whether among troops or civilians. He observed the chaos for a few hours and then tersely remarked to some acquaintances:

"I do not wish to survive the fall of Richmond."[8]

It was on March 31, 1865, that A. P. Hill took his last look at Richmond. Though he didn't like what he saw, he refused to acknowledge that the fall of the Confederacy was near. His mind kept running back to the positions then held by the Third Corps around Petersburg. The lines were thin, but there were good men down there. They'd hold for a long time. He thought of some of the tight spots that he'd been in with the Light Division. His division had always "come up" to save the day; his corps would do it this time.

Then he suddenly shook his head. For the first time doubt came into his mind. The Light Division had always come through, but there was no longer a Light Division. O'Brien Branch, Maxcy Gregg, Dorsey Pender, John Archer—all dead. His hand trembled slightly. These staunch friends had commanded four of his six brigades at Mechanicsvillle that June, which now seemed so long ago. The other brigadiers who rode out to battle with them at the start of the Seven Days, Field and Joe Anderson, were not with him either, even though they were still alive. It was the thought of the first four that caused the faint tremor of his hand. They had given their lives to preserve the Confederacy and its capital. Now they were gone. Richmond might just as well be gone too. Then a grim smile crossed his deeply lined features. Yes, Richmond was dying, but down around Petersburg the Army of Northern Virginia still held fast. That army contained the remnants of the Light Division, and there were still many great officers of the old brigades on the battle line.

[8] 19 *S.H.S.P.*, 185.

There were some, too, who had not served in the Light Division, but who were now creating distinguished records in Hill's Third Corps. They included Cadmus Wilcox, a hard fighter whom Hill admired as his type of soldier. Wilcox commanded Dorsey Pender's old division. Alfred Scales, later governor of North Carolina, had succeeded to the command of Pender's own brigade when Dorsey became a major general. He had not been considered sufficiently experienced, however, for command of the division when Dorsey sustained his fatal wound. Similarly, Jim Lane was considered too green for division command. McGowan was still disabled from the wounds of Chancellorsville. His successor as brigade leader, Abner Perrin, was a good officer who would soon join the list of generals under Hill to be killed in action. Perrin, however, like Scales and Lane, was too new a brigadier for such early promotion to the command of a division. Thomas was qualified, but he was in the unfortunate position of commanding a Georgia brigade in a North Carolina division. Lee feared that dissatisfaction might be created if he were put at the head of the division to fill the shoes of the great North Carolinian, Dorsey Pender.[9] As a result, Lee had gone outside of the division and given Pender's command to Cadmus Wilcox.

Wilcox's prior assignment was as a brigadier under Dick Anderson in the only one of Hill's three divisions that contained neither troops nor officers of the old Light Division. Wilcox had been at West Point with Powell Hill, Harry Heth, and many other old schoolmates. He could not take Pender's place as a close friend of Powell—perhaps nobody could in those late days of the war. But Powell liked him and had confidence in him. He would never attain brilliance, but he was always steady and dependable. Hill's only regret, with respect to Wilcox's Division in the lines around Petersburg, was that its ranks were terribly thin as the result of the war of attrition that finally was producing results for Grant.

Hill's other division commander, besides Harry Heth,

---

[9] Gen. R. E. Lee's *Dispatches*, p. 115.

during the last days around Petersburg, was a strange but dynamic character named William Mahone. "Little Billy," as he was known, was so slight in height and frame that Sorrel called him "a mere atom with little flesh." Mahone's wife, on one occasion, hearing that he had received a flesh wound said, "Now I know it is serious, for William has no flesh whatever."[10] Sorrel related that one of the first times he saw Mahone, Billy was protecting himself from the heat by wearing a huge Panama straw hat, while the rest of his "uniform" consisted of a boy's brown linen suit, the jacket of which buttoned to the trousers. He also displayed the eccentricity of keeping a cow and laying hens constantly near his field headquarters even on active campaigns.

There was, however, nothing eccentric about Mahone as a soldier. He had been a good brigadier. Unlike many of his contemporaries, he was even better when promoted to the rank of major general and given command of Anderson's Division, when Dick was selected by Lee to succeed the wounded Longstreet.[11] Mahone's Division immediately became the spearhead of the army. It probably was to the Army of Northern Virginia, during the last part of the war, what the Light Division had been in its great twelve-month career of 1862-63. As Powell Hill walked the streets of Richmond for the last time that grey March day, he could muster a faint smile when he thought of Billy Mahone. It was a satisfaction to have in his command a reminder of the old dash and brilliance of the Light Division, even if the men who now exhibited these traits were not the same veterans who had followed him through the Seven Days, Slaughter's Mountain, Manassas, Sharpsburg, Fredericksburg, and Chancellorsville.

Yes, and what was left of the Light Division was still valiantly carrying on in the Third Corps. Despite the despair apparent in Richmond, Grant was still at bay, and the Confederacy was still alive. Harry Heth, the unlucky general, was leading one tired, battered segment of the old Light

[10] Sorrel, p. 276.
[11] 36, *O.R.* Pt. 2, p. 967.

322

Division with as much success as conditions permitted. Heth's Division had been badly mauled three times, through no fault of his, since he assumed his command in the Third Corps. He had precipitated the battle of Gettysburg when he was merely looking for shoes for his troops with the approval of Hill. Though this is not generally remembered, the result had been the heaviest loss of men sustained by any division in Lee's army at Gettysburg.[12] Then, in The Wilderness, Heth sustained heavy casualties because he could not get Hill's permission to establish a better line the night before the big Federal attack. Finally, it was Heth's Division which fared the worst in the Bristoe Station fiasco. Here, again, however, the responsibility must be with Powell Hill. Heth was smashed while diligently following his commander's orders. Through all the misfortune, however, he remained an extremely competent and loyal officer.

Hill fully realized that Heth's apparent "disasters" were not Heth's fault, but his own. Powell had been somewhat careless in giving his assent to the shoe expedition at Gettysburg, in view of Lee's standing order to avoid a battle. He had certainly blundered at Bristoe Station and The Wilderness. It was to Heth's credit that he still had a division on the field at Petersburg with morale that could match any of them, even though its manpower was woefully weak.

Hill was closer to Heth than to any other general in the corps during the last days, although there was not quite the personal relationship that had existed between the original commander of the Light Division and his leading brigadiers, Gregg and Pender. Heth always felt that some people blamed him for the defeat at Gettysburg. With it all, however, he never lost his sense of humor and never fell from the esteem of the major figures on both sides who survived the war with him. He reminisced at length with Grant at Appomattox and was the recipient of two gallons of good whiskey from the Union commander.[13] Years later he was the prominent

---

[12] Alexander, p. 443 et seq. indicates that Pickett lost 2,888, and Rodes lost 2,853 against Heth's 2,850. Heth's report on "missing," however, is incomplete and undoubtedly would more than overcome the difference in each case.

[13] Heth Mss.

figure in ceremonies dedicating the A. P. Hill monument in Richmond.

An incident took place in Heth's Division at Gettysburg which typified the fighting spirit of the men of the Light Division, and which has been used as an anecdote by soldiers (each claiming originality) in all of our wars since that time. It occurred on the first day of the Battle of Gettysburg. The 26th North Carolina regiment of Heth's Division was wavering under terrific Union fire. An officer, unfortunately never officially identified, rode out in front of his men. Rising in his stirrups he turned toward the faltering troops and pointed his sword at the enemy.

"Come on," he shouted, "Come on! Blast your cowardly souls, do you want to live always?"[14]

There were some others of the oldtimers who were still on hand with Powell Hill to carry on the traditions of the Light Division. Sam McGowan had recovered and was back with his brigade. He had led one of the last assaults that were characteristic of the old division, when an attempt was made to break out through the Union lines at Burgess' Mill. The assault was a brilliant attempt to duplicate the old days, but it was, of course, a failure against the odds. McGowan would survive the war, to continue his successful career in politics.

Then there was Jim Lane, who stayed with his brigade to the bitter end. He had succeeded Pender temporarily on the field at Gettysburg. He later temporarily took over command of the division when Wilcox went on leave at the time of his brother's death. On both occasions, however, he was glad to get back to his own brigade, which he never failed to lead with distinction. This brigade had been O'Brien Branch's before Sharpsburg, with Lane a regimental commander. Lane's old regiment, therefore, remained with him without a break from the Seven Days to Appomattox. Lane retired to teaching school after the war.[15]

---

[14] This quote is from an old newspaper clipping, which cannot be identified as to the publication or the date, but is certainly well back into the 19th century.

[15] He also became the chronicler of the brigade's war history.

There was one other general, who had come all the way with Hill, and who would be on hand at Appomattox after Hill had fallen. Edward L. Thomas, who had succeeded J. R. Anderson during the Seven Days, led his Georgia Brigade through every campaign thereafter. There were few if any brigades to see such continuous active service under one leader. Thomas and his men not only fought on all the battlefields of the Army of Northern Virginia, but also saw some detached service in the Valley under Early during the winter of 1864. Thomas' troops were among the stalwarts of Wilcox's skeleton division of about 2,600 men who would finally receive their first real respite in nearly four years when they laid down their arms at Appomattox. Thomas' subsequent career was divided between farming and Federal government employment.

Powell Hill had been glad to see Charley Field return to harness in time for The Wilderness campaign. Field staged a remarkable recovery, but Hill did not directly benefit thereby. The War Department was worrying about a replacement necessary in Longstreet's First Corps at about the time Field was medically approved for return to duty. Hood had been transferred to the western theater of operations with a promotion. Field now was designated Hood's successor as commander of his old division.

Hill could never reflect on the men who still served with him at the start of spring 1865 without fond thoughts of Willie Pegram. Pegram was one of those universal favorites who actually was too good in his job to be spared for promotion to a higher command. Wounded on several occasions, he always displayed great resiliency in returning to his guns before the next campaign opened. Willie, barely 23 years of age, would fall in action within a few days. Neither he nor Powell Hill, the leader he most admired, would ever know that the other was killed. Pegram was eulogized by many. His memory has been kept alive by generations of orators throughout the South. An early report by Charlie Field, covering the battle at Slaughter's Mountain in August of 1862, however, when Pegram was only a battery commander, would seem to exemplify his exploits better than any funeral oration. Field wrote:

> Pegram's battery—of four guns only—was soon replied to by three batteries of the enemy. This gallant officer maintained this unequal contest for an hour and until his guns were silenced by his losses in men. * * * I have taken occasion before to speak of the distinguished services of Pegram's battery. It is sufficient to say now that it fully sustained the reputation made on other fields.[16]

It was more of those who had passed on, however, than of the living that A. P. Hill thought as his last visit to the capital came to a close. Again the names came to his mind: Branch, Gregg, Pender, Archer, and later, the promising brigadier, Perrin, killed before he could really get his teeth into his new command. Gregg and Pender brought back the dearest memories. He felt that his eulogies of these men in his reports had been inadequate; but a battle report was no proper forum for sentimentality, to his way of thinking. It was not, however, maudlin sentiment that pervaded his thoughts of Maxcy and Dorsey. Hill was sincere in all things. He had deep respect for their memory and a sense of loss at the absence of his two best generals of the old days—and his two best friends.

As Hill walked the streets of Richmond that March day, he knew that his record as a corps commander had fallen short of that of the commander of the Light Division. Bristoe Station had been a debacle. The Wilderness had been uncomfortably close to total disaster. Peculiarly, however, these occasions had resulted respectively from the exercise of A. P. Hill's two most admirable traits as a leader of troops. It had been his relentless, driving force to destroy the enemy that had made him too impetuous at Bristoe Station and led him into the ingenious Federal trap. It had been his consideration for the comfort of his tired men in The Wilderness that had prompted him to deny Heth's request to spend the night re-establishing the line, so that his and Wilcox's divisions might not remain exposed to the Union counterattack the

---

[16] 12 *O.R.*, Pt. 2, p. 218.

326

following morning. It might seem ironical that disaster befell Hill when he was displaying his greatest attributes. The failure to temper such traits with the judgment called for by the moment, was a weakness that was not apparent in him at the division command level, but which, nevertheless, prevented Powell Hill from ever becoming a really great corps commander.

Through it all, starting as a regimental commander in the early days of the war, and going right through the year of the Light Division and into the final stages of the conflict as commander of the Third Corps, Hill never stopped being an able, courageous soldier. Perfection in warfare has never been achieved. The mantle of greatness descends on the shoulders of those who achieve the most at the expense of the fewest mistakes. That applies to A. P. Hill. No general in the army achieved a greater record of constant frontline leadership.

From the Peninsula to Five Forks, Powell Hill had fought every battle of the Army of Northern Virginia even though there were two brief interludes, when a wound at Chancellorsville and sickness in the Spotsylvania campaign rendered him hors de combat. He never permitted himself to be taken to the rear, however. On each of those occasions he resumed his command in a matter of little more than hours. He felt that he was giving everything he could to the Confederacy, but to him no other course was conceivable. He was still ready and anxious for action on the eve of the fall of Richmond.

With these thoughts he prepared to return to the thin gray line representing the sector of the Petersburg defenses assigned to the woefully undermanned Third Corps. Heth, Wilcox, and Mahone were good division commanders but Hill knew that he alone was responsible for the necessary integration of the corps. Lee's advice to look out for his health notwithstanding, to Powell his only place was with the troops. And he wanted to be back at the front after viewing crumbling, morale-shattered Richmond.

CHAPTER 22

Death of a Hero

*P*OWELL HILL had somewhat miscalculated the time of the opening of the Federal spring offensive. He returned to Petersburg on the morning of April 1. Later that day there commenced what history calls the Battle of Five Forks. This was the last major engagement of the war. April 1 was also A. P. Hill's last full day on earth.

His first duty on that fateful day was an inspection of the entire tenuous line held by the Third Corps. Heth's and Wilcox's divisions were on the line with Mahone in mobile reserve. Heth's right rested on Burgess' Mill where Hill had led the corps in one of its last successes. Heth's Division extended left for three and three-quarters miles. From Heth's left, Wilcox held the next two and a half miles. At the present division strengths the entire front of the Third Corps was hopelessly undermanned. The situation was as bad or worse along the rest of the Confederate line. On Heth's right, for example, there was almost a void in the front. The entire distance of three miles from Burgess' Mill to Hatcher's Run was held only by a skirmish line of a few sharpshooters.

As Hill made his tour of inspection that morning the first indications came of the impending attack. Northern activity was evident. Lee advised A.P. Hill that he was recalling Longstreet from north of the James with everything that could possibly be spared in that sector. Hill knew that the ultimate crisis of four years of war was at hand. He directed such preparations as could be made and then returned to his headquarters on Washington Street. As evening approached he felt the mysterious illness threaten him physically and mentally. With a sigh he left his desk and turned

329

to the one source that could possibly revive him for the developments of that night and the following day. He walked across the town to the Venable cottage where Dolly and the children awaited him.

His leave had done him little good as far as his health was concerned. His last evening with his family, however, was, as usual, the one tonic that could keep him on his feet for another day. The evening was short. Powell Hill retired early to a sleep of only a very few hours. It was well before dawn on the 2nd of April that his chief of staff, Colonel William H. Palmer, called him. Palmer reported that part of the thin line had given way. The roar of artillery made it obvious that the action commenced the previous day was now being brought to climactic intensity. Powell hurriedly said goodbye to Dolly. She was accustomed to his going out in the cold dark of early morning toward the sound of the guns. She was a soldier's wife and concealed her emotions even though she was pregnant. There was no fanfare at their last parting.

At his headquarters Hill found utter confusion. No reports had come through from either Heth or Wilcox. It therefore appeared likely that they had been cut off. He had never been hesitant to take action regardless of the circumstances, and this critical moment was no exception.

"Alert the staff and all headquarters personnel," he snapped to Palmer and strode toward the couriers' quarters. Suddenly he paused and shouted another order.

"Hitch up the headquarters wagons and be ready to move out if you have to. I'm going to General Lee's."[1]

Palmer started to follow him. "Can I go with you, sir?"

Hill shook his head. "Stay here and watch things at headquarters."

When he reached the couriers' quarters he called for Sergeant G. W. Tucker.

"Follow me with two couriers to General Lee's headquarters at once," he said.

---

[1] The two most complete accounts of A. P. Hill's death and the events immediately preceding appear in 11 *S.H.S.P.* 564-569 (Sgt. Tucker) and 12 *S.H.S.P.* 185-187 (Col. Venable).

Tucker was grooming his horse. He told couriers Jenkins and Kirkpatrick to follow the general. Tucker lost only a few moments himself in saddling his horse. The others were directly behind Hill riding two horses already saddled and held ready for emergencies.

They rode the mile and a half to the Turnbull House, army headquarters at Edge Hill. Hill went directly to Lee's bedroom. The commanding general was lying on the bed partly clothed. They immediately commenced discussing the situation, the full import of the seriousness of which, neither yet realized. While they were talking, Venable burst into the room. He reported that wagons were being driven wildly down the road and that Federal skirmishers were definitely within the Confederate lines. That there had been a serious breakthrough was clear. Hill leaped to his feet. He had to be with his troops without delay. Lee told Venable to get more detailed information at once.

Kirkpatrick had already been dispatched back to Third Corps Headquarters. Powell Hill now rode out in the dim gray light, accompanied by Venable, Sergeant Tucker, and Courier Jenkins. There was light enough for Hill to make out a Confederate battery apparently inactive on a nearby hill. He told Colonel Venable to order it into action as there did not appear to be any other Confederate troops in the vicinity. Powell then rode on with only Tucker and Jenkins. Sounds of rifle fire indicated that they were cut off from returning to their headquarters by the route they had taken earlier. Hill felt he had no choice but to ride through the fields, now well infiltrated by enemy skirmishers, in an attempt to reach Heth's position.

Suddenly they came upon two Federal infantrymen. Hill and his two troopers wheeled upon them.

"Surrender!" the Confederates shouted in unison.

The Federal soldiers promptly laid down their guns.

Hill turned to Jenkins. "Take these men to General Lee. He will want the information that can be gotten from them." He then spurred his horse on toward where he supposed Heth's flank was located. Tucker alone now accompanied his general. As they rode on they saw a group of soldiers standing around some old log huts that had been used as winter quarters by Mahone's Division but which had been abandoned.

"General," asked Tucker, "what troops are those?"

"The enemy's," was the terse reply.

They rode on within rifle shot of this group of enemy. Tucker, alarmed for the general's safety, blurted out:

"Please excuse me, General, but where are you going?"

Hill answered, "Sergeant, I must go to the right as quickly as possible." Pointing southwest, he added, "We will go up this side of the branch to the woods, which will cover us until reaching the field in rear of General Heth's quarters. I hope to find the road clear."

Tucker reports that from this point he endeavored to ride slightly ahead of his general, a difficult procedure in view of Hill's determination to reach his command and his complete disregard for personal safety. Perhaps, even as they rode, A. P. Hill sensed the impending fall of Richmond and recalled his statement concerning his survivorship of that disaster. They finally emerged from the woods into a field opposite Heth's headquarters. As they rode on, the general turned to his sergeant:

"Sergeant, should anything happen to me you must go back to General Lee and report it."

Suddenly in the woods adjacent to the field through which they were riding, Hill pointed out a group of Federal soldiers. Tucker's report indicates that there were "six or eight" and that two of them were in advance of the others. Hill drew his Colt pistol and snapped:

"We must take them!"

Hill and Tucker were then within twenty yards of the two most advanced Federals, who had taken positions behind a large oak tree. Tucker attempted the old ruse of trying to make them think that a larger force of Confederates was following. He shouted at the two men:

"If you fire you'll be swept to hell! Our men are here. Surrender!"

332

Hill was at the sergeant's side, also shouting "Surrender!"

The Union soldiers thereupon fired from pointblank range. One shot went wild. The other struck Powell Hill's upraised left hand, took off his thumb, entered his heart, and passed out through his back.[2] As the Culpeper Cavalier fell from his horse he shouted to Tucker his last words and final command,

"Take care of yourself!"[3]

Thus, in the words of Colonel Venable, as he related the tragic incident some twenty years later, "fell one of the knightliest generals of that army of knightly soldiers."[4]

Tucker caught the bridle of Hill's horse and led him galloping toward the woods. Over his shoulder he caught his last glimpse of the commander of the old Light Division, lying on the ground "with his limbs extended, motionless."[5] The sergeant knew there was nothing he could do except obey his orders to report to General Lee. He switched to Hill's superior horse and was soon near headquarters.

Longstreet, who had just arrived, hailed Tucker. Old Pete was silent as the courier explained what had happened. He and A. P. Hill had not been friends since July 1862, but theirs had been a mutual respect. Now Longstreet could only stare at the empty saddle from which Tucker had just sprung. Years later he was to write of Hill's death:

"The Southern service lost a sword made bright by brave work upon many heavy fields."[6]

As Tucker started for the headquarters house, Lee quickly walked toward him. Another courier who watched the incident stated, "Never shall I forget the look on General Lee's face as Sergeant Tucker made his report."[7]

Tears welled in Lee's eyes. He spoke quietly and slowly.

"He is at rest now, and we who are left are the ones to

[2] 19 *S.H.S.P.* 185.
[3] 20 *S.H.S.P.* 383.
[4] 12 *S.H.S.P.* 187.
[5] 11 *S.H.S.P.* 568.
[6] Longstreet, p. 605
[7] 12 *S.H.S.P.* 184.

suffer."[8] Then, turning to Palmer, he continued. "Break the news to Mrs. Hill as gently as possible."

Palmer dreaded the assignment. His task did not become easier when he heard Dolly singing as he approached the cottage. He stood silently in the doorway until she saw him. Her song stopped. The first words spoken were from Dolly, not the Colonel.

"The General is dead," she said slowly. "You would not be here unless he was dead."

Word of A. P. Hill's death was quickly conveyed to Jefferson Davis. The President of the expiring Confederacy paused in the midst of the wild preparations to evacuate the capital. He remarked to his wife that General Hill had been killed with a sick-furlough in his pocket.

"He was," the President said, "brave and skillful, and always ready to obey orders and do his full duty. A truer, more devoted, self-sacrificing soldier never lived or died in the cause of right."[9]

The band did not play "Auld Lang Syne" at Appomattox until Palm Sunday, eight days later. Nevertheless, the curtain was rung down on the Confederacy that grey, dripping morning of April 2. The Petersburg-Richmond line was abandoned that day. In a short while the capital would be surrendered to the Federals. The day was at hand which Powell Hill had vowed he did not wish to survive. Then, too, the soldier whom he loved more than any other, Willie Pegram, was mortally wounded the evening of April 1 and died early on the 3rd. Neither he nor his general ever knew that the other had been shot down.

A. P. Hill's posthumous child was a girl. There were no sons to carry on the lineage, but Kitty Morgan Hill never stopped being a soldier's wife. She named the little girl Ambrose Powell Hill.

The exigencies of the last days of the war, and the hard period that was to follow, prevented Dolly from burying Powell in his beloved Culpeper. The remains were tem-

---

[8] *Ibid.*
[9] 14 *S.H.S.P.* 452.

porarily interred in the Winston burial ground at Chester-field. Later, the body was taken to Hollywood Cemetery in Richmond where A. P. Hill's grave was in the midst of so many thousands of his most illustrious and gallant comrades-in-arms. Years later, on Memorial Day, 1892, amidst great fanfare, parading and speech-making, the remains were moved to the outskirts of Richmond and placed beneath a great statue of the general, depicting A. P. Hill in full dress uniform, looking proudly and calmly south across the capital in the defense of which he died. A couple of miles away on a direct line, upon an extension of the old Hermitage Road, the famous equestrian statue of Stonewall Jackson faces north. A. P. Hill and Stonewall Jackson at last see eye to eye, an experience denied them in their brief life spans. The name of Jackson became a household word, and Stonewall a favorite subject of hero-worshippers for all time. A. P. Hill, no less honored and revered by all who know his story and his deeds, has been denied his full measure of fame.

Those who served with him, however, never forgot him. Five years after Hill's death, Robert E. Lee, who perhaps knew and appreciated A. P. Hill better than did most of his other associates in the war, died in the peace and quiet of a college campus at Lexington, Virginia. The great Southern leader's final words as he entered the delirium preceding death were:

"Tell A. P. Hill he must come up!"

Appendix

TO COMPILE a complete bibliography of everything that one may have read on a subject at some time during his life, and which may have exerted a subconscious influence upon a writer's current work, is probably impossible. This is especially true of a subject bearing upon the Civil War. I have, therefore, limited the bibliography here to two relatively small lists, including chiefly material that was constantly at hand and frequently referred to in the writing of this book. One list covers authors and titles. The other recites miscellaneous sources and compilations that are not identified with authors. In the second group are to be found the two primary sources upon which I have relied most heavily in my annotations. They are, of course, the *Official Records* and the *Southern Historical Society Papers*.

In addition to the volumes and other material appearing on the following lists, however, there were numerous reference sources made available to me through the kindness of many individuals and institutions. I shall attempt to list these kind people and organizations alphabetically at this point and, in so doing, express my deepest appreciation to each:

Dr. Francis L. Berkely for courtesies extended at the Alderman Library, University of Virginia.

Confederate Museum, Richmond, Va. for making available all material on A. P. Hill in its possession.

Confederate Memorial Institute, Richmond, for permission to examine many documents, including such matters as Jackson's court-martial specifications against Hill.

Mr. Sidney Forman, archivist at the United States Military Academy, for producing all material at West Point bearing upon Cadet A. P. Hill.

Miss Mildred T. Hill of Culpeper, Va., and her cousin, Miss Mildred T. Bispham, grand-nieces of A. P. Hill, who gave me much personal information on my subject and directed me to numerous leads resulting in the uncovering of much additional material. Without the aid of Miss Hill and Miss Bispham, the data on A. P. Hill's youth and family background would have been most incomplete.

Mrs. Emlyn H. Marsteller of Manassas, Va., who not only made the invaluable Harry Heth manuscript available, but demonstrated never-to-be-forgotten Southern hospitality to Mrs. Schenck and myself.

New York State Library, Education Building, Albany, N. Y. for many courtesies including loan of S.H.S.P. volumes and use of microfilm projectors.

The late Mr. J. L. Rutledge of Toronto, a student and analyst of the A. P. Hill story, who answered many questions that otherwise I would have had great difficulty in solving.

Colonel Willard Webb of the Library of Congress, Washington, D. C., another student of A. P. Hill, who courteously answered several inquiries and volunteered other information.

Mr. and Mrs. Edward G. Hapgood, Lynchburg, Va., for affording me a "base of operations" in the war country.

Leo W. O'Brien, newspaperman and broadcaster, as well as Member of Congress, representing the 30th District of New York, for invaluable editorial help.

One additional field of acknowledgment should not be overlooked. In the manner of A. P. Hill I found personal reconnaissance to be of great value in describing the battle scenes. As a result I toured in detail every scene of activity of the Army of Northern Virginia. I would like to thank everybody who has played a part in maintaining the various battlefields, parks, cemeteries, and museums commemorating the campaigns in Virginia, Maryland, and Pennsylvania. Most sites are so laid out that one can easily re-live the days of 1861-65.

Bibliography

Alexander, E. P., *Military Memoirs of a Confederate*
Blackford, W. W., *War Years With Jeb Stuart*
Caldwell, J. F. S., *History of a Brigade of South Carolians Known as Gregg's and Subsequently as McGowan's Brigade*
Casler, John O., *Four Years in the Stonewall Brigade*
Clark, Walter (ed.), *Histories of Several Regiments and Battalions From North Carolina in the Great War 1861-65*
Cullum, G. W., *Biographical Register of the Officers and Graduates of the United States Military Academy*
Dabney, R. L., *Life and Campaigns of Lieut. Gen. Thomas J. Jackson*
Doubleday, Abner, *Chancellorsville and Gettysburg*
Douglas, Henry Kyd, *I Rode With Stonewall*
Eisenschiml, Otto, *The Celebrated Case of Fitzjohn Porter*
Elson, Henry W., *Elson's New History*, material accompanying Brady photography, published as *Civil War Through the Camera*
English Combatant, *Battlefields of the South*
Fish, Carl Russell, *The American Civil War*
Freeman, Douglas Southall, *Lee's Lieutenants*
—*R. E. Lee*
Henderson, G. F. R., *Stonewall Jackson and the American Civil War*
Heth, Harry, unpublished manuscript (courtesy of Mrs. Emlyn H. Marsteller, Manassas, Va.)
Hotchkiss, Jed, *Field Notebook No. 4, The Sharpsburg Battlefield*
Hotchkiss, Jed, and Allan, William, *Battlefields of Virginia—Chancellorsville*
Lindsley, J. B. (ed.), *Military Annals of Tennessee—Confederate*
Long, A. L., *Memoirs of Robert E. Lee*
Longstreet, James, *From Manassas to Appomattox*
Macartney, Clarence E., *Little Mac*
Maurice, Frederick, *An Aide-de-Camp of Lee* (comprising an edition of the papers of Charles Marshall, also annotated "Marshall")
Mitchell, Joseph B., *Decisive Battles of the Civil War*
Moore, Edward A., *Story of a Cannoneer Under Stonewall Jackson*
Palfrey, F. W., *The Antietam and Fredericksburg*
Pollard, E. A., *Lee and His Lieutenants*
—*The Lost Cause*
Robertson, William J., a series of articles (published in Richmond *Times Dispatch*, October 1934)
Ropes, John C., *The Army Under Pope*
Sheridan, Philip H., *Personal Memoirs*
Sorrel, Moxley, *Recollections of a Confederate Staff Officer*
Stackpole, E. J., *Drama on the Rappahannock.*
Taylor, Richard, *Destruction and Reconstruction*
Watkins, Sam R., *Co. Aytch*
Webb, A. S., *The Peninsula*
Woodward, W. E., *Meet General Grant*

LIST OF MISCELLANEOUS SOURCES
Archives, Library of Congress, Washington, D. C.
Battles and Leaders of the Civil War (a compilation of narratives by participants in the war)
Centennial of U.S. Military Academy (1802-1902) (a history of the Academy during that period)
Confederate Veteran
Harper's Weekly, 1861-65 (bound volumes of the magazine during the entire war period)

Land We Love (Southern magazine published 1866-69 and republished in bound volumes)

Letters of Dorsey Pender to His Wife (touching and informative series of letters covering Pender's entire war career prior to his death at Gettysburg; microfilm copies obtained from University of North Carolina)

Official Records (complete authorized title: *War of the Rebellion, Official Records of the Union and Confederate Armies*)

Southern Historical Society Papers (collection of essays, articles, military reports, etc., covering the war period by contemporaries. Publication of papers commenced in 1876; last published volume, to writer's knowledge, dated 1944)

Soldier in the Civil War, edited by Mottelay & Campbell-Copeland, 1885 (a compilation of illustrated narratives by participants in the war)

Index

A

Alabama troops (5th Bn), 39
Albany, N. Y., 287
Aldie, 170, 171
Alexander, E. P., 90, 115
Alexandria, 168, 179
Anderson, Joseph R., 17, 18, 20, 40, 55, 56, 57, 65, 70, 71, 86, 88, 93, 108, 109, 119, 320
Anderson, Richard H., 11, 12, 77, 108, 133, 191, 212, 245, 246, 258, 267, 268
Antietam, Battle, creek (see also Sharpsburg), 194, 196, 199, 215, 216
Antietam Campaign, 187-203
Appomattox, 109, 289, 304
Archer, James J., 20, 38, 39, 55, 56, 57, 71, 72, 86, 108, 109, 151-3, 155-6, 168, 171, 178, 180, 182, 184, 192, 199, 202, 205, 229, 230, 231, 233, 239, 248, 254, 255, 264, 318 320, 326
Arkansas troops (2d Regt), 108
Armistead, Lewis, 265
Army of Northern Virginia, 1, 3, 20, 73, 89, 94, 95, 132, 159, 189, 191, 203, 212, 216, 236, 268, 314
Army of Virginia (Pope), 131
Army of the Potomac, 43, 131, 214, 215, 228, 235, 244, 274, 315
Ashcake Road, 52
Ashland, 18, 44, 49, 53
Atlee's Station, 52, 53, 103

B

Baltimore Crossroads, 16
Barbour, W. M., 108
Banks, N. P., 112, 113, 114, 131, 134, 144, 149, 150, 153, 154, 156
Barnes, Dixon, 200, 202
Barnett's Ford, 137, 139
Bayard's cavalry, 153
Beaver Dam Creek, 45, 55-7, 62, 63, 74, 78, 96, 113
Beauregard, P. G. T., 9, 95, 316
Berdan, Hiram (Sharpshooters), 95
Bloody Lane, 195
Blue Ridge Mountains, 189
Boatswain's Swamp, 75
Boteler's Ford, 197, 205
Boyd, W. W., 108
Branch, L. O'B., 17, 18, 20, 36, 38, 49, 51, 53, 70, 71, 72, 86, 93, 108, 109, 151-3, 155-7, 168, 171, 178, 183-4, 192, 199, 200-2, 212-13, 224, 320, 324, 326
Brandy Station, 265, 272
Braxton's Battery, 78
Bridgeford, D. B., 229
Bristoe Station, 169, 296-302
Brock Road, 248
Brockenbrough, J. M., 178, 180, 183, 192, 199, 205, 212, 223, 224, 225, 229, 261, 264, 266
Brook Church, Road, 20, 37, 51
Buford, John, 149, 155, 179, 272, 276
Bull Run, 170, 182, 183
Bull Run Mountains, 165, 166
Burgess' Mill, 317, 324, 329
Burnside, Ambrose E., 111, 141, 195, 196-7, 214-17, 221-2, 225, 227-8, 235

C

Campbell, R. P., 108
Cashtown, 273, 277
Casualties, Williamsburg, 15; Seven Pines, 19, 39; Mechanicsville, 59, 64; Gaines' Mill, 77; Frayser's Farm, 89; Seven Days, 96, 107; Slaughter's Mountain, 156; Manassas, 178, 184; Harpers Ferry, 192; Sharpsburg, 202-3; Fredericksburg, 234; Chancellorsville, 256; Gettysburg, 276; Bristoe, 299; Wilderness, 309; Crater, 316
Catharine Furnace, 248
Cavalry, Confederate, see Stuart
Cavalry, Federal (see also Buford, Stoneman), 53, 54
Cemetery Hill, 277
Central R. R. Bank, 121
Centreville, 169, 170, 182
Chambersburg, 213
Chancellorsville, 1, 142, 161, 243-259
Chantilly, 183
Charles City, road, 17, 85
Charlottesville, 131
Chickahominy River, bridges, 15, 16, 17, 18, 20, 43, 45, 49, 50, 51, 52, 67, 79, 80, 81, 91, 114
Chimneys, The, 20
Cigar incident, Antietam, 195
Cold Harbor, town, battle, 49, 62, 235, 304, 313, 314
Colston, R. E., 237, 246, 252
Confederate uniform, 103
Congressional investigations, 143, 179
Conscription Act, 238
Cooke, John R., 297, 298, 299
Cooke, P. St. George, 297
Cornelius Creek, 100
Corning, Erastus, 287
Corps organized, 132
Corse, M. D., 12, 14
Cox, Jacob, 197
Crater, 316
Crawford, S. W., 134
Crenshaw's, 52, 53
Crenshaw's Battery, 72
Cromwell and Cavalier, 142, 208, 259
Crutchfield, S., 90
Culpeper, 4, 7, 11, 54, 124, 138, 144, 149, 150, 152, 154, 155, 207, 213, 215, 216, 272, 282, 295, 316, 319, 320
Cunningham, Richard, 265

D

Daniel, John M., 117-8, 123
Darbytown Road, 100
Davidson's Battery, 93
Davis, Jefferson, 16, 58, 82, 83, 84, 99, 107, 120, 131, 211, 214, 258, 265, 266, 300, 334
Davis, Joseph, 258, 267, 268, 297
Douglas, Henry Kyd, 250, 252
Drill of troops, 102
Duke, Basil, 7

E

Early, Jubal A., 133, 152, 153, 174, 229, 233, 234, 237, 245, 269, 274, 303, 315
Economic breakdown, CSA, 285
Edwards, O. E., 27, 239, 264

341

Ellerson's Mill, 57, 58, 65
Elzey, Arnold, 9
Ely's Ford, 244, 253, 304
Evans' Brigade, 178
Evelington Heights, 96
Ewell, Richard S., 18, 49, 59, 74, 75,
  80, 94, 132, 133, 137, 148, 149, 151,
  163, 169, 171, 183, 190, 191, 229,
  257, 258, 268, 271, 272, 274, 277,
  295, 296, 314

F

Fairfax Court House, 183
Fairview, 253
Farnsworth, J. F., 53
Field, Charles W., 18, 20, 26, 28, 50,
  54, 56, 57, 71, 72, 86-8, 109, 151,
  168, 171, 177, 212, 223, 239, 266,
  320, 325
Five Forks, 304, 329
Fleet's Battery, 152
Forbes, W. A., 108
Forno, Henry, 175, 178
Franklin, W. B., 91, 114, 191, 192, 228
Frayser's Farm, 82, 83, 86, 89, 90, 93,
  96, 108, 114
Frederick 188, 189
Fredericksburg, 160, 215-237, 245
Fremont, J. C., 112, 114, 131
Furnace Road, 248

G

Gaines' farm, 63
Gaines' Mill, 65-78, 96, 109, 113, 117,
  122, 169-70
Garland, Samuel, 12-15
Garnett, Richard, 135, 137
Georgia troops, 39, 59, 74, 108
Germanna Ford, 244, 304
Gettysburg, 269-283
Gillam, W. W., 135
Gordonsville, 119, 131-3, 147-8, 155,
  159, 245
Guiney's Station, 17, 217, 256
Grant, U. S., 147, 303-4, 311-17, 323
Grapevine Bridge, 81, 82, 91, 114
Gray, R. H., 108
Gregg, Maxcy, 17-18, 20, 28, 40, 55,
  65-74, 86-8, 109, 113, 123, 149, 151,
  164-5, 168, 171-4, 178, 180-8, 190-9,
  200-05, 217-25, 229-34, 243, 261-3,
  320, 323, 326
Greenwich, 169
Groveton, 170

H

Half Sink, 51
Halleck, H. W., 143, 147, 225
Hamilton, D. H., 200, 239, 264
Hamilton's Crossing, 245-6
Hampton, Wade, 30, 39, 89, 263, 317
Hancock, W. S., 265, 304, 308, 309
Hanover Junction, 18
Hanover Court House, 20
Hanover Court House Road, 49
Hardy, W. B., 152
Harpers Ferry, 8, 188-97, 200, 225
Harrison's Landing, 85, 96, 99, 147
Haskell, W. T., 67
Hatcher's Run, 317, 329
Hatton, Robert, 19
Hayes, Harry, 133, 175
Hazel Grove, 253, 255
Health of command, 22, 23, 99, 100, 239
Heintzelman, S. P., 169
Heth, Henry, 105, 109, 111, 141, 221,
  222, 239, 253, 255, 258, 264-7, 273-4,
  277, 280, 283, 297-300, 304-8, 310-11,
  314, 317, 321-9, 330, 332

Hill, Lt. Gen. A. P., actions and operations (see campaigns); administrator,
  18, 19, 22, 24, 238; appearance, 3,
  37, 54, 57, 129, 152; appraisal of, 3,
  59, 211, 260, 327; background, 4;
  boyhood, 4, 265; cadet days, 6, 111;
  care of men, 92, 211, 236, 238;
  character, personality, 2, 15, 34, 54,
  88, 121, 154, 171, 173, 177, 193,
  198, 243, 270, 297; children, 124, 271;
  commander, 9; death and burial, 333-5;
  early service, 6-9; feud with Jackson,
  135, 137-42, 164, 188, 190, 208-10,
  240, 244; feud with Longstreet, 117-
  20; illness, 5, 128-9, 303, 305, 308,
  310, 311, 313, 315; marriage and
  family, 7, 124, 127, 207, 214, 270,
  303, 316, 319, 330; promotions, 11,
  17, 258; relations with subordinates,
  41, 217-23, 239, 243, 307, 323; relatives 4; romances 6
Hill, Ambrose Powell (daughter), 334
Hill, Daniel H., 18, 19, 44, 45, 49, 57,
  70-1, 74, 80, 94, 95, 113, 132, 133,
  159, 187, 194, 195, 212, 229, 237,
  257
Hill, Frances Russell, 124
Hill, Frances Russell Baptist, 4-5
Hill, Henrietta, 7, 124
Hill, Capt. Henry, 4
Hill, Katherine Morgan (Dolly), 7, 92,
  127, 189, 207, 214, 219, 220, 269,
  270, 295, 303, 316, 319, 330, 334
Hill, Lucy Lee, 269, 270, 271, 301
Hill, Maj. Thomas, 4
Hogan house, 67
Hoke, R. F., 52
Hoke, W. J., 108
Holmes, T. H., 80, 85, 86, 94, 132
Hood, J. B., 39, 75, 77, 86, 163, 178,
  212, 237, 325
Hooker, Joseph, 114, 169, 195, 228, 236,
  244, 245, 246, 253-4, 271, 272
Hotchkiss, Jed, 237
Howard, O. O., 1
Huger, Ben, 18, 80, 82, 85, 94, 113
Hundley's Corner, 60, 113

I

Illinois Cavalry (8th), 53
Ironclads, 16
Insignia, Confederate, 104

J

James River, 16, 80, 85, 89, 91, 94, 96,
  100, 132, 159, 313, 315, 329
Jackson, Thomas J. (Stonewall), character, 110; actions (see campaigns);
  cadet, 111, 141; compared with Hill,
  110-112; as Cromwell, 140-1; discipline, 136; feud with Hill (see Hill);
  harsh treatment of subordinates, 135,
  166, 188, 190, 240, 251; inadequacy
  during Seven Days, 60-3, 71-5, 79, 82,
  89-91, 109-115; independent type, 46-7;
  religion and piety, 35, 135, 232;
  wounding and death, 2, 249 ff.
Jenkins' Brigade, 86
Jenkins, Private, 331
Jones, D. R., 133, 200
Jones, J. William, 54, 152, 236
Jones, John R. 133
Jones, William E. (Grumble), 155, 315
Johnston, A. S., 26
Johnston Joseph E., 8, 11, 16, 18, 19, 39,
  317
Johnny Reb, description, 105
Johnson, Edward, 269

Johnson, Allegheny Ed, 314
Johnson, T. C., 108

K

Kelly's Ford, 244
Kearny, Philip, 114, 173-5, 179, 184-5
Kemper, J. L., 12-15
Kirkland, W. W., 298-9
Kirkpatrick, Pvt., 331
King, Rufus, 170-1, 178

L

Lane, James H., 2, 205, 212-13, 224, 228, 230, 233, 240, 243, 249, 251, 261, 262, 263, 264, 321, 324
Lawton, A. R., 133, 149
Lee, C. C., 108, 212
Lee, Fitzhugh, 133, 160-1
Lee, Lighthorse Harry, 4
Lee, Robert E.
Actions (see specific campaign); appraisal of Hill, 3, 211; appearance, 30, 68; assumes command of ANV, 19; character, personality, 34, 43; mediator, 205-11; mentioned, 7, 20, 44, 58-61, 67, 73-5, 82-5, 89, 94-6, 107, 109, 111, 119, 120-9, 131-6, 140-3, 156, 159-64, 179, 181, 194, 197-8, 203, 213, 216, 219, 227-8, 236-7, 246-7, 255-8, 265-9, 271, 276-80, 286, 289, 292, 301, 304, 308, 311, 313, 319, 330-5
Leesburg, 190, 213
Libbey Prison, 193
Light Division (see also A. P. Hill) Actions (see specific campaign); activated, 17; brigades, 17, 25-41; casualties, (see Casualties); initial location, 18-20; named, 19; organization and composition, 17-25, 27; qualities, 3, 19, 41, 59, 73-4, 77, 97, 155, 253; reorganized as 2 new divisions, 258, 264; strength, 25, 106, 133, 240
Lincoln, Abraham, 131, 143, 213, 286
Little River Turnpike, 183
Little Round Top, 280
Long Bridge, 16
Longstreet, James (Old Pete), 11-18, 45, 66-8, 71-5, 77-99, 109, 113-25, 133-5, 163, 169, 170, 175, 178-9, 180-84, 196, 207, 215-17, 227-8, 237, 257, 268, 271-2, 276, 279-82, 303-9, 317, 329, 333
Loring, W. W., 135
Louisa Court House, 132
Louisiana Brigade, 133, 178

M

Madison Court House, 155
McAllister, Julian, 221
McCall, George A., 63, 86, 88, 114
McClellan, George B., 5, 6, 11, 17-18, 43, 45, 49, 62-3, 73, 79, 80, 89, 91-9, 110, 131, 141-2, 144, 147-8, 189, 191, 194-6, 205, 215-16, 222
McDowell, Irvin, 17, 131, 142, 155, 169-70
McGowan, Samuel, 173, 178, 203, 233, 239, 240, 258, 261, 263-4, 308, 324
McGuire, Hunter, 256
McIntosh, David, 239
McLaws, Lafayette, 17, 133, 159, 187, 191-4, 212, 245-6
Magruder, John, 20, 80, 82, 85-6, 88, 93-4, 133
Mahone, William, 268, 317, 322, 327, 329
Mallory, Francis, 87
Malvern Hill, 91-6, 102, 109, 112
Manassas, First Battle, 9, 39

Manassas, Second Campaign, 159-185
Manassas, Junction, 164, 168-70, 194
Marcy, Ellen (Nellie), 6, 92, 207
Marcy, Randolph B., 6
Marshall, Charles, 89, 246
Martinsburg 190-1
Marye's Heights Hill, 227-9, 234, 235, 254
Maryland troops, 9
Mayo, Robert, 88
Meade, George G, 63, 230, 233, 246, 274, 295
Meadow Bridges, 18, 20, 50, 55
Mechanicsville, 18, 45, 49, 53, 55-9, 103, 109, 100
Miles, Dixon, 192
Milroy, Robert, 148
Miller, E. H., 108
Mine Run, 302
Morgan, John, 7
Morgan, Katherine (see Hill, Dolly)
Monroe, Fort, 9
Munford's cavalry, 90

N

Napoleon guns, 87
Naval Blockade, 285
New Bridge, 82
New Cold Harbor, 66-9
New Jersey Brigade, 168
New Orleans, 143
New York troops, 197
Nine Mile Road, 20, 49
North Anna River, 216, 314
North Carolina troops, 2, 3, 30, 58, 108, 249, 263, 324

O

Old Cold Harbor, 70
Old Church Road, 57
Orange and Alexandria R. R., 149, 299
Orange Court House, 11, 132, 137, 139, 140, 149, 164, 302, 305
Orange-Culpeper Road, 137
Orange Plank Road, 246
Orr's regiment, 231, 234
Ox Hill, 183

P

Palmer, William H, 330
Pamunkey River, 43
Plank Road, 245, 304-5, 308
Pegram, John, 265
Pegram, William, Pegram's Battery, 72, 78, 93, 94, 152, 203, 213, 223, 230, 234, 239, 317, 318, 325-6
Pender, Mary Frances (Fanny) 125
Pender, William Dorsey, 5, 20, 29, 31, 34, 40, 55, 57, 65-6, 70-4, 87-8, 108-9, 123-7, 151-6, 168, 171, 178, 180-4, 192, 199, 205, 206, 217-8, 220-25, 229, 233-4, 239, 243, 251, 254-5, 258-61, 268, 274, 276, 280, 282, 320, 323, 326
Pendleton, W. N., 205, 212, 238
Peninsular campaign, 9-97
Pennsylvania troops, 168, 206
Perrin, Abner, 264, 321, 326
Perry, E. A., 268
Petersburg campaign, siege, 270, 304, 315-20
Pettigrew, Johnson, 30, 258, 267, 297, 298
Pettus, J. W., 262
Pickett, George E., 5, 11, 77, 135, 212, 237, 282
Pleasant Valley, 183
Pole Green Church, 53
Pope, John, 119, 124, 131-2, 137-9, 143-5, 148, 155, 159-175, 179-191

343

Porter, Fitz John, 5, 18, 43, 45, 55, 63, 65, 77-8, 95, 113, 169, 179, 181-5, 205
Port Royal, 237
Posey, Carnot, 268
Potomac River, 188, 197, 205-6
Powell, Capt. Ambrose, 4
Powell, Ann, 4
Powhite Creek, 67, 74-5
Price's farm, 20
Prince, Henry, 154

Q

Quaker Road, 82
Quartermaster supply, 22

R

Rapidan River, 155, 160, 161, 163, 244, 304
Rappahannock River, 132, 160, 163, 164, 165, 185, 215-17, 236-7, 245
Rations, 102
Ream's Station, 317
Retreat from Yorktown, 11-12
Review of six campaigns, 290 ff
Reynolds, J. F., 63, 169
Rhode Island, 196
Richmond, 8, 9, 11, 17, 80, 83, 93, 96, 100, 117, 124, 131-4, 147-8, 213-19, 237-8, 315-20
Richmond, Fredericksburg, and Potomac R. R., 217
Ricketts, James B., 178
Riddick, R. H., 108
Ripley, Roswell, 57-8
Rodes, Robert E., 1, 248, 252-3, 269, 277, 279
Romney, 8

S

Salem, 165
Savage Station, 81-2
Scales, A. M., 321
Second Manassas, 148, 159-185
Sedgwick, John, 86, 114, 244-5, 254, 302, 308
Seven Days battles, 43-97; aftermath, 99 ff
Seven Pines, battle, 19-20
Shackleford, J. C., 108
Sharpsburg, campaign, 187-203, 215, 224
Shenandoah, 111, 131
Shepherdstown, 197
Sheridan, P. H., 270, 313
Shields, James, 112
Siege artillery on R. R. cars, 22
Sigel, Franz, 131, 148-9, 155, 169
Slaughter's Mountain, battle, 147-157, 208, 255
Smith, G. W., 16-19
Slocum, H. W., 85, 114
Sorrell, G. Moxley, 12, 103, 118-121, 277, 279, 318
South Carolina troops, 1, 17, 29, 87, 173, 200, 201, 239, 263
Spotsylvania Court House, 304, 311
Stackpole, Edward J., 225
Stafford, Leroy, 151, 154, 157
Starke, W. E., 87
Stevens, I. I., 184-5
Stevens, W. H., 22
Stone Bridge, 182
Stonewall Brigade, 152, 264
Stoneman, George, 245
Stony Run, 37
Strengths, 63-4, 106, 211-12, 240, 245
Strong, H. B., 178
Stuart, J. E. B., 28, 37, 93, 96, 132-3, 160-1, 179, 212-3, 252, 253, 255-6, 272, 273, 277, 295, 300, 309, 313-14
Sumner E. V., 216, 228

Sunken Road, 227, 235
Snydor, T. W., 58-9
Sykes, George, 72-3, 85

T

Taliaferro, W. B., 133, 150-2, 163, 169, 170-1, 190-1, 212, 229
Taylor, George, 168
Taylor, Richard, 133
Tabernacle Church, 245-6
Tennessee troops (see Archer)
Tenth Maine Regiment, 156
Thomas, E. L., 57, 74, 93, 108-9, 134, 151, 153, 155, 168, 171, 173, 178, 180, 184, 190, 197, 205, 212, 229-33, 240, 248, 258, 261, 325
Thoroughfare Gap, 163, 165, 169, 175, 178-9
Toombs, Robert, 196-8
Training troops, 23
Traveller, 67, 269
Tredegar Iron Works, 41, 108
Trimble, Isaac, 133, 237
Tucker, G. W., 331-3
Turney, P., 108
Turnbull house, 331

U

United States Military Academy, 4, 26, 103
U. S. Ford, 249, 253-4

V

Vallandigham, 268, 286-9
Venable, 331-3
Verdiersville, 161
Virginia Central R. R., 131
Virginia, ironclad, 16
Virginia Military Institute, 212, 262
Virginia troops, 8, 11-14, 25, 87-8, 103, 108, 178

W

Walker, Henry, 298
Walker, John, 191-2
Walker, R. Lindsay, 72, 151, 163, 192, 229, 258, 318
Walnut Grove Church, 66
War Department (U. S.), 142, 215
Warren, Gouverneur, 300
Washington, D. C., 142-3, 147, 161, 183, 185, 187, 213, 215
Wellford's, 248
White, Julius, 192-3
White Oak Swamp, 80, 85, 89, 90, 109, 114
Whiting's Division, 18, 44, 48, 75, 80, 90-1, 133
Wilcox, C. M., 12, 88, 268, 299, 305, 306-8, 321, 324, 326-30
Wilderness Church, 246, 248-9, 304, 313-14
Williamsburg, battle, 12-16
Williams, L. B., 12
Williamsport, Md., 190
Wilson, Emma, 6
Winchester, 213
Winder, Charles, 133, 136, 138, 149-51
Wooding's Battery, 90
Wright, A. R., 268
Wise, Henry E., 133

Y

Yellow Tavern, 37, 313
Yerby's Station, 217
York River R. R., 16
Yorktown, 11

Z

Zouaves, 33

344